CONNECTING FAMILIES?

Information & Communication Technologies, generations, and the life course

Edited by Barbara Barbosa Neves
and Cláudia Casimiro

First published in Great Britain in 2018 by

Policy Press
University of Bristol
1-9 Old Park Hill
Bristol
BS2 8BB
UK
t: +44 (0)117 954 5940
pp-info@bristol.ac.uk
www.policypress.co.uk

North America office:
Policy Press
c/o The University of Chicago Press
1427 East 60th Street
Chicago, IL 60637, USA
t: +1 773 702 7700
f: +1 773-702-9756
sales@press.uchicago.edu
www.press.uchicago.edu

© Policy Press 2018

British Library Cataloguing in Publication Data
A catalogue record for this book is available from the British Library

Library of Congress Cataloging-in-Publication Data
A catalog record for this book has been requested

ISBN 978-1-4473-3994-6 hardcover
ISBN 978-1-4473-3996-0 ePub
ISBN 978-1-4473-3997-7 Mobi
ISBN 978-1-4473-3995-3 epdf

The right of Barbara Barbosa Neves and Cláudia Casimiro to be identified as editors of this work has been asserted by them in accordance with the Copyright, Designs and Patents Act 1988.

Cover design by Robin Hawes
Front cover image: 123RF

Contents

List of figures and tables

Figures

Tables

Notes on contributors

Alexandra Sanders is a research and teaching associate in sociology at the School of Social and Political Sciences, University of Melbourne. She holds a Bachelor's degree in Gender and Cultural Studies from Murdoch University, and is a qualified counsellor and art therapist. Alexandra manages a private practice and also works in the public mental health sector, delivering programmes for people recovering from mental illness. She recently completed research examining genealogists' narratives of self and Other, and is currently collaborating on research on social isolation and loneliness among older Australian adults. Her research interests include life narratives, the sociology of mental illness, and the politics of identity and representation.

Alexia Maddox (PhD) is Lecturer in Communications in the School of Communications and Creative Arts, Deakin University. As a practising sociologist, her research interests are in research methods and digital community studies with a focus on social change and social inclusion. Her recent book, *Research Methods and Global Online Communities: A Case Study*, with Routledge combines these areas to illustrate the application of existing and emerging research methods to modelling collective social behaviours, particularly those adapting and augmenting through digital networked technologies.

Amanda du Preez (PhD) is Professor in the Department of Visual Arts at the University of Pretoria, where she teaches Visual Culture Studies. She obtained a DPhil in English from the University of South Africa on the topic of cyberfeminism and embodiment in 2003. She has coedited *South African Visual Culture* (2005); edited *Taking a Hard Look: Gender and Visual Culture* (2009) and authored *Gendered Bodies and New Technologies: Rethinking Embodiment in a Cyber-Era* (2009). She served as assistant editor of two accredited journals, *Image & Text* and *De Arte*. Currently, she serves on the Advisory Board of *Gender Questions* and the international journal *Persona Studies*. She is also a member of the Governing Board of the International Association for Visual Culture.

Anabel Quan-Haase (PhD) is Professor of Information & Media Studies and Sociology at the University of Western Ontario. She is the Director of the SocioDigital Media Lab. Her focus is on social change, social media, ageing, and social networks. She is the author of *Technology and Society* (Oxford University Press, 2016), co-editor of the *Handbook of Social Media Research Methods* with Luke Sloan (Sage, 2017), and co-author of *Real-Life Sociology* with Lorne Tepperman (Oxford University Press, 2018). Her work has appeared in *New Media & Society*, *Journal of Computer-Mediated Communication*, and *Information, Communication & Society*.

Barbara Barbosa Neves (PhD) is Lecturer/Assistant Professor in Sociology at the University of Melbourne, Australia. She is also an elected board member of the International Sociological Association Committee on Family Research (RC06-ISA). For the 2014–2018 term, she is the secretary and treasurer of the committee. Prior to her appointment at the University of Melbourne, she was Associate Director and Researcher at the 'Technologies for Aging Gracefully Lab' (TAGlab), the University of Toronto, Canada. Her research has been examining determinants and social effects of adoption and non-adoption of digital technologies in a life course perspective. In particular, she is interested in the links between digital and social inequalities. More recently, Barbara has been studying the role of digital technologies in addressing issues of social isolation and loneliness in later life. Her work has been published in a range of top-tier outlets in sociology and human–computer interaction, including *Social Science Research*, *Information, Communication & Society*, *CHI*, and *MobileHCI*.

Barry Wellman (PhD) co-directs the NetLab Network and is the Distinguished Visiting Scholar of Ryerson University's Social Media Lab. Wellman is a Fellow of the Royal Society of Canada and the past president of the Sociological Research Association honour society. He has published more than 200 articles, with more than 80 co-authors. His most recent book is *Networked: The New Social Operating System*, with Lee Rainie (MIT Press).

Bernadette Kneidinger-Müller (PhD) is Assistant Professor for Sociology with special focus on the internet at the Otto-Friedrich-University of Bamberg in Germany. Her work is focused on the fields of media and internet sociology. Her research projects analyse the interplay of technological and social changes, especially in the contexts of mobile and computer-mediated communication.

Brianna Routh has a Master's in Public Health Nutrition from the University of Minnesota and is a Registered Dietitian. She is currently a PhD candidate at Iowa State University in Human Development and Family Studies. Her research focuses on how families across the lifespan influence behaviour development and health outcomes, primarily exploring this phenomenon for low-income and minority families. She is also particularly interested in exploring how technology is used as a potential intervention or programme delivery method.

Catalina Arango Patiño is a Colombian social researcher who lives in Montreal, Canada, and holds a Master's degree in Communications from the University of Ottawa. She has led several research projects in the USA, Canada and Colombia on public opinion, civic journalism, deliberative democracy, the use of ICTs by diaspora communities, and the transformation of communication processes in urban communities. Four of these projects have been published by Colombian publications. Her passion is teaching, empowering communities, researching, and writing short stories.

Cláudia Casimiro (PhD) is an Invited Assistant Professor at ISCSP, University of Lisbon, and full research member at the Interdisciplinary Centre for Gender Studies (CIEG). Her PhD is in Social Sciences, with a speciality in sociology. She is co-coordinator of the 'Families and Life Course' network of the Portuguese Sociological Association. Recent publications include the co-edition of a themed number, 'Famílias e Curso de Vida: Potencialidades, limites e desafios metodológicos', for *Sociologia* (Universidade do Porto, 2016), and 'Self-presentation in the Portuguese online dating scene: does gender matter?' (Institute of Network Cultures, 2015). Cláudia's current research interests include families, gender, ICTs, and online dating.

Diana Carvalho is a PhD student in Sociology at the School of Social and Political Science, University of Lisbon (CAPP/ISCSP-ULisboa). She is developing a thesis on youth, work and transitions to adulthood. Additionally, she is a research fellow at the Centre for Administration and Public Policies of the University of Lisbon. Diana has collaborated in several research projects on family, children and youth, and has published work in these areas. She holds a Bachelor's (2010) and a Master's (2013) degree in Sociology from the University Institute of Lisbon (ISCTE-IUL). She also has a postgraduate degree in Data analysis in social sciences from the same university.

Elizabeth Bortolaia Silva is Professor of Sociology at the Open University. Her recent publications include journal special issues: 'Habitus beyond Sociology?', *Sociological Review* (2016), 'Fields, boundaries and social inequalities', *Cultural Sociology* (2013), *Poetics* in *Cultural Capital: Histories, Limits and Prospects* (2011); and books: *Technology, Family, Culture: influences on home life* (Palgrave 2010), *Cultural Analysis and Bourdieu's Legacy* (co-edited, Routledge 2010) and *Culture, Class, Distinction* (co-authored, Routledge 2009). Professor Silva's research derives from engagements with the work of Bourdieu and materialities in social life, with current research on Brazil focusing on 'Exhibiting social change: narrating the past, imagining the future'.

Geoffrey Mead (PhD) is a research fellow in the School of Social and Political Sciences at the University of Melbourne, Australia. His research interests are centred on the concept of symbolic capital in the work of Pierre Bourdieu and the place of perspectivism in the history of sociological thought.

Hua Wang (PhD) is Associate Professor of Communication at the State University of New York at Buffalo. Her research focuses on leveraging digital and interactive media for health promotion and social change, and has been published in journals such as the *American Journal of Public Health*, *Journal of Medical Internet Research*, *Communication Research*, *American Behavioral Scientist*, and *Computers in Human Behavior*. She was the 2014 International Communication Association conference theme chair and theme book editor on technologies and well-being. In 2016, she received University's Exceptional Scholars – Young Investigator Award.

J. Jill Suitor (PhD) is Professor of Sociology and a Faculty Associate of the Center on Aging and the Life Course at Purdue University. Across the past 35 years she has studied middle and later-life families, with emphasis on ties between older parents and adult children, the experiences of adult children during caregiving, and the consequences of family relations for well-being. Since 2000, she has led the Within-Family Differences Study, a NIH-funded panel investigation of the ways in which parents' differentiation among their adult children shapes intergenerational relations and patterns of caregiving and well-being in more than 500 multigenerational families.

Jolynna Sinanan (PhD) is a Research Fellow in Digital Media and Ethnography at the University of Sydney. Prior to this position, she was a Vice Chancellor's Postdoctoral Research Fellow at RMIT University and a Research Fellow in Anthropology at University College London. She is the author of *Social Media in Trinidad* (UCL Press, 2017) and co-author of *Visualising Facebook* (UCL Press, 2017) and *Webcam* (Polity, 2014) with Daniel Miller.

Karolina Kazimierczak (PhD) holds a Master's degree in Sociology from the University of Warsaw and a PhD from the Department of Sociology at Lancaster University. She currently works as Lecturer in Management Studies at the University of Aberdeen Business School. Karolina's research draws on feminist science studies, material semiotics, posthumanism and poststructuralism and explores the performativity of everyday practices. Her recent work has looked at clinical interactions and relations, and at mundane sociotechnical practices at home, as boundary-making projects, which help materialize specific inclusions and exclusions and contribute to the enactment of specific objects/ bodies and attributes/identities.

Larissa Hjorth (PhD) is an artist, digital ethnographer, and Distinguished Professor at RMIT University. Since 2000, she has been researching the gendered and sociocultural dimensions of mobile media and gaming cultures in the Asia–Pacific regions, which are outlined in her books, *Mobile Media in the Asia-Pacific* (Routledge, 2009), *Games & Gaming* (Berg, 2010), *Online@AsiaPacific* (with Michael Arnold, Routledge, 2013), *Understanding Social Media* (with Sam Hinton, Sage, 2013), *Gaming in Social, Locative and Mobile Media* (with Ingrid Richardson, Palgrave, 2014), *Digital Ethnography: Principles and Practice* (with Sarah Pink, Heather Horst, John Postill, Tania Lewis and Jo Tacchi, Sage, 2016), *Screen Ecologies* (with Sarah Pink, Kristen Sharp & Linda Williams, MIT, 2016) and *Haunting Hands* (with Kathleen M. Cumiskey, Oxford, 2017).

Magda Nico (PhD) is a researcher at CIES-IUL and Invited Assistant Professor at the University Institute of Lisbon. She is a representative of the Society for Longitudinal and Life Course Studies, a member of the Pool of European Youth Researchers, and a co-coordinator of the 'Families and Life Course' network of the Portuguese Sociological Association. Among her latest publications are 'Romantic turning points and patterns of leaving home' (*European Societies*, 2016), *Young*

People of the 'Austere Period': Mechanisms and Effects of Inequality over Time (Palgrave Macmillan, 2016) and 'Young individuals as microcosms of the Portuguese crisis' (*Contemporary Social Science Journal*, 2017).

Megan Gilligan (PhD) is an Assistant Professor of Human Development and Family Studies and a Faculty Associate of the Gerontology Program at Iowa State University. Her research focuses on family relationships and well-being, with particular interest in parent-child and sibling relationships in the middle and later years.

Merril Silverstein (PhD) is Professor in the Departments of Sociology and Human Development and Family Science, and inaugural holder of the Marjorie Cantor Chair in Aging Studies, at Syracuse University. In over 150 research publications, he has focused on ageing in the context of family life, with an emphasis on life course and international perspectives on intergenerational relationships and exchanges. He serves as principal investigator of the Longitudinal Study of Generations and has had projects in China, Sweden, the Netherlands, and Israel. He is a Brookdale Fellow and Fulbright Senior Scholar and between 2010 and 2014 served as editor-in-chief of *Journal of Gerontology: Social Sciences.*

Natasha Mauthner (PhD) is Professor of Social Science Philosophy and Method at the University of Aberdeen Business School and a Fellow of the Academy of Social Sciences. She holds an undergraduate degree in the natural sciences and a PhD in social and political science from the University of Cambridge. Following a postdoctoral fellowship at the Harvard University Graduate School of Education, she moved to Scotland where she has held research and lecturing posts at the Universities of Edinburgh and Aberdeen. Her current work seeks to articulate a posthumanist philosophy, methodology, ethics and politics of social science drawing on feminist philosophy of science, feminist science studies, new materialist philosophies, and poststructuralism.

Renwen Zhang is a PhD student in the Media, Technology, and Society programme at Northwestern University. Her research focuses on how technologies facilitate health behaviour change and patient-provider communication; in particular, the role of online health communities in helping people obtain health information and social support. Her publications have appeared in *Computers in Human Behavior* and *Telematics and Informatics.*

Ron Baecker (PhD) is the Director of the Technologies for Aging Gracefully Lab (TAGlab), Department of Computer Science, University of Toronto, Canada. He is Emeritus Professor in Computer Science and one of the most influential scholars in human-computer interaction: he has been named one of the 60 Pioneers of Computer Graphics by ACM SIGGRAPH, has been elected to the CHI Academy by ACM SIGCHI, and has been given the Canadian Human Computer Communications Society Achievement Award.

Sondra Cuban (PhD) is a Professor in the Department of Health & Community Studies at Western Washington University. Her research focuses on the nexus of gender, migration, care and new technologies. Her books are: *Deskilling Migrant Women in the Global Care Industry* (Palgrave Macmillan, 2013) and *Transnational Family Communication: Immigrants and ICTs* (Palgrave Macmillan, 2017). She undertook a Fulbright Core Scholar award in Chile in 2017 to study immigrant women's adaptations.

Sangbo Nam is a doctoral candidate in the department of Human Development and Family Studies with a minor in Gerontology at Iowa State University. His research focuses on older adults' technology use of various kinds, such as information technology, communications technology, entertainment technology, and health technology in the context of family and home environment. He is currently involved in a number of projects on the topic of technology use among older adults using several longitudinal datasets – the Health and Retirement Study, the Within-Family Differences Study, and the Wisconsin Longitudinal Study.

Siyun Peng is a dual title PhD candidate in Sociology and Gerontology, and a member of the Center on Aging and the Life Course at Purdue University. His research focuses on life course, ageing, health, family, and marriage with a particular interest in the role of family relationships in the process of ageing.

Woosang Hwang is a doctoral candidate in the Department of Human Development and Family Science at Syracuse University. During the doctoral programme, he took a Certificate of Advanced Study in Public Management and Policy from the Department of Public Administration and International Affairs. Currently, he is working in the Aging Studies Institute as a research assistant. His research focuses on low fertility, population ageing, and family policies. He received his BA in Child and Family Studies/Mass Communication and his MA in Child and Family Studies from Yonsei University, South Korea.

Yuka Sakamoto (PhD) is Associate Professor of Family and Consumer Sciences at the Graduate School of Natural and Living Sciences Education in Naruto University of Education, Japan. Her main areas of expertise include alternative work arrangement and work–family life, female labour participation, children's lifestyle and consumer studies. She has directed three family lifestyle research projects funded by the Japan Society for the Promotion of Science. She has extensive experience in working in both quantitative and qualitative research projects and is especially familiar with quantitative research methods, study design and statistical data analysis.

Acknowledgements

The editors gratefully acknowledge the work and dedication of all contributors, particularly considering the tight deadlines. We also thank the outstanding Policy Press team, particularly Isobel Bainton, Shannon Kneis, Helen Davis, Rebecca Tomlinson and Ruth Wallace – what an extraordinary group of women! Finally, we are grateful to our families and friends. Barbara would like to thank Marcos Caceres, Maria Helena Silva Barbosa, Tiago Neves, Ane Neves, Orlando Neves, Manuela Neves, Jorge Neves, the Caceres family, Barbara & Alex Noriega, José Luís Reis, Carla Brás, Barry and Bev. Wellman, Fausto Amaro, Romana Xerez, Mr. Oily, and the wonderful ISA-RC06 community. All help me 'doing' and 'feeling family' every single day. Cláudia would like to thank all those with whom she maintains strong 'kinship ties' and 'bonds of affection' and who have been her personal and professional inspiration and motivation. A special thanks to the Coordinator of the Interdisciplinary Center for Gender Studies (CIEG), Professor Anália Torres, for her decisive and genuine support. May each one of you find in this book the testimony of my gratitude and recognition.

The family has become a network

Barry Wellman

Once upon a time, many families in the developed world lived in little boxes surrounded by white picket fences. For example, *Fun with Dick and Jane* was the school primer I read as a child in 1947. In this first book for any of us six-year-olds, breadwinner 'Dad' went off to work every morning, leaving his housewife 'Mom' at home to do household chores and look after their children – 'Dick' and 'Jane' – along with their dog 'Spot'.

As Bob Dylan tells Mr Jones, stuck in an old paradigm, the times are changing in how families are constituted and connect: The old road is rapidly aging for mothers and fathers. Something is indeed happening, and this challenging book provides a good handle on what contemporary families are like.

Change does not happen in a vacuum. To gain perspective on the present nature of families, it is useful to think about the profound social, cultural, financial, political, and technological transformations that have occurred since Dick and Jane's 1950s. Although most of the specific phenomena I discuss will seem obvious to contemporary readers, taken together they describe a profound change from the solidary family groups of the 1950s (and before) to the networked families of today. I draw on evidence principally from North America to illustrate these changes, although I believe they are more widely applicable elsewhere.

Composition

In the twenty-first century, Dick and Jane are each likely to link up with several other Dicks and Janes. The taboo on premarital sex has weakened. For example, in 2005 nearly half (43%) of Canadians aged 15-19 had had premarital sex, and it is likely that much of the laggard half had sexual relations sometime afterward (Rotermann, 2008). This is quite a change from the 1950s' quixotic attempt to preserve premarital chastity.

It is now common to live together as 'partners' without exchanging marital vows or filing legal documents. While some states recognize this as 'common-law marriage' after a few years, in practice it has less legal or moral force than marriage. Being 'partners' is often a half-way house for young adults between dating (or what old-time Dick and Jane would have called 'going steady') and marriage, but it is also a common practice for divorced or widowed adults who have moved in with new partners without going through the formality of marriage. Indeed, nearly one-quarter (22%) of Canadian couples were in common-law relationships in 2016 (Grenier, 2017).

Even when marriage occurs, it is often not a lifetime experience. The 1950s' normative scorn regarding divorce and remarriage has so lessened that US President Trump – with his three wives and multiple affairs – is strongly supported in 2017 by evangelical Christians supposedly committed to the sanctity of a single lifetime marriage (Worthen, 2017).

It is not just Dick and Jane who are getting married; it is Dick with Dick as well as Jane with Jane. The past decade has seen a rush to legalize and legitimize what had hitherto been the illicit, underground practice of same-sex marriage – or what eager practitioner Oscar Wilde called 'the love that dares not speak its own name'. Since Canada legalized gay marriage in 2005, the percentage of gay couples has zoomed, up 61% from 2006 to 2016 (Grenier, 2017). The current Premier of Ontario is a lesbian with a wife, while seven members of the United States Congress are openly gay, lesbian, or bisexual (Wikipedia, 2017).

Large families are rare; zero or one child is becoming the norm (plus a cat or dog). The children in a home are more likely to be Dick *or* Jane rather than Dick *and* Jane. For example, 28% of Canadians lived alone in 2016, up from only 7% in 1956 (Grenier, 2017). Spot is less of a family pet and more of a beloved companion of single or childless couples. Part of the reason is birth control, which has moved from unreliable condoms to pills, IUDs, and other reliable and non-obtrusive devices. A friend tells me: 'My husband wants to have kids, but I don't tell him that I always have an IUD inside.' My aforementioned friend is a hard-working career woman, which leads to another aspect of changing families: *a higher percentage of women are leaving the home to do paid work.* More than half of all North American women do paid work (Rainie and Wellman, 2012). No longer is Mom staying at home to mind Dick and Jane during the daytime. She needs to do paid work that will help pay for family housing.

Bit work has taken over from atom work, making it easier for many women to find paid employment. More than half the work in North America has shifted from growing, making, mining, and transporting things – *atom work* in the 1950s' material economy – to selling, describing, and analysing things via words and pictures – *bit work* in the information economy (Florida, 2014; Rainie and Wellman, 2012). Less manual labour and more computer-based labour physically empowers more Moms to do work away from home – and in some cases to do paid work at home.

An appreciable amount of the new forms of work is done by women for women. With homemakers also becoming breadwinners outside the home, paid worker substitutes abound. The frequency of family dinners at home has declined sharply (Putnam, 2000; Walton et al, 2016). Fast food and family restaurants take the place of home cooking; the 37,000 McDonald's outlets (14,155 in the United States, 22,744 elsewhere) make it the world's biggest chain (Statista, 2017). Daycare centres care for Dick and Jane after school, and dog-walkers care for Spot's needs. Local pedestrian-focused stores for daily shopping have given way to shopping centres with large parking lots that get most business after work or on weekends.

Connectivity

Moms did not magically decide to leave the home to do paid work. Several affordances have been needed to accompany the demands of paying for hefty mortgages or rents. Consider how *family mobility has become personal mobility.* In the 1950s, my family piled into the sedan most weekends to drive to visit one of my parents' siblings. It was the family group that made these journeys: Mom and Dad and Barry meeting another nuclear family of close kin. But affluence and suburbanization led to a need for Mom to get her own car. Personal mobility plus economic need led to Moms leaving home during the day to do paid work.

Personal mobility often means air travel. When we drove to our relatives' homes in the winter, we used to sing 'over the river and through the woods, to grandmother's house we go'. We are likely now to shudder 'over to the airport check-in kiosk and through the metal detector'. My relatives now live in Los Angeles, 4000 kilometres away from my Toronto home. Fortunately, the real cost of long-distance travel has decreased from a rare luxury to a routine travel cost. And when we do not have the time or money to fly to Los Angeles, we can always telephone them. It's free now, where it cost $1.00 per minute in the 1950s. And we can even see them via Skype, a technology that in the 1950s was only dreamed of in science fiction.

Personal communication has replaced household communication. In the 1950s, my family used to gather around the single household phone to talk collectively to our Los Angeles relatives. It was black and the handset was coil-wired to the body. When we called someone, we did not know which family member was answering (and they did not know who was calling), spawning random conversations before we asked to speak to the wanted person. But family phone togetherness has gone the way of the rotary dial. Personal mobile phones vastly outnumber fixed landlines (Rainie and Wellman, 2012). (To the amazement of younger colleagues, my wife and I still keep a landline at home so that we can talk jointly to our Los Angeles relatives.) Mom and Dad (and often Dick and Jane) each have a phone in their pocket or bag, great for being always connected but awful for collective phone conversations. This makes telephonic relationships basically one-on-one. Mobile phones also help parents track their children's whereabouts as they wander far from home.

Each individual has their own personal computer, with their own private login and password. Communities have moved from neighbourhoods to networks. To be sure, social media helps relationships to persist at long distances, but individuals maintain their own unique networks – neighbours know what Dick and Jane are up to only if they are 'friends' on social media.

Personal information gathering has replaced family sharing. My wife and I still try to watch TV network news most nights, just as Mom and Dad did in the 1950s. But now we come forearmed, having each read online new media and blogs during the day. These media are personalized, so we have different pieces of information to share, and sometimes different interpretations. Not only have print newspapers rapidly dwindled in number and subscriptions, television watching is way down and whole-household TV watching is down even more. What used to be seen on the family TV has become individualized streaming on personal computers, smartphones, and TVs that have moved out of the family room into individual bedrooms. Family members who may watch violent shows such as *Game of Thrones* may be developing different interpretations of the world than those chuckling through *Seinfeld* reruns.

Networked households

Such structural changes in developed countries have weakened traditional families but increased their connectivity as individuals. In Hillary Clinton's 1996 book, *It Takes a Village*, she recognized that families do not operate as gated households but as networks. Although the trend to networked families began before the advent of digital media, their intrinsically *personal* nature has encouraged the transmutation of solidary households behind white picket fences into networks. Family members use their cars, phones, and the internet to stay connected, even as Dad, Mom, Dick, and Jane go their physically separate ways. (And even Spot can wear a tracker.)

Older adults, the most reluctant to be digitally connected, are now using the internet and mobile phones. Those with limited physical mobility especially value being connected with local and far-flung family members of both their own and younger generations. Dick and Jane have weekly Skype chats with their grandparents, who often find joy in watching them on webcams.

Each family member operates as a semi-autonomous individual, with their own agenda, using a multitude of transportation and personal communication media to coordinate with each other. Rather than being lonely and isolated, families continue to be thickly connected at anytime and anywhere, with in-person contact supplemented by the internet and smartphones. Not only have families changed in composition and connectivity, they have changed in their lifestyles. Digital media have become thoroughly embedded in their lives. Paradoxically, digital media – in conjunction with personal automobiles and low-cost airfares – have empowered family members with the ability to go their separate ways while at the same time keeping them more connected. Dick and Jane – and Mom and Dad – are still having fun as networked individuals in networked families.

Acknowledgements
I appreciate the advice of the editors of this book as well as Brent Berry, Anabel Quan-Haase, Lee Rainie, Hua Wang, Renwen Zhang, and Beverly Wellman. This research was supported by the Social Sciences and Humanities Research Council of Canada.

References

Dylan, B. (1964) *The Times They Are A-Changin'*, Los Angeles: Warner Brothers.

Florida, R. (2014) *The Rise of the Creative Class – Revisited* (revised edn), New York: Basic Books.

Grenier, E. (2017) 'More Canadians living alone and without children, census figures show', *CBC News*, 2 August, www.cbc.ca/news/politics/census-2016-marriage-children-families-1.4231163

Putnam, R. (2000) *Bowling Alone: The Collapse and Revival of American Community,* New York: Simon and Schuster.

Rainie, L. and Wellman, B. (2012) *Networked: The New Social Operating System*, Cambridge, MA: MIT Press.

Rotermann, M. (2008) 'Trends in teen sexual behaviour and condom use', *Health Reports*, 19(3): 53–57.

Statista. (2017) 'McDonald's – Statistics & facts', www.statista.com/topics/1444/mcdonalds/

Walton, K., Kleinman, K. P., Rifas-Shiman, S. L., Horton, N. J. , Gillman, M. W., Field, A. E., Austin, S. B., ... Haines, J. (2016) 'Secular trends in family dinner frequency among adolescents', *BMC Research Notes*, 9(35): 1–5. https://doi.org/doi:10.1186/s13104-016-1856-2

Wikipedia. (2017) 'List of LGBT members of the United States Congress', https://en.wikipedia.org/wiki/List_of_LGBT_members_of_the_United_States_Congress

Worthen, M. (2017) 'A match made in heaven', *The Atlantic*, May, www.theatlantic.com/magazine/archive/2017/05/a-match-made-in-heaven/521409/

ONE

Connecting families?
An introduction

Barbara Barbosa Neves and Cláudia Casimiro

Context

This edited collection seeks to critically examine the intersection of family life and the use of information and communication technologies (ICTs) within generations and in a life course perspective. Over the past two decades, ICTs such as the internet and personal mobile computing have started to permeate everyday family life in industrialized countries (Eurostat, 2017; Hughes and Hans, 2001; Pew Research Center, 2017; Rainie and Wellman, 2012). Yet we still lack a thorough understanding of the interplay of ICTs and family dynamics in different regions and contexts. To address this gap, we invited researchers examining this interplay to submit their work to two sessions at conferences of the International Sociological Association (ISA). These sessions were organized for the ISA Family Research Committee (RC06), the last of which was held at the 2016 ISA Forum in Vienna. The outstanding number and quality of submissions highlighted the increasing relevance of this topic for sociologists. Our sessions aimed to address the following questions:

- Are ICTs connecting families?
- What does this connectedness mean in terms of family routines, relationships, norms, work, intimacy, and privacy?
- How do family members envision the role of ICTs in connecting families?

This book emerged from these questions, and from new angles identified in the conference sessions. Despite the growing interest in the subject (Kennedy and Wellman, 2007), as well as influential sociological work on families and domestic technologies (Cowan,

1983; Silva, 2010; Wajcman, 2010), current sociological research on ICTs and families remains scant and scattered.

There are, of course, a few notable exceptions. The seminal issue of *Marriage & Family Review* by Marvin B. Sussman in 1985 on 'Personal Computers and the Family' – also published as a book by Haworth Press in 1985 – presented groundbreaking articles on computer use within families, its implications for children's development and family life, and its role in family therapy, counselling, and empowerment. In the introduction to the book, Sussman considers changes occurring in professional environments and occupational systems as a consequence of the introduction of computers to reflect upon 'microcomputers' (home computers) and families. He also enquires about the relationship between social stratification and technology, and explores the use of personal computing to diagnose and treat patients in areas such as marriage and sex. Sussman recognizes, however, that the edition was based on scarce empirical data, only warranting rich descriptions and conjectures about the impact of home computers on family life. He concludes that the collection:

> Should be viewed as the opening of a new vineyard for empirical work on the meaning and significance of a revolutionary telecommunication device upon the organization, values, ideologies, and behavioral practices of family systems. The various authors have birthquaked multitudinous ideas, issues, and problems. It will take a decade to research them appropriately. The technology is changing so fast and changes in families lag not too far behind, [which] means that some of the queries and concerns expressed by our authors may not be germane or may have already been answered at the time this issue is read. (Sussman, 1985, p 5)

Despite extraordinary advances and uptake in ICTs, some of the topics explored by the authors of this 1985 collection (with the exception of some grand predictions) still resonate in 2018 – particularly in terms of critical themes, such as work–life balance, family conflicts, gender inequalities, social class, social connectedness, and intergenerational families. Nevertheless, as shown in the literature, family life has been characterized by both changes and continuities over time (Adams and Trost, 2004; Casper and Bianchi, 2001; Lück et al, 2017).

Twenty-five years later, *Marriage and Family Review* presented a collection on 'Families and Communication' edited by Lynn Blinn-

Pike (2009). This new issue includes a variety of articles examining digital technologies and family life, covering important themes such as online methods, eHealth, social networking sites (MySpace), and internet dating. In her introduction, Blinn-Pike offers an overview of the role of home computer and internet use in the family from the 1980s to the 2000s, showing that computers only became prevalent in American homes in the 2000s. She emphasizes two central points: (i) we are still trying to understand how ICTs affect family interaction over time, and (ii) we still need to deconstruct utopian versus dystopian visions of technology.

These points continue to be relevant today – the interrogation in our title 'Connecting Families?' captures this tension. But since Blinn-Pike's edited issue was published, the number of households with computers and internet access has increased in the US and across the globe. According to the US Census Bureau (2014), in 2013, 84% of households had a computer (compared to 51% in 2000) and 74% had some form of internet access. In 2009, 62% of American adults had broadband internet service at home, while in 2016 that average reached 73% (Pew Research Center, 2017). In the European Union (28 countries, 2016), 85% of households had a computer and 83% had a home broadband internet service (Eurostat, 2017). A number of Latin American countries had a comparably high average of households with a computer in 2014: 72% in Chile, 58% in Argentina, and 55% in Brazil (Pew Research Center, 2015). In the same period, 59% of Chinese households had a computer (Pew Research Center, 2015). The lowest computer ownership rates are found in sub-Saharan African countries – approximately 25% in 2014 (Pew Research Center, 2015). Nonetheless, considering other ICTs, the number of mobile phone and internet users has been growing globally: in 2017, 50% of the world's population was online – which represents a growth of 936% since 2000 (Internet World Stats, 2017) – and 66% of the global population had a mobile phone (We Are Social and Hootsuite, 2017).

Even though both *Marriage and Family Review* issues (Sussman in 1985 and Blinn-Pike in 2009) were cutting-edge, they were mostly restricted to North America. The 2009 issue does include one article on international adoption by US families (Gill, 2009), and a pioneering study on transnational Turkish families and their telephone and email communication (Şenyürekli and Detzner, 2009). Interestingly, work on transnational families and ICTs has been advancing considerably in the last two years (see Baldassar et al, 2016). Notwithstanding the two international articles, the geographical focus was especially limited.

In this context, our conference sessions were tasked with assembling scattered research on the topic, with a focus on international studies and more diverse approaches to ICTs and families. With these sessions, we realized that the interest in the subject by family scholars was growing and there was a need for a sociological space of discussion. We also realized that existing research tends to focus on studies of a particular age group or life stage, from children and young adults (Blair et al, 2015; Ito et al, 2009; Livingstone and Haddon, 2009) to older adults (Blaschke et al, 2009; Neves et al, 2013, 2017a, 2017b). As such, a life course perspective is widely lacking in the literature. This is a critical perspective for ICTs and families, as it can ensure that we are taking into account different roles, positions, meanings, and contexts over an individual's life span. A life course perspective emphasizes a continuum of social events and transitions over time – a continuum that both affects and helps make sense of family life and ICTs. Hence, the original questions that guided our conference sessions motivated our subsequent exploration of a life course perspective. This book is the result of those sessions, specifically of identified gaps and needs.

To provide a comprehensive approach to the subject, our edited collection brings together theoretical, methodological, and empirical work on family life and ICTs in a life course perspective. This combination offers students, researchers, and practitioners a variety of tools to analyse and understand how ICTs are used, appropriated, and domesticated in family life. These tools allow for an informed and critical study of ICTs and family dynamics, practices, management, conflicts, intimacy, care, solidarity, and intergenerational relations.

Conceptualizing family, generations, ICTs, and the life course

Family and generations

The concept of 'family', used so often throughout this book, may have different interpretations since the term is polysemic. As McCarthy (2012, p 69) points out, a diversity of terms to delineate the connotations 'family' can assume have 'been proposed and discussed (Morgan, 2003), including "family" as an adjective (as in "family practices", Morgan, 1996, 2011), or an alternative language altogether, such as "intimacy" (discussed in Jamieson, 1998, 2004), "relatedness" (Carsten, 2004), or "relationships" (discussed by Brynin and Ermisch, 2009)'. Such multiplicity of meanings corresponds to the changes occurring in the family in the last few decades, particularly in the Western world.

We have witnessed the affirmation of new trends in the emergence of modern forms of family organization and legitimacy – such as the family's deinstitutionalization (Beck and Beck-Gernsheim, 1995). Practices, values, and social attitudes regarding family life changed substantially over the last few decades (Torres et al, 2013): building a family, living in it, undoing or rebuilding it, has become increasingly diversified and informal (Casimiro, 2015), particularly when compared to more homogeneous models from the past. The Parsonian family model (in which a father, mother, and children were placed in a rigid hierarchy with socially fixed roles) has shifted to more flexible, diverse, multifaceted, and democratic family models in which family members' power and roles tend to be negotiated (Casimiro, 2011; Torres et al, 2008).

Of course, nuclear heterosexual families continue to exist, but there has been a pluralization of the composition and modes of family functioning and bonding: the social construction of family ties is becoming versatile as changes operate in the 'boundaries between kinship ties and a wider array of affinities' (Wall and Gouveia, 2014, p 352). As such, David Morgan (2011) reframes family as a process rather than a fixed institution, and argues that contemporary families can be 'defined more by "doing" family things than by "being" a family' and the 'diversity of family composition and the fluidity of family relationships' means that those we consider 'our family' can change across the life course (Finch, 2007, pp 66-67). Although sociologically and in everyday life the term 'family' may have acquired various meanings, it remains a central social concept as well as an object of study. In fact, 'while concepts of personal lives and intimacy have much to offer they can not capture the full range and nature of relations raised through the lens of family' (Gillies, 2011, p 1). This book is based on such comprehensive understanding of family and its social role(s).

Related to family is the concept of generations (Koller, 1974), insofar as families are composed by and based on intergenerational ties and dynamics (for example, relationships between parents and children). The term 'generation' is, however, multidimensional and has different meanings (Neves and Fernandes, 2016). For instance, one can find a plethora of labels and interpretations for generations, including the popular: millennials, consumerist, welfare, 1968, Gulf War, X, economic, yuppie, MTV, Facebook (Szydlik, 2016). In addition, different definitions abound in this 'jungle of generational terminology'

(Szydlik, 2016, p 9). Nonetheless, two types of generations are frequently used in the sociological literature: (i) a *familial* or *family generation*, based on kinship (micro level), and (ii) a *social generation*, based on a birth cohort that experiences similar social, cultural, economic, and political events at the meso and macro levels (Neves and Fernandes, 2016; Szydlik, 2016). Yet there are several challenges with delimiting social generations as discussed by sociologist Karl Mannheim in his influential essay 'The Sociological Problem of Generations' (1952). These challenges go beyond agreeing on chronological periods as shared experiences/characteristics and their lifelong effects are hard to categorize; even today there are no set criteria to identify social generations (Szydlik, 2016). Mannheim (1952, p 297) also explores the familiar generation; according to him, the family is not a social generation but a 'concrete social group' that encompasses different levels of kinship and where presumably members acknowledge each other and/or share common interests and goals. This understanding is still useful for contemporary sociologists (see Szydlik, 2016). In this book, the concept of generations corresponds mainly to familial generations.

Information and communication technologies (ICTs)

Since the term information and communication technologies has no universally agreed-upon definition, it is important to address it at the outset of this collection. ICTs are an extension of the concept information technology (IT), which seems to have first appeared in an essay by Harold Leavitt and Thomas Whisler (1958) on how business would change with electronic tools (Stafford and Hillyer, 2012). In this essay, Leavitt and Whisler (1958) state that information technology includes instruments that: (i) quickly process large amounts of information (computers), (ii) are based on the use of statistical and mathematical techniques for problem-solving (mathematical programming), and (iii) result in simulations and reasoning through computational programs. It was only later, in 1986, that Everett Rogers considered the role of social communication in the study of technological innovations by advancing the term communication technology (CT) (Stafford and Hillyer, 2012). He broadly defined it as 'the hardware equipment, organizational structures, and social values by which individuals collect, process, and exchange information with other individuals' (Rogers, 1986, p 2). Examples of CT include the invention of spoken language and computer-based communication systems (Rogers, 1986). As noted by Stafford and Hillyer (2012), these authors did not pair their concepts, but their combination was unavoidable with the evolution of computer technologies; as such, the concept became popular in the 1990s as scholarship on the uses and impacts of ICTs increased.

Conceptually, ICTs are based on the convergence of technological development in terms of space, time, and digital devices (Aebischer and Hilty, 2015). Because digital technologies seem to be constantly changing and being reshaped in contemporary societies, providing a comprehensive definition of ICTs is challenging. Faced with this problem, Aebischer and Hilty (2015) suggest that enumerating types of devices might be easier than aspiring to craft a precise definition. We follow their lead by indicating the devices/tools that are usually associated with ICTs, namely computers (including laptops and tablets), the internet (the web, email, social media, social networking sites), and mobile phones. The chapters in this book draw on the study of these ICTs. This enumeration matches the United Nations' ICT Development Index, which collects a set of 11 internationally agreed ICT indicators since 2009 (United Nations International Telecommunication Union, 2016). In terms of access, the Index considers the following devices: computers, the internet, mobile phones, and fixed-telephone subscriptions. In terms of use, it only considers computers, the internet, and mobile phones (not telephones). Fixed-telephone subscriptions are incorporated in the index because of their role in providing internet access – however, in some studies the telephone is categorized as an ICT precisely due to that infrastructure and diffusion value, particularly in developing nations (Sassi and Goaied, 2013). One of the authors of this collection presents a study of long-distance calls through landline telephones and a thought-provoking discussion of this device as an ICT.

The life course perspective

The life course perspective represents a 'theoretical orientation' (Elder et al, 2003) as well as an analytical tool. The general aim of a life course approach is to analyse how historical, socioeconomic, cultural, and demographic changes, influence and shape biographical trajectories of individuals and groups such as generations. This perspective, popular in various social and behavioural sciences, has been facilitated by longitudinal and panel studies (Elder, 2000). Specifically, the life course approach focuses on important events, stages, and transitions experienced by individuals or generations in various domains of life (that is, family and social relations, education, work, leisure, health). The interdependence of these spheres is at the heart of life course research, as captured by the following questions: how do people live their lives from childhood to old age? How do life events and stages – childhood, adulthood, marriage, parenthood, unemployment, and migration, for instance – influence the course of ageing? How do historical, social, and economic contexts impact on the development and evolution of individual or generational pathways?

However, understanding 'life course' as a construct and not as a 'theoretical orientation' often leads to conceptual confusion (Nico et al, 2016). This conceptual confusion has resulted in an undifferentiated use of terms such as 'life span', 'life history', and 'life cycle' (Elder et al, 2003; O'Rand and Krecker, 1990). This 'linguistic economy' (Adams, cited by O'Rand and Krecker, 1990, p 242) is challenged by Elder and colleagues (2003, pp 4–5):

> Life span… specifies the temporal scope of inquiry and specialization. Thus, a life-span study is one that extends across a substantial portion of life, particularly one that links behavior in two or more life stages …. Life history, on the other hand, typically indicates the chronology of activities or events across the life course (residence, household composition, family events) and is often drawn from age-event matrices or retrospective life calendars… Lastly, life cycle has been used to describe a sequence of events in life, but in population studies it refers to the reproductive process from one generation to the next. (Elder et al, 2003, pp 4–5)

Life course is a more complex concept that encompasses three organizing axes, namely trajectory, transition, and turning points (Elder and Shanahan, 2006). Additionally, the life course perspective is based on five paradigmatic principles (Elder, 2000; Elder and Giele, 2009). The first one is *development throughout life*: the need to have a long-term perspective in research and analysis that takes into consideration that the biological, psychological, and social development of an individual is a process ranging from birth to death. The second principle is *time and historical place*. This directly points to the importance of context: the course of individuals is integrated and shaped by the time and place within which their lives unfold. The third principle is *social timing of lives*, and it refers to the moment in which core events happen – the moment and the order of such events have an impact on the rest of the individual or generational life course. The interdependence of lives, or *linked lives*, is the fourth principle. Such a principle holds that the course of a person's life is directly connected to the life course of those around them: 'lives are lived interdependently and social and historical influences are expressed through this network of shared relationships' (Elder, 2000, p 1620). The last principle, *human agency in choice-making and action*, emphasizes that individuals are not passive entities upon whom social and historical structural elements are unconditionally imposed, but rather active agents that make choices and act, thus shaping their own life course.

This book draws on the aforementioned axes and five principles to conceptualize the life course. However, the reader will notice that 'generations' is also part of the title. This was used to signify the strong focus on intergenerational linked lives and transitions in our life course approach. For instance, research has been showing the role of intergenerational relations in stimulating adoption of new technology at turning points (that is, retirement, institutionalization) and the potential of ICTs to build generational bridges (Neves and Amaro, 2012; Neves and Fernandes, 2016; Neves et al, 2013). But most current research on ICTs and family is still limited by short-term longitudinal data. As longitudinal data begins to be collected more systematically, we will be able to employ the perspectives and instruments discussed in this collection to advance our understanding of the relationship between ICTs, families, and all dimensions of the life course. As such, another core motivation of this book was to reflect on possibilities and challenges. Furthermore, as noted by Bengtson and Allen (2009, p 469), in applying the life course to families we need to move beyond the individual and the micro family level of analysis to 'examine the unfolding history of intimate connections in families and the social context of such long-term relationships in terms of social structure and historical location'. Our edited collection takes this broader approach to family, linked lives, and transitions.

Aims of the collection

- This publication aims to fill a gap in family and ICT studies by bringing together innovative theoretical, methodological, and empirical work using a life course perspective (intergenerational linked lives and transitions).
- It aims to disseminate new sociological and related research that is relevant to researchers, students, and practitioners interested in family and technology studies.
- It also aims to challenge isolated understandings of ICTs and family life to inform research, practice, and social policy.

Overview of the book

This book is organized in two main parts. The first collects and reflects upon different theoretical and conceptual perspectives to help frame research in the field, and on methodological techniques and contributions to study family life and ICTs in a life course perspective. The second presents empirical research from different regions around the world. It features groundbreaking empirical research based on current cross-cultural studies and best practices that combine family and technology studies. Each chapter ends with a set of highlights ('In brief') that summarizes key points, concepts, theories, and methodologies. The collection is introduced with a foreword by Professor Barry Wellman, a pioneer in the sociological study of technology, community, and networks; and concludes with an afterword by Professor Elizabeth Silva, a sociologist with internationally recognized research on family, gender, and domestic technologies.

Part I starts with a critical overview of four theoretical perspectives on technology and society (technological determinism, social constructivism, actor–network theory, and posthumanism) by Natasha Mauthner and Karolina Kazimierczak. They eloquently cover these perspectives, situate them within current empirical research on ICTs and family dynamics, and advance our understanding of the emerging posthumanist framework that originated from feminist studies of science and technology. Building on this general outline, we then move to Mead and Neves' chapter on two recursive (situational and integrative) approaches to study technology adoption within family and the life course. The authors explore assumptions, applications, opportunities, and challenges of actor–network theory and the new strong structuration theory to frame and explain relationships between technology use, family life, and life transitions. Next, Quan-Haase, Wang, Wellman, and Zhang offer a discussion of networked individualism as a conceptual and analytical model to shed light on social and network transitions affecting families and communities since the 1990s. These include moving from bounded groups established by locality and social class to various far-flung networks based on common interests and sociability, the pervasiveness of internet-based communication, and the ubiquity of mobile devices that allow for the constant availability of personalized communication. The authors use research on older adults and digital media use to connect with family and friends (from the famous East York project in Toronto) to illustrate those transitions and their implications. Amanda du Preez then reflects on the affordances of ICTs and the different intergenerational practices of sharing (or 'oversharing') online, using the concepts of 'aesthetics of appearance' (representation that endures over time and space) and 'aesthetics of disappearance' (constant presentism), as developed by French theorist Paul Virilio. This is a provocative, reflective piece that introduces new concepts to explore digital practices and family life. Taken together, these chapters present both well-established and innovative frameworks to theorize about the relationship between ICTs, family, and the life course.

The next chapters take the reader through research methods and strategies to design and study the subject. Authors go beyond a description of available techniques to actively engage with the practicalities and limitations of each method. We begin with Maddox's contribution on digital methods. This chapter matches the analytical elements of a life course approach in the study of ICTs and families to the emerging affordances and applications ('tropes') of digital methods (including data scraping and visualization, Big Data analysis, among others). It concludes with a critical discussion on the limitations and ethical issues of employing these methods. Next, Neves, Baecker, Carvalho, and Sanders address the design and implementation of a cross-disciplinary (sociology and computer science), mixed methods project to investigate technology adoption in later life and family dynamics. They reflect on the benefits and challenges of combining sociological (interviews, field observations) and human-computer interaction (usability and accessibility testing) techniques in their research and its implications for technology, family, and life course studies. Part I finishes with Casimiro and Nico's chapter on a dual relationship between technology and family. The authors show that technologies can be envisaged both as an object of study – technology usage and its impact on family relationships in a life course perspective – and as an instrument – technology as a tool. In the latter, they focus on computer assisted qualitative data analysis software (CAQDAS) to tackle problems of comparability and triangulation of qualitative and quantitative data in life course research.

Part II begins with a chapter investigating the use of communication technologies (emailing and texting) for the maintenance of intergenerational solidarity. Peng, Silverstein, Suitor, Gilligan, Hwang, Nam, and Routh compare data from two US sources and from different years (the 2008 Within-Family Differences Study and the 2016 Longitudinal Study of Generations) to analyse patterns and predictors of older mothers' digital solidarity. The temporal distance between studies – almost a decade – allows the authors to conclude that mothers in the 2016 sample are more likely to use communication technology with their offspring than are mothers in the 2008 sample. The next chapter by Jolynna Sinanan and Larissa Hjorth shows how digital media practices, relating to care and intimacy (the 'intimate surveillance'), are being played out in the daily lives of intergenerational and cross-cultural families in Melbourne, Australia. Catalina Arango Patiño then provides a vivid picture of the positive and negative impacts of ICTs in the storytelling processes among transnational families (Colombian migrants residing in Montreal, Canada). More than constraining storytelling, the use of ICTs to share photographs, texts, emoticons, and videos emerges as a catalyst. Nevertheless, that digital mediation seems to be altering family storytelling. Also exploring the theme of transnational families, Cuban's chapter focuses on how Mexican migrants in the US provide support to distant older family members, namely their left-behind parents affected by health problems. The author proposes an interesting shift in the way we investigate the interplay between ICTs and transnational families, suggesting that besides technology affordances we should consider the role family members play in the establishment of care-based communication ('rescue chains'). Next, Bernadette Kneidinger-Müller's study carried out among young German adults (aged 20–30), demonstrates how smartphones may function as a relevant digital tool for maintaining both family and romantic relationships. Analysing interviews and diary research, the author reaches a set of important conclusions: many of the interviewees cannot imagine a life without mobile phones; text messages are used for different reasons depending on relationship types; and when in the physical presence of ties, texting with family members or a romantic partner happens less than with friends or acquaintances. This second part of the book concludes with a chapter by Yuka Sakamoto on the impact ICTs are having in Japan, especially its effects (for example through telework) on the permeability of work-family borders, and consequently on work-family conflicts over childcare. Through the use of structural equation modelling, Sakamoto illustrates how intensive use of ICTs is increasing work-family conflicts.

These carefully curated chapters, from five different continents, offer theoretical, methodological, and empirical approaches to understand and study: (i) how ICTs relate to family life (including intergenerational relationships, routines, norms, work, intimacy, and privacy), (ii) how ICTs are used and integrated in family dynamics, and (iii) what opportunities and challenges arise from that use in a life course perspective. In particular, they provide foundational knowledge to support students, researchers, and practitioners in the analysis of current and emerging technologies – the insights, guidelines, and practices presented herein transcend specific technologies and can be applied in different settings. It is our hope that scholars can test and expand on these perspectives to examine novel and more diverse contexts. We believe this book lays the ground for future research and new directions in the burgeoning area of ICTs, family, and the life course.

References

Adams, B. N. and Trost, J. (2004) *Handbook of World Families*, Thousand Oaks, CA: Sage.

Aebischer, B. and Hilty, L. M. (2015) 'The energy demand of ICT: A historical perspective and current methodological challenges', in L. Hilty and B. Aebischer (eds) *ICT Innovations for Sustainability*, New York: Springer, pp 71-103.

Baldassar, L., Nedelcu, M., Merla, L. and Wilding, R. (2016) 'ICT-based co-presence in transnational families and communities: Challenging the premise of face-to-face proximity in sustaining relationships', *Global Networks*, 16(2): 133-144, https://doi.org/10.1111/glob.12108

Beck, U. and Beck-Gernsheim, E. (1995) *The Normal Chaos of Love*, Cambridge: Polity Press.

Bengtson, V. L. and Allen, K. R. (2009) 'The life course perspective applied to families over time', in P. Boss, W. J. Doherty, R. LaRossa, W. R. Schumm and S. K. Steinmetz (eds) *Sourcebook of Family Theories and Methods*, New York: Springer, pp 469-504.

Blair, S. E., Claster, P. N. and Claster, S. M. (eds) (2015) *Technology and Youth: Growing Up in a Digital World*, New York: Emerald Group.

Blaschke, C. M., Freddolino, P. P. and Mullen, E. E. (2009) 'Ageing and technology: A review of the research literature', *British Journal of Social Work*, 39(4): 641-656. https://doi.org/10.1093/bjsw/bcp025

Blinn-Pike, L. (2009) 'Technology and the family: An overview from the 1980s to the present', *Marriage & Family Review*, 45(6-8): 567-575, https://doi.org/10.1080/01494920903224459

Casimiro, C. (2011) 'Tensões, tiranias e violência familiar: Da invisibilidade à denúncia', in J. Mattoso and A. N. de Almeida (eds) *História da Vida Privada*, Lisboa: Círculo de Leitores, pp 112-140.

Casimiro, C. (2015) 'Self-presentation in the Portuguese online dating scene: Does gender matter?', in I. A. Degim, J. Johnson and T. Fu (eds) *Online Courtship – Interpersonal Interactions Across Borders*, Amsterdam: University of Amsterdam, pp 71-95.

Casper, L. M. and Bianchi, S. M. (2001) *Continuity and Change in the American Family*, Thousand Oaks, CA: Sage.

Cowan, R. S. (1983) *More Work for Mother: The Ironies of Household Technology from the Open Hearth to the Microwave*, New York: Basic Books.

Elder, G. H. (2000) 'The life course', in E. F. Borgatta and R. J. V. Montgomery (eds) *Encyclopedia of Sociology* (2nd edn), vol. 3, New York: Macmillan, pp 1614-1622.

Elder, G. H. and Giele, J. Z. (2009) 'Life course studies: An evolving field', in G. H. Elder and J. Z. Giele (eds) *The Craft of Life Course Research*, New York: The Guilford Press, pp 1-24.

Elder, G. H. and Shanahan, M. J. (2006) 'The life course and human development', in W. Damon and R. M. Lerner (eds) *Handbook of Child Psychology. Theoretical Models of Human* Development (6th edn), New York: Wiley, pp 665–715.

Elder, G. H., Johnson, M. K. and Crosnoe, R. (2003) 'The emergence and development of life course theory', in J. T. Mortimer and M. J. Shanahan (eds) *Handbook of the Life Course*, New York: Kluwer Academic/Plenum Publishers, pp 3-19.

Eurostat (2017) 'Digital economy and society statistics', http://ec.europa.eu/eurostat/statistics-explained/index.php/Digital_economy_and_society_statistics_-_households_and_individuals

Finch, J. (2007) 'Displaying families', *Sociology*, 41(1): 65-81, https://doi.org/10.1177/0038038507072284

Gill, J. (2009) 'Constructing and enhancing the international adoptive family through communication technology', *Marriage & Family Review*, 45(6-8): 783-806, https://doi.org/10.1080/01494920903224376

Gillies, V. (2011) 'From function to competence: Engaging with the new politics of family', *Sociological Research Online*, 16(4): 1-11, https://doi.org/10.5153/sro.2393

Hughes Jr, R. and Hans, J. D. (2001) 'Computers, the internet, and families: A review of the role new technology plays in family life', *Journal of Family Issues*, 22(6): 776-790, https://doi.org/10.1177/019251301022006006

Internet World Stats (2017) 'World internet penetration', www.internetworldstats.com/stats.htm

Ito, M., Baumer, S., Bittanti, M., Cody, R., Stephenson, B. H., Horst, H. A., ... and Perkel, D. (eds) (2009) *Hanging Out, Messing Around, and Geeking Out: Kids Living and Learning with New Media*, Cambridge, MA: MIT Press.

Kennedy, T. L. and Wellman, B. (2007) 'The networked household', *Information, Communication & Society*, 10(5): 645-670, https://doi.org/10.1080/13691180701658012

Koller, M. R. (1974) *Families: A Multigenerational Approach*, New York: McGraw-Hill.

Livingstone, S. M. and Haddon, L. (eds) (2009) *Kids Online: Opportunities and Risks for Children*, Bristol: Policy Press.

Leavitt, H. J. and Whisler, T. L. (1958) 'Management in the 1980's', *Harvard Business Review*, November, https://hbr.org/1958/11/management-in-the-1980s

Lück, D., Widmer, E. D. and Česnuitytė, V. (2017) 'Conclusion: Changes and continuities in European family lives', in V. Česnuitytė, D. Lück, and E. D. Widmer (eds) *Family Continuity and Change*, London: Palgrave Macmillan, pp 313-328.

Mannheim, K. (1952) 'The Sociological Problem of Generations', in *Essays on the Sociology of Knowledge: Collected Works of Karl Mannheim*, New York: Routledge, pp 276–322 (Original work published 1927–28).

McCarthy, J. R. (2012) 'The powerful relational language of "family": Togetherness, belonging and personhood', *The Sociological Review*, 60(1): 68-90, https://doi.org/10.1111/j.1467-954X.2011.02045.x

Morgan, D. (2011) *Rethinking Family Practices*, London: Palgrave Macmillan.

Neves, B. B. and Amaro, F. (2012) 'Too old for technology? How the elderly of Lisbon use and perceive ICT', *The Journal of Community Informatics*, 8(1), http://ci-journal.net/index.php/ciej/article/view/800/904

Neves, B. B. and Fernandes, A. A. (2016) 'Generational bridge', in *The Wiley Blackwell Encyclopedia of Family Studies*, https://doi.org/10.1002/9781119085621.wbefs212.

Neves, B. B., Amaro, F. and Fonseca, J. R. (2013) 'Coming of (old) age in the digital age: ICT usage and non-usage among older adults', *Sociological Research Online*, 18(2): 1-14, https://doi.org/10.5153/sro.2998

Neves, B. B., Franz, R. L., Munteanu, C. and Baecker, R. (2017a) 'Adoption and feasibility of a communication app to enhance social connectedness amongst frail institutionalized oldest old: An embedded case study', *Information, Communication & Society*: 1-19, https://doi.org/10.1080/1369118X.2017.1348534

Neves, B. B., Franz, R., Judges, R., Beermann, C. and Baecker, R. (2017b). 'Can digital technology enhance social connectedness among older adults? A feasibility study', *Journal of Applied Gerontology*, https://doi.org/10.1177/0733464817741369

Nico, M., Cunha, V. and Casimiro, C. (2016) 'Nota de apresentação. Famílias e curso de vida. potencialidades, limites e desafios metodológicos', *Sociologia, Revista da Faculdade de Letras da Universidade do Porto*: 8-19, http://ler.letras.up.pt/uploads/ficheiros/14607.pdf

O'Rand, A. M. and Krecker, M. L. (1990) 'Concepts of the life cycle: Their history, meanings, and uses in the social sciences', *Annual Review of Sociology*, 16: 241-262, https://doi.org/10.1146/annurev.so.16.080190.001325

Pew Research Center (2015) 'Communications technology in emerging and developing nations', www.pewglobal.org/2015/03/19/1-communications-technology-in-emerging-and-developing-nations/

Pew Research Center (2017), 'Internet/broadband fact-sheet', www.pewinternet.org/fact-sheet/internet-broadband/

Rainie, L. and Wellman, B. (2012) *Networked: The New Social Operating System*, Boston: MIT Press.

Rogers, E. M. (1986) *Communication Technology: The New Media*, New York: Simon and Schuster.

Sassi, S. and Goaied, M. (2013) 'Financial development, ICT diffusion and economic growth: Lessons from MENA region', *Telecommunications Policy*, 37(4-5): 252-261, https://doi.org/10.1016/j.telpol.2012.12.004

Şenyürekli, A. R. and Detzner, D. F. (2009) 'Communication dynamics of the transnational family', *Marriage & Family Review*, 45(6-8): 807-824, https://doi.org/10.1080/01494920903224392

Silva, E. (2010) *Technology, Culture, Family: Influences on Home Life*, London: Springer.

Stafford, L. and Hillyer, J. D. (2012) 'Information and communication technologies in personal relationships', *Review of Communication*, 12(4): 290-312, https://doi.org/10.1080/15358593.2012.685951

Sussman, M. B. (1985) *Personal Computers and the Family*, New York: Haworth Press, .

Szydlik, M. (2016) *Sharing Lives: Adult Children and Parents*, London: Routledge.

Torres, A., Mendes, R. and Lapa, T. (2008) 'Families in Europe', *Portuguese Journal of Social Science*, 7(1): 49-84, https://doi.org/10.1386/pjss.7.1.49_1

Torres, A., Coelho, B. and Cabrita, M. (2013) 'Bridge over troubled waters', *European Societies,* 15(4): 535-556, https://doi.org/10.1080/14616696.2013.836403

United Nations International Telecommunication Union (2016) 'Measuring the Information Society Report', www.itu.int/en/ITU-D/Statistics/Documents/publications/misr2016/MISR2016-w4.pdf

US Census Bureau (2014) 'The 2013 American Community Survey: Computer and internet access', www.census.gov/newsroom/press-releases/2014/cb14-170.html

Wajcman, J. (2010) 'Domestic technology: Labour-saving or enslaving?', in C. Hanks (ed) *Technology and Values: Essential Readings*, Richmond: John Wiley & Sons, pp 272-288.

Wall, K. and Gouveia, R. (2014) 'Changing meanings of family in personal relationships', *Current Sociology*, 62(3): 352-373, https://doi.org/10.1177/0011392113518779

We Are Social and Hootsuite (2017) 'Digital in 2017 global overview report', https://wearesocial.com/special-reports/digital-in-2017-global-overview

PART I

Theoretical and methodological approaches

Theoretical perspectives on technology and society: implications for understanding the relationship between ICTs and family life

Natasha S. Mauthner and Karolina A. Kazimierczak

Introduction

Recently there has been growing academic interest in the ways in which emerging information and communication technologies (ICTs) are changing family practices and relations. Particular focus has been given to the potential detrimental and/or beneficial effects of these technologies on family functioning across different dimensions, including family communication and cohesion; family roles, rules and intergenerational conflicts; relationship formation; intimacy patterns; and work-home and family boundaries (Arnold, 2004; Bittman et al, 2004; Carvalho et al, 2015; Hertlein, 2012; Hughes and Hans, 2001; Jamieson, 2013; Lanigan, 2009; Lanigan et al, 2009; Mesch, 2006; Nansen et al, 2009, 2010, 2011; Wajcman et al, 2008, 2010). There has been additional interest in how these effects vary according to age, gender, social class and nationality (Cuban, 2017; Lim, 2016). Underlying these studies are particular theoretical conceptualizations of the relationship between technological and social change, which implicitly or explicitly frame the specific ways in which ICTs are understood to relate to family dynamics. For example, ICTs might be seen as driving changes in family life or, conversely, family members' intentional uses of technologies can be understood as mediating their effects. In this chapter we examine how the technology–society relation has been theorized and consider how this has influenced research on ICTs and family life. We begin by outlining four conceptual approaches to understanding the relationship between technology and society. The first three – 'technological determinism', 'social constructivism', and 'actor network theory' – have left a clear mark on the field, while the fourth, 'posthumanist', perspective is emergent and results from a recent 'posthumanist turn' associated with feminist studies of science (see Barad, 2007).[1] Drawing on recent research, we then go on to illustrate how these approaches inform theoretical and empirical investigations of ICTs and family life. We conclude by suggesting that these theoretical formulations are important resources through which people, families, organizations, governments, educational systems, the media, and much more, experience and make sense of the role of technology in contemporary life, and devise interventions accordingly.

Theoretical perspectives on technology and society

Technological determinism

Technological determinism is a way of thinking about the relationship between technological and social change that informs academic, policy and popular accounts about the place of technology in everyday life (Marx and Smith, 1994; Wyatt, 2008). Its foundations are generally traced back to the work of Karl Marx and his historical materialist analysis of the role of technology in labour processes.[2] Technological determinism is not a unified approach.[3] However, it is possible to discern some common principles.

Technological determinism conceptualizes technology as hard material objects. As Marx and Smith (1994, pp x–xi) explain, 'technology is conceived in almost exclusively artefactual terms, and its materiality serves to reinforce a tangible sense of its decisive role in history'. This understanding is present in Marx's definition of the machine as 'a mechanism that, after being set in motion, performs with its tools the same operations as the worker formerly did with similar tools' (Marx cited in MacKenzie, 1984, p 486). The idea of technology as a material artefact makes it possible to conceptualize it as an 'autonomous force or entity that is independent of social processes' (Marx and Smith, 1994, p xi). As Wyatt (2008, p 168) further explains, the assumption is that 'technological developments take place outside society, independently of social, economic, and political forces'. Moreover, these developments are understood to follow a particular teleological trajectory which is sequential in nature and which in turn prescribes 'a necessitous path over which technologically developing societies must travel' (Heilbroner, 1967, p 336). Elaborating on Marx's classical example of the move from the hand- to steam-mill, Heilbroner (1967, p 336) notes how 'the steam-mill follows the hand-mill not by chance but because it is the next stage in a technical conquest of nature that follows one and only one grand avenue of advance'. Importantly, this trajectory is seen as naturally given, with its own logic, rationale and law-like properties. Technological determinism, then, is 'a view of history in which human will has no real role – in which culture, social organization and values derive from laws of nature that are manifest through technology' (Bimber, 1994, p 99). In this account, technology stands in as a proxy for nature, which determines history and culture, or provides the material constraints within which human agency and will are exercised. As Heilbroner (1994, p 69) notes, 'Machines make history by changing the material conditions of human existence'. Heilbroner (1994) argues that the 'acquisitive mindset' – which he defines as human economic behaviour or the principle of 'maximizing', and which he sees as a fundamental 'rule' or 'law' of behaviour in societies – is the 'mediating mechanism' through which technology acts as the primary causal agent in history and social change.

Social constructivism

Social constructivist approaches to technology were developed in the 1980s in direct reaction to some of the assumptions underpinning technological determinism, and as an extension of a broader social constructivist movement in the social sciences (Berger and Luckmann, 1966). Examples of such approaches include 'social shaping of technology' (MacKenzie and Wajcman, 1985), 'social construction of technology' (also known as SCOT) (Pinch and Bijker, 1984) and 'technological systems' perspectives (Hughes, 1987). Social constructivist approaches contest the key assumption underpinning technological determinism that technology is an independent, exogenous and autonomous entity or force that drives social change. Authors such as Pinch and Bijker (1984) and Grint and Woolgar (1997) challenge the essentialist notion that technologies have inherent features that determine their nature, use and effects. They suggest that the attributes, workings and successes of technologies are not derived from their internal characteristics but rather from the broader sociopolitical contexts in which they are designed, developed and adopted. In his account of SCOT, Sismondo (2010, p 98) illustrates this with the example of the watch, which he suggests can be 'simultaneously constructed to tell time, to be attractive, to make profits, to refer to a well known style of clock, to make a statement about its wearer, etc.'. He furthermore explains that even the practice of telling the time serves multiple purposes such as keeping time, measuring length of time, or recording the timing of an event. Given this diversity of use, he contends that 'there is no essence to a watch. And if the watch has no essence, then we can say that it has systematic effects only within a specific human environment' (Sismondo, 2010, p 98). The argument then is that the social contexts in which technologies are designed and taken up determine their nature and effects. Consequently, the development and use of technology are understood as negotiated and contingent *social* processes rather than reflections of some inherent, natural, internal or teleological trajectory and logic. Bringing a feminist perspective to social constructivist accounts, Wajcman (2010), for example, argues that gender identities and power relations influence the development, design and use of domestic and workplace technologies. Equally, she suggests, 'our relationship to technology is integral to the constitution of subjectivity for both sexes' (Wajcman, 2010, pp 144-145). In this sense, technology and gender can be seen as mutually shaping one another. Another example comes from Pinch and Bijker (1984), who suggest that there is nothing inevitable about the development of the modern bicycle. Its design and uptake, they argue, is not due to its intrinsically superior design compared to rival models. Rather, it is the result of a negotiated process involving competing interpretations (what they call 'interpretive flexibility') by different 'relevant social groups' of what bicycles are, and of their purposes, problems and solutions. The eventual form of technological artefact that is stabilized – the modern-day bicycle in this example – emerges through a process of 'closure' in which certain interpretations of the bicycle, and the solutions that it is seen to provide to specific problems, come to be accepted. As Sismondo (2010, p 98) puts it, 'the development of technologies is the result of rhetorical operations, defining the users of artefacts, their uses, and the problems that particular designs solve'. On this account, the success of the artefact is not dependent on its effective design; rather, it is the very success of the artefact that allows us *retrospectively* to claim some designs as more effective than others. While social constructivist approaches consider technology to be a '*sociotechnological ensemble*' (Bijker, 1995) in which the social and the technical interact and mutually shape one another (MacKenzie, 1984), priority is given to human actors and their intentional meaning-making processes (Pinch, 2010). Technologies might shape and influence human actions, but ultimately human actors are the main locus of agency and drivers of sociotechnical change.

Actor network theory

Actor network theory (ANT) approaches to technology and society are both a continuation of, and a break from, social constructivist accounts. They continue to see technology as embedded in social relations and processes. However, they try to overcome the separation between technology and society by rejecting the notion that these are two separate, yet interacting and mutually shaping, spheres. In this regard they are trying to move beyond both technological determinism and social constructivism. ANT rejects both the idea that technology is a given fixed material entity that drives social change, and the notion that technology is simply a socially constructed effect. Instead, ANT conceptualizes technologies, social institutions and relations as comprised of both material and cultural elements. As Latour (1991, p 110) argues, 'We are never faced with objects or social relations, we are faced with chains which are associations of humans and non-humans'. Or, in Law's (1992, p 381) words, the material and the social are nothing other than networks of heterogeneous elements. Callon (1986) illustrates this point through the example of the electric car. On his account, the existence of this 'technical object' is reliant on the construction of 'its concomitant actor-world', understood as a combination of many associated and heterogeneous entities including 'consumers, social movements and ministries... accumulators, fuel cells, electrodes, electrons, catalysts and electrolytes' (Callon, 1986, p 22). ANT therefore takes as its starting point these networks of human and nonhuman 'actants' (Latour, 1994) and investigates how these sociotechnical assemblages are established and their relational effects. Importantly, this approach seeks to treat the human and the nonhuman in a symmetrical way as equal participants in the world, refusing to privilege one over the other. For instance, in his example of the gun and the gunman, Latour (1994) draws attention to the way in which human and nonhuman actants are brought together in specific actions in which they share and exchange their properties, and are thereby modified to become '*someone else*, the hybrid actor composed... of gun and gunman' (Latour, 1994, p 33). Latour therefore redistributes actions within human–nonhuman or sociotechnical networks: 'action is a property of the whole association, not particularly of those actants called humans' (Latour, 1994, p 36). Callon and Muniesa (2005, p 1236) further illustrate this point in their analysis of economic markets as dependent on 'distributed calculative agencies'. As they argue, these agencies 'are not human individuals but collective hybrids', where 'knowledge and action are never individual', but 'distributed between humans and nonhumans', including – in the case of financial markets – such tools as double-entry bookkeeping or computer assisted trading systems (Callon and Muniesa, 2005, pp 1236-1237). ANT is therefore sometimes conceptualized as grounded within a 'relational materialist' ontology, which is regarded as one of its distinctive features compared to other versions of materialism within sociology (Law, 1992). As well as rejecting the dualist tendency to treat the material and the social (and related binaries such as agency/structure and micro/macro) as essentially different, ANT treats all kinds of entities, 'people, machines, "ideas" and all the rest – as interactional effects rather than primitive causes' (Law, 1992, p 389). Agency is therefore located with interactions of heterogeneous elements, and the capacity of these elements to modify each other through their associations. On this account, reality is made up of sociotechnical networks which continuously reconstitute themselves and are therefore the prime agents of change. As Law (1992, p 389) suggests, 'to the extent that "society" recursively reproduces itself it does so because it is materially heterogeneous. And sociologists that do not take machines and architectures as seriously as they do people will never solve the problem of reproduction'.

ANT seeks to treat nonhumans (the technological) and humans (the social) symmetrically and refuses to accord analytical importance to the difference between the nonhuman and the human (Law, 2009, p 147). Its key theoretical concern is to extend agency to nonhuman entities in the same way that humans have been granted agency. To engage in this project, it necessarily designates (and therefore differentiates) various actants in the world as either 'nonhuman' or 'human' in order to consider how these come together in heterogeneous networks. For instance, in Latour's (1994) example of the gun-and-gunman 'collective', the gun is taken to represent the 'nonhuman' while the gunman stands for the 'human' element. Similarly, in Callon's (1986) study, the production of the electric car is seen as dependent on an assemblage of elements that are described as 'human' (for example, consumer markets, social movements, ministries) or 'nonhuman' (for example, accumulators, fuel cells, electrodes, electrons, catalysts and electrolytes). ANT conceives itself as a 'posthumanist' project (Law, 2009, p 147) in that it seeks to dismiss ontological differences between human and nonhuman actants, thereby allowing their equal participation in the world. This is just one specific understanding of 'posthumanism'. In the section that follows, we discuss a distinctive posthumanist approach in which the key focus is not so much on how to eradicate analytical distinctions between the nonhuman and the human, or the technological and the social, but rather on understanding how nonhuman and human entities, and the divisions between them, come into being.

Posthumanism

A number of feminist science studies scholars, such as Haraway, Barad, Suchman and Castañeda, are putting forward alternative 'posthumanist' approaches to understanding the relationship between technology and society. Whereas ANT investigates how technology and culture come together in heterogeneous human–nonhuman networks to produce reality, these feminist authors are interested in the ontologically prior question of how 'technology' ('the nonhuman') and 'culture' ('the human') come to be constituted as ontologically distinct entities and domains *in the first place* (Barad, 2007; Castañeda and Suchman, 2014; Haraway, 1989, 1991, 1994, 1997, 2008, 2016; Suchman, 2007). It is in this sense that we consider these approaches to be 'posthumanist', following Barad's (2007, p 136) understanding of posthumanism as 'the practice of accounting for the boundary-making practices by which the "human" and its others are differentially delineated and defined'.

On this posthumanist approach the project of understanding the relationship between technology and society consists in investigating how it is that 'the technological' and 'the social' come to be configured as separate and separable. No a priori dualistic distinctions are made between technology/society, nonhuman/human, object/subject, nature/culture, and so on. Rather, the nature of the world is taken to be ontologically indeterminate outside of specific practices. As Haraway (1997, p 62) explains: 'The bifurcated categories themselves are reifications of multifaceted, heterogeneous, interdigitating practices and their relatively stable sedimentations, all of which get assigned to separate domains for mainly ideological reasons'. Importantly, these practices (for example, those that constitute the division between 'technology' and 'society') are also conceptualized in a non-dualist way as 'material-semiotic' (Haraway, 1988) or 'material-discursive' (Barad, 2007). Crucial here is the specific conceptualization of materiality and discourse as mutually constituted and articulated. The former is not seen as a fixed substance, or an inherent property of independently existing objects, but rather as referring to ongoing processes of materialization; while the latter is not considered as synonymous with language, but as constituting 'the material conditions for making meaning' (Barad, 2007, p 335). Just as discursive practices are always already material (they are an ongoing materialization of the world), so too materiality is discursive: material phenomena come into being through, and are inseparable from, discursive practices. As Barad (2014, p 175) explains: 'Meaning is not an ideality; meaning is material. And matter isn't what exists separately from meaning. Mattering is a matter of what comes to matter and what doesn't'. Material-discursive practices, then, dynamically enact specific objects, meanings and boundaries that are constitutive of the world.

Posthumanist approaches focus neither on the ways in which technology and society mutually shape one another, nor on how technology and society come together in relational networks that include interacting heterogeneous elements. Rather, they investigate how the entities 'technology' and 'society', 'nonhuman' and 'human', and the boundaries between these, are dynamically produced and reproduced through historically, culturally and materially contingent and specific material-semiotic practices. Suchman (2007) illustrates this approach through her work on human-machine relations. She explores the development of 'humanlike machines', also known as 'humanoid, android, social, and personal' robots (Castañeda and Suchman, 2014, p 316) as fertile ground for investigating the ways in which human/ nonhuman and social/technological entities and boundaries are constituted. For example, she shows how these artificial intelligence robotics projects already enact the human/machine binary, as they seek to develop and study 'models of human intelligence by constructing them on a physical robot' (Menzel and D'Aluisio, 2000, p 58, cited in Suchman, 2007, p 235). The starting point of these projects is that there exist certain qualities, attributes and capacities (such as intelligence, the ability to interact with the environment, embodied sensory-motor interactions, learning through interaction, sociality, development) that are understood to be *essentially* 'human', and that these can be grafted onto what is regarded as 'nonhuman', inert and inorganic matter. Suchman's point is that these robots are not so much bringing together human/social and nonhuman/technological properties and capabilities. Rather, the development of these robots, and their underpinning dualist assumptions, are actively implicated in the very constitution of human/nonhuman and social/technological entities and binaries.[4] On this posthumanist understanding of the relationship between the human/social and the nonhuman/technological, agency resides neither with one of these binary terms, nor with their interacting associations, but rather with the materialization and making of these binary entities and boundaries. On this approach, both 'persons' and 'machines' are understood 'as entities achieved only through the ongoing enactment of separateness and always in relation with others' (Suchman, 2007, pp 257-258), where this relation with 'others' is understood as 'intra-active' (Barad, 2007, p 33). Barad's concept of 'intra-action' is key to understanding the relationship between the social and the technological that is being proposed by posthumanist approaches. Unlike 'interaction', which assumes the existence of separate individual agencies prior to their relation, 'intra-action' recognizes the inherent inseparability of entities from one another and from the specific practices and relations in which they are constituted. Entities do not pre-exist these practices and relations, but are their constitutive effects. Therefore, on a posthumanist account, the world makes and remakes itself through dynamic materializations of differences – such as the human/society and nonhuman/technology distinction – where these differences and boundaries are open to ongoing reconfiguration.

These distinctive theoretical perspectives on the relationship between technological and social change provide important conceptual resources for studies investigating interactions between ICTs and family life. In the following section we explore how the first three positions (technological determinism, social constructivism and actor network theory) have implicitly or explicitly shaped empirical research on ICTs and family life, and we outline possibilities for using the fourth, posthumanist, approach as a framework through which to investigate this problematic.

Implications for research on ICTs and family life

Technological determinism

While few studies explicitly align themselves theoretically with technological determinism, many carry deterministic overtones in their concern with the specific effects that ICTs have on different aspects of family life. One example is research conducted by Lanigan and colleagues (Lanigan, 2009; Lanigan et al, 2009) in which they explored the impact of home computer use on family communication, cohesion and adaptability. Results from their online survey indicated that:

> Most participants (68%) said computer use increased their sense of connection to friends and family, resulting in improved communication and cohesion. One third said e-mail encouraged more frank communication, which was perceived as good for the family. Family time increased due to efficiencies gained through computer use. The computer was seen as an enticement to keep children home as well as a source of mutual interest, interaction, and tool to plan

family activities. Several respondents used the computer to pursue education, enhance personal growth, and support important life roles such as spouse or parent. (Lanigan, 2009, p 603)

Their conclusion is that 'The computer altered adaptability by functioning as a change agent' (Lanigan, 2009, p 603). The relationship between ICTs and the family is conceptualized in a deterministic way to the extent that the computer is understood as an autonomous material device carrying inherent 'technology characteristics with the potential to influence family usage patterns' (Lanigan, 2009, p 597). These properties of technology include accessibility (user friendliness and convenience of use), scope (multifunctionality), obtrusiveness (physical properties and pervasiveness), resource demand (financial cost) and gratification potential (fashion, style and entertainment of the ICT in question) (Lanigan, 2009). By virtue of these fixed and given features, technology is seen as providing 'alternative means of fulfilling existing family functions and needs' (Lanigan et al, 2009, p 27), thereby affecting the ways in which families operate. It is in this sense that technology is understood to act as a key 'change agent'.

Social constructivism

Wajcman's research on the role of ICTs on the work/home boundary is an example of a social constructivist approach to conceptualizing the relationship between technology and society (Wajcman, 2008; Wajcman et al, 2008, 2010). This project is a continuation of her pioneering work in science and technology studies challenging technological determinism (MacKenzie and Wajcman, 1985), and of her longstanding interest in theorizing the interaction between gender and technology (Wajcman, 1991, 2004, 2010; Bittman et al, 2004). In this recent research, Wajcman and her colleagues reject the technologically deterministic notion that 'people have little control over the effects of technology and must largely accept its impact' (Wajcman et al, 2010, p 258). Instead, they are interested in exploring 'user decisions about the way they incorporate the Internet in their daily lives, specifically in relation to the purpose – be it for work or personal purposes – and time of use' (Wajcman et al, 2010, p 259). In their discussion of Australian households' use of ICTs to manage the division between work and home, they emphasize that people are not passively accepting the capacity of technologies to blur temporal and spatial boundaries between these two spheres. Rather, they are 'actively making decisions about how they incorporate the technology into their lives in ways that are beneficial to them' (Wajcman et al, 2010, p 271) and that allow them to manage work and home life. For example, while some employees in their study interpreted the internet as 'a tool that may assist them to attend to personal matters while at work' (Wajcman et al, 2010, p 270), or – on the other hand – as 'a work extension technology' (Wajcman et al, 2010, p 270), most participants appeared to maintain the boundary between work and family life, despite the specific technical capabilities, or affordances, of the technology to connect work and home. This study is an illustration of a social constructivist approach to the relationship between ICTs and family to the extent that it rejects the notion of technology as a determinant of family life and work–home boundaries and conceptualizes it as the effect of human intentional actions and interpretations.

Actor network theory

Actor network theory is a further theoretical resource for researchers studying interactions between ICTs and family life. For example, Arnold, Davis, Gibbs and Nansen (Arnold, 2004; Nansen et al, 2009, 2010, 2011) draw on insights from ANT and material culture studies in sociology, anthropology and cultural geography to explore the proliferation and use of ICTs in domestic and familial everyday life in Australian homes. Their interest is in developing a 'symmetrical approach to the study of home life through analysis of the physical encounters and cultures formed within the home – the entanglements of spaces, objects, and subjects' (Nansen et al, 2011, p 694). Their research considers the ways in which people, domestic architectures and material artefacts – including ICTs – 'are materially and temporally woven together to constitute the particular kind of place called home' (Nansen et al, 2011, p 694). Consequently, they treat the social and the material, the human and the nonhuman, and the social and the technological as mutually shaped emergent 'sociotechnical phenomena' (Arnold, 2004, p 185) rather than separate entities. A major focus of their work is the agency of technologies, which they argue 'are not simply neutral tools, but active participants in constructing the familial, the organisational, and the social' (Nansen et al, 2010, pp 139–140). For example, they explore how technology-mediated practices shape domestic rhythms and the temporal organization and experience of contemporary life. They argue that family routines and schedules are inflected by new technologies through their involvement in everyday practices (Nansen et al, 2009). Importantly, they locate agency not simply with ICTs and their affordances but rather with their interactions with domestic and family life (Nansen et al, 2010, p 147). In this sense technology is neither an agent of change in family practices and relations, nor is it a passive tool that is simply domesticated by human actors (Arnold, 2004, p 185). Rather, technology has effects through its participation in networks of domestic practices, architecture and material artefacts (Nansen et al, 2011).

Posthumanism

On the posthumanist approach that we outlined above, the study of the relationship between ICTs and the family entails a way of doing research that takes neither 'ICTs' nor 'the family' as already constituted entities, but rather sees these domains, and the separation between them, as dynamically constituted through historically, culturally and materially contingent and specific material-semiotic practices (Mauthner and Kazimierczak, 2014). These include, among others, technology design, development and marketing; family practices, relations and ideologies; government policies and legislation around technology (surveillance, privacy, trust, safety and security), family and work-life balance; organizational policies and practices around technology, family and work-life interactions; educational policies and institutions; notions of childhood including their intersection with conceptions of nature and its role in child development; and various public discourses on these matters, including the media, popular culture and academia. A posthumanist study could focus on one or several of these aspects. The important point is that it would specifically investigate and account for how practices across these various domains are implicated in the constitution of the boundary between ICTs (the technological) and family (the social). Our earlier discussion of the different theoretical conceptualizations of the relationship between technological and social change (technological determinism, social constructivism and actor network theory), as well as our outline of the empirical studies above, are examples of how academic practices have been involved in (re)producing the ICT/technology and family/society binary. Our argument is that a posthumanist study of ICTs and family life is one that accounts for the *constitution* of these entities (and their separation), rather than assuming that these entities are pre-existing starting points for the investigation. On this posthumanist approach, agency lies with multiple historically, culturally and materially contingent and specific practices that materialize 'ICTs', 'family' and the separation between them.

Conclusion

In this chapter we have highlighted the links between specific studies of ICTs and family life and broader conceptualizations of technological and social change present in social theory. In doing so, we want to emphasize that what is at stake in these empirical projects is not only the issue of how families are shaped by, engage, form networks, or come into being with ICTs. Rather, embedded in these investigations, and the theoretical perspectives that underpin them, are more fundamental assumptions about the nature of the world, and how it is made and sustained. For technological determinism, it is the laws governing technological developments and human behaviours that act as causal mechanisms driving the world forward. Social constructivism, on the other hand, positions human intentional actions as the main locus of change. ANT conceptualizes the world as produced and reproduced through operations of heterogeneous sociotechnical networks. On a posthumanist account, the world makes and remakes itself through dynamic materializations of difference – such as the distinction between technology and society – where these differences and boundaries are open to ongoing reconfiguration.

These distinctive approaches have implications for how we conceptualize the nature of time and its relation to technological, social and family change. On our reading, the first three perspectives all treat time as an ontological given, but differ in their understanding of how time relates to technological and social change and progress. Technological determinism takes time as a fixed external parameter and backdrop against and within which transformations unfold. The future both temporally and causally follows from the past according to a teleological trajectory that promises ever-increasing progress, knowledge and understanding. Social constructivism conceptualizes change as an effect of human meaning-making processes. Here, the past can only be understood through a present that renders it meaningful, and progress is attributed retrospectively. Actor network theory rejects the notion of progress understood as inevitable movement from a less developed and informed past to a more advanced and enlightened future. Instead, it suggests that the direction of change proceeds from complexity to ever-increasing complexity in the form of entangled networks (Latour, 1998, 2004). A posthumanist perspective, as outlined in this chapter, does not treat time as a pre-existing container or marker of 'what already is' (Barad, 2007, p 430). Rather, it conceptualizes time as constituted *with* social, technological and family change. While this approach rejects a teleological notion of progress, it nevertheless retains a version – albeit reconfigured – of causality. In this understanding of causality, distinctions between cause and effect, past and future, are not taken as given but rather as relational outcomes of dynamic processes of materialization through which other binaries such as society/ technology are constituted. This means that, for instance, technological developments, social change and family practices across the life course are not seen as separate and pre-existing phenomena, each unfolding over time independently of, but in interaction with, one another. Instead, the posthumanist proposal is that technology, society and the family intra-actively (re)constitute themselves dynamically not through time but together with time.

The theoretical formulations presented in this chapter and their conceptualizations of technology, society, family and time are important because they provide resources through which people, families, organizations, governments, educational systems, the media, and much more, make sense of the role of technology in contemporary life, and devise interventions accordingly. For example, while technological determinism is one of the most critiqued ways of understanding the technology/society relationship, this perspective nevertheless underpins many popular and policy accounts of how technology has changed society, as well as everyday experiences of technology (Marx and Smith, 1994; Wyatt, 2008). It is in this sense that, as Suchman (2007, p 1) suggests, the ways in which the 'human–machine' relation is configured matter and have material-semiotic effects because they provide possibilities for seeing, imagining, intervening and indeed making the world.

In brief

1. Underlying studies of ICTs and family life are particular conceptualizations of the relationship between technological and social change, which frame how ICTs are understood to relate to family dynamics: 'technological determinism', 'social constructivism', 'actor network theory' and 'posthumanism'.

2. Technological determinism views the laws governing technological developments and human behaviours as causal mechanisms driving the world forward. This perspective informs studies in which ICTs are understood as autonomous material devices carrying inherent properties which influence family life.

3. Social constructivism rejects the assumption that technology drives social change and gives priority to human actors and their intentional meaning-

making processes. This entails conceptualizing ICTs as effects of human actions and interpretations, rather than as determinants of family life.

4. Actor network theory conceptualizes heterogeneous sociotechnical networks (rather than either technology or humans) as prime agents of change. ICTs are seen as having effects through their participation in networks comprising family members, technological artefacts, domestic practices and the material home.

5. Posthumanism regards the world as constituting itself through dynamic materializations of difference, including the technology/society distinction. This approach investigates and accounts for how practices across various domains are implicated in the constitution of the boundary between ICTs and family.

Notes

[1] The authors and approaches included within each of the four perspectives are not unified in their understanding of the relationship between technology and social change. However, their conceptualizations share some key common principles and characteristics which warrant grouping them together.

[2] There are different interpretations as to whether Marx's work constitutes a technological determinist account of history (Bimber, 1990; Heilbroner, 1967, 1994; MacKenzie, 1984).

[3] See Marx and Smith (1994) for a discussion of 'hard' and 'soft' versions of technological determinism.

[4] There are other practices and projects that are also implicated in the making of these boundaries, for example, developmental psychology, evolutionary biology, etc (Castañeda and Suchman, 2014; Suchman, 2007).

Acknowledgements

This chapter draws on a research project funded by the UK's Engineering and Physical Sciences Research Council (grant number EP/K025392/1). We thank the editors, Barbara Barbosa Neves and Cláudia Casimiro, for inviting us to contribute to this collection and two anonymous reviewers for comments on an earlier version.

References

Arnold, M. (2004) 'The connected home: Probing the effects and affects of domesticated ICTs', *Proceedings of the Participatory Design Conference*, 2: 183–186, http://ojs.ruc.dk/index.php/pdc/article/view/345/337

Barad, K. (2007) *Meeting the Universe Halfway: Quantum Physics and the Entanglement of Matter and Meaning*, London: Duke University Press.

Barad, K. (2014) 'Diffracting diffraction: Cutting together-apart', *Parallax*, 2(3): 168–187, https://doi.org/10.1080/13534645.2014.927623.

Berger, P L. and Luckmann, T. (1966) *The Social Construction of Reality: A Treatise in the Sociology of Knowledge*, New York: Anchor Books.

Bijker, W. E. (1995) *Of Bicycles, Bakelites, and Bulbs: Toward a Theory of Sociotechnical Change*, Cambridge, MA: MIT Press.

Bimber, B. (1990) 'Karl Marx and the three faces of technological determinism', *Social Studies of Science*, 20(2): 333–351, https://doi.org/10.1177/030631290020002006

Bimber, B. (1994) 'Three faces of technological determinism', in M. R. Smith and L. Marx (eds) *Does Technology Drive History? The Dilemma of Technological Determinism*, Cambridge, MA: MIT Press, pp 79–100.

Bittman, M., Rice, J. M. and Wajcman, J. (2004) 'Appliances and their impact: The ownership of domestic technology and time spent on household work', *The British Journal of Sociology*, 55(3): 401–423, 10.1111/j.1468-4446.2004.00026.x

Callon, M. (1986) 'The sociology of an actor-network: The case of the electric vehicle', in M. Callon, J. Law and A. Rip (eds) *Mapping the Dynamics of Science and Technology: Sociology of Science in the Real World*, London: Palgrave Macmillan, pp 19–34.

Callon, M. and Muniesa, F. (2005) 'Peripheral vision: Economic markets as calculative collective devices', *Organization Studies*, 26(8): 1229–1250, https://doi.org/10.1177/0170840605056393

Carvalho, J., Francisco, R. and Relvas, A. P. (2015) 'Family functioning and information and communication technologies: How do they relate? A literature review', *Computers in Human Behavior*, 45: 99–108, https://doi.org/10.1016/j.chb.2014.11.037

Castañeda, C. and Suchman, L. (2014) 'Robot visions', *Social Studies of Science*, 44(3): 315–341, https://doi.org/10.1177/0306312713511868

Cuban, S. (2017) *Transnational Family Communication: Immigrants and ICTs*, London: Palgrave Macmillan.

Haraway, D. (1988) 'Situated knowledges: The science question in feminism and the privilege of partial perspective', *Feminist Studies*, 14(3): 575–599, https://doi.org/10.2307/3178066

Haraway, D. (1989) *Primate Visions: Gender, Race, and Nature in the World of Modern Science*, New York: Routledge.

Haraway, D. (1991) *Simians, Cyborgs, and Women: The Reinvention of Nature*, London: Free Association Books.

Haraway, D. (1994) 'A game of cat's cradle: Science studies, feminist theory, cultural studies', *Configurations*, 2(1): 59–71.

Haraway, D. (1997) *Modest_Winess@Second_Millenium.FemaleMan©_ Meets_OncoMouse™*, New York: Routledge.

Haraway, D. (2008) *When Species Meet*, Minneapolis: Minnesota University Press.

Haraway D. (2016) *Staying with the Trouble: Making Kin in the Chthulucene*, Durham, NC: Duke University Press.

Heilbroner, R. L. (1967) 'Do machines make history?', *Technology and Culture*, 8(3): 335-345.

Heilbroner (1994) 'Technological determinism revisited', in M. R. Smith and L. Marx (eds) *Does Technology Drive History? The Dilemma of Technological Determinism*, Cambridge, MA: MIT Press, pp 67-78.

Hertlein, K. M. (2012) 'Digital dwelling: Technology in couple and family relationships', *Family Relations*, 61: 374-387, https://doi.org/10.1111/j.1741-3729.2012.00702.x

Hughes, T. P. (1987) 'The evolution of large technological systems', in W. E. Bijker, T. Hughes and T. J. Pinch (eds) *The Social Construction of Technological Systems*, Cambridge, MA: MIT Press, pp 51–82.

Hughes, R. and Hans, J. D. (2001) 'Computers, the internet, and families: A review of the role new technology plays in family life', *Journal of Family Issues*, 22(6): 776-790, https://doi.org/10.1177/019251301022006006

Grint, K. and Woolgar, S. (1997) *The Machine at Work: Technology, Work and Organization*, Oxford: Polity Press.

Jamieson, L. (2013) 'Personal relationships, intimacy and the self in a mediated and global digital age', K. Orton-Johnson and N. Prior (eds) *Digital Sociology: Critical Perspectives*, London: Palgrave Macmillan, pp 13-33.

Lanigan, J. D. (2009) 'A sociotechnological model for family research and intervention: How information and communication technologies affect family life', *Marriage & Family Review*, 45(6-8): 587-609, https://doi.org/10.1080/01494920903224194

Lanigan, J.D., Bold, M. and Chenoweth, L. (2009) 'Computers in the family context: Perceived impact on family time and relationships', *Family Science Review*, 14(1): 16–32.

Latour, B. (1991) 'Technology is society made durable', in J. Law (ed) *A Sociology of Monsters: Essays on Power, Technology and Domination*, New York: Routledge, pp 103-132.

Latour, B. (1994) 'On technical mediation: Philosophy, sociology, genealogy', *Common Knowledge*, 3(2): 29-64.

Latour, B. (1998) 'Essays on science and society: From the world of science to the world of research?', *Science*, 280(5361): 208-209.

Latour, B. (2004) *The Politics of Nature: How to Bring the Sciences Into Democracy*, Cambridge, MA: Harvard University Press.

Law, J. (1992) 'Notes on the theory of the actor-network: Ordering, strategy, and heterogeneity', *Systems Practice*, 5(4): 379–393, https://doi.org/10.1007/BF01059830

Law, J. (2009) 'Actor network theory and material semiotics', in B. S. Turner (ed) *The New Blackwell Companion to Social Theory*, Oxford: Wiley-Blackwell, pp 141–158.

Lim, S. S. (ed) (2016) *Mobile Communication and the Family: Asian Experiences in Technology Domestication*, London: Springer.

MacKenzie, D. (1984) 'Marx and the machine', *Technology and Culture*, 25(3): 473–502, https://doi.org/10.2307/3104202

MacKenzie, D. and Wajcman, J. (eds) (1985) *The Social Shaping of Technology. How the Refrigerator Got Its Hum*, Milton Keynes: Open University Press.

Marx, L. and Smith, M. R. (1994) 'Introduction', in M. R. Smith and L. Marx (eds) *Does Technology Drive History? The Dilemma of Technological Determinism*, London: MIT Press, pp ix–xv.

Mauthner, N. S. and Kazimierczak, K. (2014) 'Technology and the (re)making of work and family', *MobileHCI '14: Proceedings of the 16th International Conference on Human–Computer Interaction with Mobile Devices and Services*, Toronto, 23–26 September.

Mesch, G. S (2006) 'Family characteristics and intergenerational conflicts over the internet', *Information, Communication & Society*, 9(4): 473–495, https://doi.org/10.1080/13691180600858705

Nansen, B., Arnold, M., Gibbs, M. R. and Davis, H. (2009) 'Domestic orchestration: Rhythms in the mediated home, *Time and Society*, 18(2/3): 181–207, https://doi.org/10.1177/0961463X09338082

Nansen, B., Arnold, M., Gibbs, M. R. and Davis, H. (2010) 'Time, spaces and technology in the working-home: An unsettled nexus', *New Technology, Work and Employment*, 25(2): 136–153, https://doi.org/10.1111/j.1468-005X.2010.00244.x

Nansen, B., Arnold, M., Gibbs, M. and Davis, H. (2011) 'Dwelling with media stuff: Latencies and logics of materiality in four Australian homes', *Environment and Planning D: Society and Space*, 29(4): 693–715, https://doi.org/10.1068/d11709

Pinch, T. (2010) 'On making infrastructure visible: Putting the non-humans to rights', *Cambridge Journal of Economics*, 34(1): 77–89, https://doi.org/10.1093/cje/bep044

Pinch, T. E. and Bijker, W. E. (1984) 'The social construction of facts and artefacts: Or how the sociology of science and the sociology of technology might benefit each other', *Social Studies of Science*, 14(3): 399–441.

Sismondo, S. (2010) *An Introduction to Science and Technology Studies*, Oxford: Wiley-Blackwell.

Suchman, L. (2007) *Human–Machine Configurations: Plans and Situated Actions*, Cambridge: Cambridge University Press.

Wajcman, J. (1991) *Feminism Confronts Technology*, Cambridge: Polity Press.

Wajcman, J. (2004) *TechnoFeminism*, Cambridge: Polity Press.

Wajcman, J. (2008) 'Life in the fast lane? Towards a sociology of technology and time', *Sociology*, 59(1): 59–77, https://doi.org/10.1111/j.1468-4446.2007.00182.x

Wajcman, J. (2010) 'Feminist theories of technology', *Cambridge Journal of Economics*, 34(1): 143–152, https://doi.org/10.1093/cje/ben057

Wajcman, J., Bittman, M. and Brown, J. E. (2008) 'Families without borders: Mobile phones, connectedness and work-home divisions', *Sociology*, 42(4): 635–652, https://doi.org/10.1177/0038038508091620

Wajcman, J., Rose, E., Brown, J. E. and Bittman, M. (2010) 'Enacting virtual connections between work and home', *Journal of Sociology*, 46(3): 257–275, https://doi.org/10.1177/1440783310365583

Wyatt, S. (2008) 'Technological determinism is dead; Long live technological determinism', in E. J. Hackett, O. Amsterdamska, M. Lynch and J. Wajcman (eds) *The Handbook of Science and Technology Studies*, Cambridge, MA: MIT Press, pp 165–180.

THREE

Recursive approaches to technology adoption, families, and the life course: actor network theory and strong structuration theory

Geoffrey Mead and Barbara Barbosa Neves

Introduction

While numerous models are used to explain technology adoption (such as the widely used technology acceptance model and its several variants), we still await a comprehensive framework that integrates technological materiality, the situation of its implementation, and users' expectations and experiences. The absence is especially glaring when we consider technology domestication in the sphere of the family and adoption across the life course (Dourish, 2004; Chuttur, 2009; Neves et al, 2017a, 2017b). This chapter seeks to address this absence by considering two 'recursive' approaches, which examine the reciprocal relationship between social structure and agency in the context of technology use over time. The recursive approaches under consideration are particularly useful given their integrative and situational sensitivity, focusing as they do on the intersection of users, contexts, and technologies (Greenhalgh and Stones, 2010). Here, we consider two approaches, adapted to the domain of digital technology: actor network theory (ANT) and strong structuration theory (SST).

ANT has emerged under the social shaping theories approach, within science and technology studies, as a response to technological determinism (MacKenzie and Wajcman, 1999). Technological determinism posits that technology is the cause of social change and that its development occurs independently of social, economic, cultural, and political forces, that is, 'outside of society' (MacKenzie and Wajcman, 1999; Wyatt, 2008). For instance, to define a civilization by its dominant technological artefacts (such as stone, iron, cars, microelectronics,) is to treat technology as independent of societal forces except insofar as it generates them (Wyatt, 2008). ANT draws on this critique but goes further by rejecting any form of determinism, whether technological or social (particularly those studies undertaken from a 'social construction of technology' perspective). The focus of ANT is on the tracing of associations between entities – whether these entities are human or non-human. The 'symmetrical' approach that actor network theorists adopt entails the avoidance of any such discrimination. Hence, it informs a non-dualist account of technology and society that avoids essentialized notions of 'the social' or technology. Our second approach, SST, begins in a formal sociological inquiry into recurrent patterns or structures and the place of agency therein. The rise of ANT compelled strong structuration theorists to consider the role of technology among the relations between agency and social structure. Despite following ANT in paying serious attention to the materiality of technology, it does not pursue it in postulating any 'symmetry' between people and technology. They remain assured that these 'actants' effect change differently and should therefore be studied differently (Greenhalgh and Stones, 2010). By combining structure, agency, and context, SST allows for a comprehensive analysis of users, technologies, and their situational dimensions.

In this chapter, we outline each approach, describing the theoretical commitments it entails for the researcher. Following an initial outline, we sketch the ways in which these approaches have been, and can be, applied in the domains of family and life course studies. Finally, we consider the opportunities and challenges that these approaches bring with them for the empirical study of technology adoption in these domains. To our knowledge this is the first attempt to discuss these recursive approaches as theoretical and analytical models to frame the relationship between technology use, family life, and life course dynamics. Due to their comprehensive nature in studying society and technology, ANT and SST are useful theoretical resources for family and life course researchers.

Recursive approaches

Actor network theory (ANT)

Located beyond both social and technological determinism, and rejecting any dualism between society and technology, is actor network theory (Latour, 1992). It takes its point of departure in a resolutely 'relational' approach (Law, 1999, p 4): what is important is not any one entity, whether human or nonhuman, social group or technological artefact, but the relations in which they are enmeshed. Crucially, the sociologist deploying this 'symmetrical' approach is discouraged from discriminating among the *kinds* of relations and entities that together comprise a network. Whether the points of the network relate on the basis of political or familial relations, cellular relations, or technological relations should not concern the sociologist. Actor network theorists often begin by noting that the social and the technological are 'inextricably' bound and inseparable (Law and Callon, 1988, p 285). Technology and society do not merely constitute one another (as a weak constructionism would have it). Rather, a stronger claim is being made: society *is* technological, just as technology is social. No line between the technological and the social can be drawn in a consistent and confident fashion, because technological apparatuses are inextricably entangled in, and so constitutive of, social relations. Networks are thus irreducibly 'hybrid' in character, comprised of elements that only appear separate in retrospect, after they have been 'purified' and separated out into technological elements, on the one hand, and social elements, on the other (Latour, 1993, p 78). Latour (1990, p 129) notes that '[s]ociety and technology are not two ontologically distinct entities but more like phases of the same essential action'. While technologies might be 'inscribed' with certain interests and intended ends, their place within a network of heterogeneous actants imposes certain 'translations' on their being. Conversely, their inscribed ends oblige other actants to adjust – including the users of the technology (Latour, 1992).

Considering technology itself as a kind of teacher, Latour (2014, p 209) asks what we can learn if we give up the pretension of presuming to know the nature and causal properties of an actor like technology before we even begin to study it. The solution is to bracket our ordinary preconception of what an actor is: '*any thing* that does modify a state of affairs by making a difference is an actor' (Latour, 2005, p 72). By resisting the temptation at the outset to separate human from nonhuman entities, or the social from the technological, we are able to trace differences or effects by *following* these actors, wherever they might lead us.

Perhaps the most audacious claim such authors make is the methodological one that nonhuman entities ought to be treated as having 'agency'. This is to apply a 'symmetrical' approach to humans and nonhumans, making no wager at the outset on each of their respective abilities to act. While many have taken this to be a statement lacking in usefulness or, at worst, an example of mere obscurantism (Bloor, 1999, p 97), there is another reading that can orient us in a productive direction – though it does neutralize ANT's apparently radical character (see Gingras, 1995): the ostensible 'agency' of things can be taken as a weaker statement of the *obstinacy* of the technological world. Rather than being socially determined or constructed in a unilateral manner, the simple projection of human technical ingenuity, technology rebounds on its creators and confounds the will of its users, producing surprises and other unexpected effects.

Applications

ANT has been used in a wide range of fields of only general relevance to those studying technological use and adoption within the family. Its more specific pertinence belongs to the sociology of technology, and other fields from organization studies to information systems (Hanseth et al, 2004; Cresswell et al, 2010). In particular, ANT is seen as a valuable model for information systems (IS), a field which was in the early 2000s still grappling with the lack of a 'theoretical understanding of [its] key object': the technological artefact (Hanseth et al, 2004, p 117). Furthermore, researchers also became interested in 'technology-in-practice', that is, 'the specific structure routinely enacted as we use the specific machine, technique, appliance, device, or gadget in recurrent ways in our everyday situated activities' (Orlikowski, 2000, p 408). By conceptualizing technology as sociotechnical networks (with human and technological components), ANT elucidates both the relationship between technology as an 'artefact' and as 'practice' and the process by which they shape each other (Hanseth et al, 2004). ANT has been employed in a variety of topics from computerized baggage handling in airports (Mähring et al, 2004) to medical technologies (Prout, 1996; Cresswell et al, 2010).

To our knowledge there is still no sociological application of ANT to digital technology adoption and family dynamics. Nor does a study rigorously deploy ANT within a life course perspective. Nevertheless, by reflecting on empirical applications in proximate domains we can identify dimensions of relevance to our subject. We selected one case study for this discussion, as it relates to family life and domestic technologies: Silva (2000) examines the historical evolution of the British cooker (1920s–1990s), in the midst of upheavals of assumptions about the gender division of labour within the home. She does this from a primarily actor network perspective, employing ANT instrumentally, as a lens (seeing technology as 'doing', following the 'relational materiality' and 'performativity' of ANT) to study the involvement of actants in the development and use of both the thermostat oven control (1920s-1930s) and the microwave oven (1980s-1990s). However, acknowledging the limitations of ANT in accounting for gendered power and subjectivities, Silva also draws on feminist poststructuralist analysis to explore the link between those technologies and notions of women and families in everyday life practices over time.

Using ANT, Silva uncovers scripts (and different interpretations) of gender identity and family living by examining manuals that instruct the user to set up the cooker or microwave oven and guidelines concerning the cooking process of food and recipes. The thermostat oven control in the 1920s and 1930s was designed for the housewife, and for a particular type of housewife: the middle-class one who had no servants. This oven is presented as clever and independent, dismissing the cook in the cooking process. Contradicting this presentation, the instructions requested continuous checking, evaluation, and modification of the cooking process which demanded improvised adaptations according to circumstantial variation in food, weight, and fuel. Despite this narrative, the cook – the housewife – was never invisible and could not be attending to 'sewing' or 'gardening' as suggested. Innovative as the technology was, the cooker remained attached to, and demanded, the conventional female role. This attachment was redoubled by an industry which assumed that housewives could not deal with more advanced methods. When the microwave oven appeared in the 1970s, it was introduced as a 'saviour of the busy housewife' (Silva, 2000, p 619). As women entered the labour market and family lifestyles started to adapt, microwaves were developed to defrost and reheat pre-prepared food. In fact, because they were mostly used for that and not for cooking, changes occurred in the technology design, including simplification of buttons and instructions, and the implementation of sensors. As with the thermostat oven, the machine was not fully independent and demanded checking and evaluation of the cooking process as well as the cook's tacit skills (for example, types of food that work best with the technology). While the microwave oven recognized a more heterogeneous conception of the cook (beyond gender patterns), from the busy professional to the exhausted parent, more advanced combination cooking was still thought of as a female affair (instructions to prepare and freeze food, so it could then be heated by children and men). Both technologies were embedded with notions of users and their performance. But the processes of technology and family life shaped the ovens as usage did not match the rigid script, and also reflected new patterns of care and gender boundaries.

Implications: opportunities and challenges

The opportunities and challenges that ANT presents to the study of technology adoption and use within the family are illustrated well by Silva's work mentioned above. Its first benefit can be seen in its disregard for setting the scale of analysis in advance, as sociologists often do when referring to the 'micro', 'meso', and 'macro' levels. ANT, on the contrary, by advocating that we follow actors, attends to how the latter themselves produce these scales (Latour, 2005, p 186). In Silva's deployment of ANT, the family is not abstracted and counted as a 'micro' structure enfolded within something larger, like a community or society, but is defined pragmatically, by the kinds of associations the family makes to its surrounding world: 'Some families or households may at different times be micro or macro, depending on the social connections that can be traced from their stories' (Silva, 2010, p 22). Since no scale is set in advance, a flexible analytical frame enables Silva to make the important point that families are not isolated from the world 'around' them, operating with 'consensual internal dynamics', but are 'intermeshed' in the world in surprising ways (Silva, 2010, p 32). So, an ANT perspective does not distinguish between relations within the household and those 'outside' it. Technological artefacts are exemplary here: imported from outside, they have roles *within* the familial division of labour delegated to them. So, the cooker that Silva examines is both a foreign piece of technology and, at least ideally, a representative for the labour ordinarily undertaken by the housewife. Moreover, just as members of the intergenerational family negotiate their relations with one another in ways commonly studied by sociologists of the family, so too do technical artefacts impose demands, 'inscribed' in them by their producers, irreducible to the desires of their users (demands that are, as Silva shows, at the root of difficulties for working-class and working wives). Taking this diachronic view, can we perhaps employ ANT to ask whether the particular 'life cycle' of a technology corresponds to different human life stages?

In its attempt to *follow* actants, trying to avoid becoming 'obsessed... by the gesture of "placing things in their wider context"' (Latour, 2005, p 186), ANT arguably loses the gains that other theoretical approaches possess precisely on account of their attention to context. Namely, in Silva's (2000, p 613) work we see the need for recourse to other means, namely Joan Scott's poststructuralist feminism, to produce a properly 'gendered analysis'. Here, while the ANT approach enables us to understand how certain gendered expectations and relations become inscribed in a technological artefact at a given time, it does not address the particular manner of appropriation, which always varies somewhat from its inscription (Couldry, 2008). In particular, Silva argues that historical changes to gender dynamics mean that the technology itself lacks the potency that ANT accords it. The actor network theorist could respond by noting that historical changes simply require us to take account again of the reshuffled network and the new place of the technology therein. Yet this arguably returns us to a mere description or tracing of associations and their effects, and does not try to get us closer to *explaining* observable changes or the interactions between the technology and those who adopt it. In a similar vein, it is finally unclear whether, by emphasizing description and analysis at the expense of explanation (Latour, 1988, p 163), ANT functions as a theory that is itself able to offer and accumulate insights transposable from one domain to another, or whether it remains a generic method tailored to tracing associations in isolated cases (Gingras, 2013, p 114). Its efficacy and appeal depend, nevertheless, on precisely what one wishes to use it for.

Strong structuration theory (SST)

If the attention to context remains a challenge in using ANT, it constitutes the point of departure for our second recursive approach: strong structuration theory. Born out of Giddens' structuration theory, SST was developed to remedy what were perceived to be the main defects of structuration theory. Its focus 'on issues of ontology at a high level of abstraction' ensured neglect of methodological and epistemological questions, hampering the ability of researchers to deploy it in empirical study (Stones, 2005, p 32). Giddens' overall aim was to reconcile subjectivist and objectivist points of view in sociological theory. Subjectivism here refers to an approach in which the subject or 'human agent is treated as the prime center for social analysis' (Giddens, 1986, p 530), with causal supremacy over its objective, structural conditions. Objectivism implies the converse, in which objective structure makes a puppet or plaything of the agent. By considering them as two independent series, Giddens (1984) argued, the sociologist renders into a 'dualism' what is in fact 'duality of structure'. An 'objective' structure is not something 'external' to individuals or interaction, but is implicated in both: 'as memory traces, and as instantiated in social practices, it is in a sense more "internal" than exterior to [individuals'] activities' (Giddens, 1984, p 25). The structure constitutes the very dispositions individuals deploy in interaction, where they either reproduce the conditions that encourage the structure to flourish or subvert this reproduction. Thus, in Giddens' phrase, structure is both the medium and the outcome of material practice. In a surprising parallel with ANT (see Johnston, 2001), Giddens sought to begin his analysis from the study of 'micro' practices, or 'situated activities' of actors, asserting such a context as the site where agency and structure intersect.

Notwithstanding this acknowledgement of situated activity, some have claimed that this is the precise domain where structuration theory lacks. For this reason, Stones (2005) resolved to elaborate SST, distinguishing it from its predecessor by moving away from 'the ontology-in-general of "structures" and "agents"' towards the 'ontology-in-situ' of *particular* structures and agents (Greenhalgh and Stones, 2010, p 1288). For Stones, Giddens remains satisfied with detecting in particular cases the mere presence of entities that he generally postulates – rules, resources, structures, and outcomes – without doing the work of examining the relations between these general elements and the modifications that specific situations and empirical cases impose on them (Stones, 2005, p 38). To overcome this limitation, while refining the theory for empirical application, SST orients itself by taking Giddens' abstract approach in the direction of 'particular concrete and/or situated entities in the world with their particular qualities, relations, shapes, tone, texture, colour and so on' (Stones, 2005, p 76). The obligation to reconcile these two levels of analysis leads Stones to propose for SST a revision of Giddens' 'duality of structure'. For Stones (2005, p 84), to properly conceptualize this situation in which structure is both the medium and the outcome of practice, a 'quadripartite' model is necessary. First, a social structure is posited, something that pre-exists and survives individuals, and provides the conditions for their practice. Second, it is 'internalized' in the form of a general worldview, on the one hand, and a specific 'conjunctural' knowledge and skill for acting in a certain realm, on the other. Third, on the basis of these internalized resources, social agents are afforded the ability to act in immediate situations, either deliberately or routinely, and in response to circumstances for which they might not be adequately disposed. Fourth, agents' action in these very situations results in outcomes that either reproduce or revise the social structure that served as an initial condition for their practice. Together, these elements of the model are labelled external structures, internal structures, active agency, and outcomes.

More recently, Stones (along with Greenhalgh) has sought to nourish SST with a technological modality (Greenhalgh and Stones, 2010). Recognizing 'the material properties of technology within interaction', and the instantiation or 'inscription' of social structures in technologies, they have assimilated a technological dimension to the second element of SST's quadripartite structure (Greenhalgh and Stones, 2010, p 1290). Like human actors, 'actants' (human agents and forms of technology) now internalize social structure, in the form of general material properties and particular, functional relations to specific situations (Greenhalgh and Stones, 2010).

Applications

Adapted to technology studies, SST helps to examine technologies as they are used 'in the wild', combining social context, human agency, and technology. As a preliminary, we should note that Giddens' own structuration theory (1984) has itself been applied within technology studies, particularly in information systems; yet because here technology is merely conceptualized as a structure that facilitated or restricted human actions, it led to a total disregard of technology and a materialization of structures (Hanseth et al, 2004). This is precisely the kind of approach that led to ANT's emphasis on the materiality of technological actors. SST seeks to overcome these issues by considering the place of technology amongst processes involving external and internal structures, active agency, and outcomes.

SST has been particularly popular in the study of health technologies (Greenhalgh and Stones, 2010; Greenhalgh et al, 2016; Jeffries et al, 2017) and organizational information systems (Jack and Kholeif, 2008; Kabanda and Brown, 2017). Still, to our knowledge it has not been applied at the intersection of technology, family, and the life course. As such, as with ANT, we will focus here on a related case study to inspect and sketch possible relationships and opportunities for application. This case study refers to our own study of technology adoption and use of a novel communication app (InTouch) among older adults (aged 65+) living in care homes in Canada. InTouch was developed with and for older adults who are frail, institutionalized, and concerned with or at risk of social isolation and loneliness. The accessible app (running on Android and iOS devices) allows users to send audio, video, picture, and pre-set text messages to relatives and friends, who can then reply using their own devices and email accounts. As informed by our field studies, drawing on a participatory design process, the app is asynchronous (users showed a clear desire to control time of communication due to health impairments and living context) and based on large icons (to adapt to users with visual limitations) and a touchscreen interface (there is no typing, only swiping and tapping, as developed for people with motor and dexterity issues) (Baecker et al, 2014).

To test adoption and use of this app, as well as its potential to address issues of social isolation and loneliness, we conducted two- and three-month deployments of the technology in a long-term care facility and a multi-care retirement community in Toronto, Canada (Neves et al, 2015, 2017a, 2017b). These studies included 16 older adults (ages ranged from 74 to 95; M = 83.9; *SD* = 5.5; ten identified as female and six as male) and their study partners (relatives or friends). The research design was based on pre-, mid-, and post-deployment stages with semi-structured interviews, psychometric scales (social support and loneliness), usability and accessibility tests, log analysis, and field observations. By using SST, we were able to examine the interplay of users, contexts, and technology. Findings highlighted the complexity of technology adoption among frail and institutionalized older adults, uncovering a set of critical factors that can facilitate or hinder adoption, namely social (family support, living arrangements), attitudinal (learning dispositions), digital literacy (prior and current level of digital skills), physical (type of motor impairment), and usability factors (ease of use of the app and tablet). More importantly, these factors were interrelated. For example, on the one hand, participants who had family deeply involved in the project were able to overcome previous digital illiteracy and quickly adopt the app. On the other hand, we found different communication preferences, norms, and expectations for family and participants. Family preferred synchronous communication and video and picture messages, whilst our participants had a preference for asynchronous communication and audio and text messages. Additionally, reply times were an issue as grandchildren were expecting quicker responses and participants would often take more than a day to reply (Neves et al, 2017a, 2017b).

With the SST approach, we discovered that context is simultaneously a condition for and an outcome of adoption. Bringing together those adoption factors and our specific technology, we can see their relationship through SST's elements: external structures (conditions of action) encompassed social factors (family norms and expectations, living arrangements, cultural signifiers) and the pre-existing functions of the technology. Internal structures (knowledge and capabilities) included digital literacy, attitudes, physical conditions and personal-based usability of the technology. Agency encompassed different adoption and usage of InTouch and outcomes were mostly linked to social interaction and social connectedness. For 13 participants, InTouch increased their sense of social interaction (communication frequency and type) with family and friends. For six participants, those who had relatives living abroad or far away, their social connectedness – which is more than social interaction; it is meaningful social interaction – increased with InTouch. However, for two of our participants, the technology had the potential to make them more aware of their social isolation and loneliness as relatives and friends did not reply to their messages (Neves et al, 2015, 2017a, 2017b).

Implications: opportunities and challenges

Strong structuration theory provides opportunities for empirical work that are especially visible when we contrast it to actor network theory. Recall that the latter rejected making recourse to the 'context' of a phenomenon as a way to explain it. For actor network theorists, such abstractions as society, group, or structure put forth as an explanation the very thing that first needed to be explained. We saw this philosophical attitude come up against the limits of empirical study in Silva's case, as she was forced to turn to feminist theory to explain the changing relation over time between technological artefacts and their users. SST offers an explanation at this level, encouraging us to think of these relations within a dilated perspective that includes historical and social structures. Still, by recognizing its own tendency toward abstraction (inherited from Giddens' theory), it also seeks to integrate micro-sociological insights. So, not only are abstract variables like 'agency' and 'structure' at play, but attention must also be paid to the various causal properties of many kinds of immediate situations and actors, including those of family dynamics and technological artefacts. By considering the four elements of the quadripartite model (internal and external structures, active agency, and outcomes), we can better flesh out the interplay of agency and structure in the context of family life. For our participants, maintaining a connection with family was the main motivator to adopt the InTouch app, but family preferences and expectations also deeply influenced their uptake and use.

Emphasizing the role of these artefacts in the 'recursive' framework, strong structuration theorists offer us a way to formally capture what Silva (1999, p 57) described as the 'technological nexus'. That is, the intersection of structures, technologies, and their immediate contexts of deployment:

> [T]he technological component of social structures may be positively instantiated when people choose, using interpretive flexibility, to use the technology in a particular

way both within and outside the intended scripts, and also negatively instantiated when they either actively refuse to use it or, importantly, are unable to use it either at all or in the ways they would like. (Greenhalgh and Stones, 2010, p 1290)

Implicit here is a distinction between the ways in which humans and technologies act. By adopting an asymmetrical approach, SST does not treat its actors as nodes subsumed within a flat network, as in ANT, but as qualitatively distinct. While Actor-Network Theorists proclaim their networks to be comprised of 'heterogeneous' entities, they ultimately distinguish actors from one another by their capacity to produce effects within a given network and not on account of any ontological differences between them. Since SST takes such differences seriously, asking how the agency of technologies differs from that of humans, it is perhaps even more 'radical' than its counterpart. In particular, its use of phenomenology to attend to the relation between the immediate situation and an agent's embodied dispositions brings us closer to understanding the peculiar, asymmetrical experience that humans have with objects, particularly in a life course perspective (Greenhalgh and Stones, 2010, p 1290).

This nevertheless requires some wager on the nature of things, committing Greenhalgh et al (2014, p 211) to declare at the outset that technology 'can only "act" in a limited way'. This ultimately means relinquishing the gains that come with ANT's symmetrical scepticism. As Michael (2017, p 87) puts it, with any such a priori sorting of entities, we potentially 'miss out on the complexity of the actants and their hybridity'. Indeed, we risk returning to a humanistic version of the agent: reflective and deliberate in opposition to the built and technological environment.

Conclusion

In line with the pluralistic pragmatism of Abbott (2004, p 76), the relation between methods like ANT and SST should not be thought of in terms of progress from one to the other, but of mutual elucidation of empirical realms that the other does not – and perhaps cannot – consider. ANT makes the important point that we should not begin by assuming that we can explain particular things by reference to abstractions, while SST offers an approach to situated empirical study that does not become trapped in the endless tracing of associations. These different approaches are difficult to reconcile in practice and so require assumptions at the outset on the part of the researcher about the nature of the things in question: do we assume a significant qualitative difference between humans and technological artefacts? What do we lose with such an assumption? What does the researcher sacrifice in siding with actor network theorists and making an assumption of symmetry?

While each, to some extent, exposes the blind spots of the other, our two case studies have demonstrated that both have their own uses, depending to a great extent on the empirical material the researcher is examining. This is to say that even in the realm of technology, family relations, and the life course there is no single and sure approach. So, to adopt one theoretical approach means relinquishing certain gains that can only be obtained by adopting another approach. The upshot of this observation is that the study of ICTs and family relations across the life course is particularly ripe for inquiry by a combination of approaches, such as those surveyed here. We have demonstrated that recursive approaches can be productive given the nature of this topic.

In brief

1. Recursive approaches to sociological study are considered as means to address the absence of a comprehensive approach to technology adoption.
2. Actor network theory and strong structuration theory are offered as exemplary approaches given the particular characteristics of the form of technology adoption in question.
3. Actor network theory is shown to be methodologically useful but nevertheless committed to analytical description over synthetic explanation and unlikely to incorporate accounts of historical change into its micro tracing of associations.
4. Strong structuration theory pays due attention to context but is forced to relinquish the gains that come from actor network theory's radical approach to agency.
5. Two case studies are presented as a way of illustrating the opportunities and limitations afforded by these approaches.

References

Abbott, A. (2004) *Methods of Discovery: Heuristics for the Social Sciences*, New York: W. W. Norton and Co.

Baecker, R., Sellen, K., Crosskey, S., Boscart, V., and Neves, B.B. (2014) 'Technology to reduce social isolation and loneliness', in *Proceedings of the 16th International ACM SIGACCESS Conference on Computers and Accessibility*, New York: ACM, pp 27–34, http://dx.doi.org/10.1145/2661334.2661375

Bloor, D. (1999) 'Anti-Latour', *Studies in History and Philosophy of Science*, 30(1): 81–112.

Chuttur, M. (2009) 'Overview of the technology acceptance model: Origin, developments and future directions', *Working Papers on Information Systems*, 9(37): 9–37.

Couldry, N. (2008) 'Actor network theory and media: Do they connect and on what terms?', in A. Hepp, F. Krotz, S. Moores and C. Winter (eds) *Connectivity, Networks and Flows: Conceptualizing Contemporary Communications*, Cresskill: Hampton Press, pp 93–110.

Cresswell, K. M., Worth, A. and Sheikh, A. (2010) 'Actor-network theory and its role in understanding the implementation of information technology developments in healthcare', *BMC Medical Informatics and Decision Making*, 10(67): 1–11.

Dourish, P. (2004) *Where the Action Is: The Foundations of Embodied Interaction*, Cambridge, MA: The MIT Press.

Giddens, A. (1984) *The Constitution of Society: Outline of the Theory of Structure*, Los Angeles: University of California Press.

Giddens, A. (1986) 'Action, subjectivity, and the constitution of meaning', *Social Research*, 53(3): 529–545.

Gingras, Y. (1995) 'Following scientists through society? Yes, but at arm's length!', in J. Z. Buckwald (ed) *Scientific Practice: Theories and Stories of Doing Physics*, Chicago: Chicago University Press, pp 123–148.

Gingras, Y. (2013) *Sociologie des sciences*, Paris: Presses Universitaires de France.

Greenhalgh, T. and Stones, R. (2010) 'Theorising big IT programmes in healthcare: Strong structuration theory meets actor-network theory', *Social Science and Medicine*, 70(9): 1285–1294, https://doi.org/10.1016/j.socscimed.2009.12.034

Greenhalgh, T., Stones, R. and Swinglehurst, D. (2014) 'Choose and book: A sociological analysis of "resistance" to an expert system', *Social Science and Medicine*, 104: 210–219, https://doi.org/10.1016/j.socscimed.2013.12.014

Greenhalgh, T., Shaw, S., Wherton, J., Hughes, G., Lynch, J., A'Court, C., ... and Stones, R. (2016) 'SCALS: A fourth-generation study of assisted living technologies in their organisational, social, political and policy context', *BMJ Open*, 6(2), e010208, https://doi.org/10.1136/bmjopen-2015-010208

Hanseth, O., Aanestad, M. and Berg, M. (2004) 'Guest editors' introduction: Actor-network theory and information systems. What's so special?', *Information Technology and People*, 17(2): 116–123, https://doi.org/10.1108/09593840410542466

Jack, L. and Kholeif, A. (2008) 'Enterprise resource planning and a contest to limit the role of management accountants: A strong structuration perspective', *Accounting Forum*, 32(1): 30–45, https://doi.org/10.1016/j.accfor.2007.11.003

Jeffries, M., Phipps, D., Howard, R. L., Avery, A., Rodgers, S. and Ashcroft, D. (2017) 'Understanding the implementation and adoption of an information technology intervention to support medicine optimisation in primary care: Qualitative study using strong structuration theory', *BMJ Open*, 7(5), e014810.

Johnston, R. B. (2001) 'Situated action, structuration and actor-network theory: An integrative theoretical perspective', in *Proceedings of the 9th European Conference on Information Systems, Global Co-operation in the New Millennium*, Bled, Slovenia, 27–29 June, pp 232–42.

Kabanda, S. and Brown, I. (2017) 'A structuration analysis of small and medium enterprise (SME) adoption of e-commerce: The case of Tanzania', *Telematics and Informatics*, 34(4): 118–132, https://doi.org/10.1016/j.tele.2017.01.002

Latour, B. (1988) 'The politics of explanation: An alternative', in S. Woolgar (ed) *Knowledge and Reflexivity: New Frontiers in the Sociology of Knowledge*, London: Sage, pp 155–176.

Latour, B. (1990) 'Technology is society made durable', *The Sociological Review*, 38(S1): 103–131, https://doi.org/10.1111/j.1467-954X.1990.tb03350.x

Latour, B. (1992) 'Where are the missing masses? The sociology of a few mundane artifacts', in W.E. Bijker and J. Law (eds) *Shaping Technology/Building Society: Studies in Sociotechnical Change*, Cambridge, MA: MIT Press, pp 225–258.

Latour, B. (1993) *We Have Never Been Modern*, Cambridge, MA: Harvard University Press.

Latour, B. (2005) *Reassembling the Social*, Oxford: Oxford University Press.

Latour, B. (2014) *An Inquiry into Modes of Existence: An Anthropology of the Moderns*, Cambridge, MA: Harvard University Press.

Law, J. (1999) 'After ANT: Complexity, naming and topology', *The Sociological Review*, 47(S1): 1–14, https://doi.org/10.1111/j.1467-954X.1999.tb03479.x.

Law, J. and Callon, M. (1988) 'Engineering and sociology in a military aircraft project: A network analysis of technological change', *Social Problems*, 35(3): 284–297, https://doi.org/10.2307/800623

MacKenzie, D. and Wajcman, J. (1999) *The Social Shaping of Technology*, Buckingham: Open University Press.

Mähring, M., Holmström, J., Keil, M. and Montealegre, R. (2004) 'Trojan actor-networks and swift translation: Bringing actor-network theory to IT project escalation studies', *Information Technology and People*, 17(2): 210–238, https://doi.org/10.1108/09593840410542510

Michael, M. (2017) *Actor Network Theory: Trials, Trails and Translations*, London: Sage.

Neves, B. B., Franz, R. L., Munteanu, C., Baecker, R. and Ngo., M. (2015) '"My hand doesn't listen to me!": Adoption and evaluation of a communication technology for the "oldest old"', in *Proceedings of the 33rd Annual ACM Conference on Human Factors in Computing Systems*, Seoul: ACM, pp 1593–1602, https://doi.org/10.1145/2702123.2702430

Neves, B. B., Franz, R. L., Munteanu, C. and Baecker, R. (2017a) 'Adoption and feasibility of a communication app to enhance social connectedness amongst frail institutionalized oldest old: an embedded case study', *Information Communication & Society*, https://doi.org/10.1080/1369118X.2017.1348534

Neves, B. B., Franz, R., Judges, R., Beermann, C. and Baecker, R. (2017b) 'Can digital technology enhance social connectedness among older adults? A feasibility study', *Journal of Applied Gerontology*, https://doi.org/10.1177/0733464817741369

Orlikowski, W. J. (2000) 'Using technology and constituting structures: A practice lens for studying technology in organizations', *Organization Science*, 11(4): 404–428, https://doi.org/10.1287/orsc.11.4.404.14600.

Prout, A. (1996) 'Actor-network theory, technology and medical sociology: An illustrative analysis of the metered dose inhaler', *Sociology of Health & Illness*, 18(2): 198–219.

Silva, E. B. (1999) 'Transforming housewifery: Dispositions, practices and technologies', in E. B. Silva and C. Smart (eds) *The New Family*, London: Sage, pp 46–65.

Silva, E. B. (2000) 'The cook, the cooker and the gendering of the kitchen', *The Sociological Review*, 48(4): 612–628, https://doi.org/10.1111/1467-954X.00235

Silva, E. B. (2010) *Technology, Culture, Family: Influences on Home Life*, Basingstoke: Palgrave.

Stones, R. (2005) *Structuration Theory*, London: Palgrave.

Wyatt, S. (2008) 'Technological determinism is dead; Long live technological determinism', in E. J. Hackett, O. Amsterdamska, M. Lynch and J. Wacjman (eds) *The Handbook of Science and Technology Studies*, Cambridge, MA: The MIT Press, pp 165–180.

FOUR

Weaving family connections on- and offline: the turn to networked individualism

Anabel Quan-Haase, Hua Wang, Barry Wellman, and Renwen Zhang

Introduction

Older adults (65+) are now flocking to information and communication technologies (ICTs) in North America after decades of lower usage than that of younger adults (Anderson and Perrin, 2017). With a significant majority of older adults now using ICTs to engage in a range of activities (Anderson and Perrin, 2017), it is important to understand how they use them to shape family life and dynamics. We investigate:

1. What role do ICTs play in supporting family networks in general, and the position of older adults in them?
2. Is ICT use helping to maintain and strengthen social ties within – and across – generations?

These questions are especially important as families in the Global North are in the midst of a societal shift from group-based interaction in a single, local, and often solidary family and community to multiple, loosely knit networks. Such networked individuals have partial membership in multiple networks and rely less on permanent membership in settled groups. They must meet their social and emotional needs by tapping into these loosely knit, often diverse networks rather than relying on tight connections with a relatively small number of family and friends. The shift to networked individualism helps us to understand connectivity across the lifespan, including the role of family connections in the lives of older adults. These are important research and policy matters, especially as some older adults report social isolation and feelings of loneliness (Neves et al, 2017).

We contribute to this understanding by examining the role of ICTs in family life from the perspective of older adults.

ICTs are facilitating new forms of social network connections for immediate and extended families, whether it is through email, texting, or more interactive forms of engagement such as video chat. In this chapter, we show how the shift from group-based analysis to examinations of loosely knit networks can help us understand connectivity across the lifespan. We specifically examine how older adults adopt and engage with ICTs and how these technologies are helping to connect families in novel ways. Scholars often include a wide range of technologies under the umbrella term of 'ICTs' (Selwyn et al, 2003; Heart and Kalderon, 2013; Chayko, 2017). For this chapter, we broadly define ICTs as the devices (that is, computers, tablets, and mobile phones) and applications (such as Facebook, Skype, and Twitter) used to access, produce, consume, and exchange information in a digital form, especially for supporting social interactions in the older adults' social networks. To provide a more fine-grained investigation, we compare their use of ICTs with other types of communication. Such nuanced analysis is particularly relevant for this demographic because older adults often own a mobile phone but use it exclusively as a phone, and many grew up before ICTs became widespread (Neves et al, 2013).

To study older adults, we draw on 41 in-depth interviews conducted in 2013–2014 with participants aged 65+ in the fourth East York (Toronto) project, and show how their use of ICTs affects family socializing, coordination, and closeness (see also Quan-Haase et al, 2016a, 2017, 2018a, 2018b; Wang et al, 2018). We use pseudonyms to protect the identity of our interviewees and add basic demographic information (gender and age) about each participant for context.

Our interviews show that while older adults own a number of ICTs, most rely primarily on using now-traditional email and are less apt to use newer types such as social media (Facebook) and video chat (Skype). When it comes to device ownership, almost all (90%) owned a computer, and nearly as high a percentage (85%) owned a mobile phone (see Table 4.1). Despite the high ownership of mobile phones among East York older adults, only one-fifth (20%) used them for texting, with the remainder (65%) using them exclusively for phone calls, often in cases of emergencies (see also Neves et al, 2013). In our sample, 17% of participants reported not having used any kind of digital communication channel such as email, social media, or video chat. Interestingly, of those older adults who had not adopted a digital communication channel, 10% owned a mobile phone that they used only for calls. This suggests that only three individuals in our sample (7%) were non-users of any type of ICT – including mobile phones.

Table 4.1 Devices owned by older adults in East York (*N* = 41)

Device	Number of participants	Percentage
Computer	37	90
– Desktop only	14	34
– Laptop only	10	24
– Both desktop and laptop	13	32
Landline telephone	40	98
Mobile phone (basic/smart)	35	85
Tablet	9	17

East York older adults have engaged in a variety of activities with ICTs, according to the kinds of social networks that they are involved in, their digital skill level, and comfort with ICTs (Quan-Haase et al, 2018a). Previous research has suggested that the oldest among the population of older adults – those who were introduced to the internet late in life – are the least likely to adopt the internet, have limited digital skills, and use the internet for a limited number of activities (Hargittai and Dobransky, 2017; Schreurs et al, 2017). For older adults, the benefits of adopting ICTs, such as convenience in facilitating activities, outweigh the detriments including concerns around security and cost (Mitzner et al, 2010). While some have small, closely knit, relatively homogeneous networks, others are *networked individuals* with multiple, partial connections to relatives and friends (Quan-Haase et al, 2018b; Rainie and Wellman, 2012). ICTs help to mobilize different kinds of social support – the East Yorkers use them for coordination, maintaining ties, and casual conversations – and to strengthen family ties with both nearby and faraway kin. The use of ICTs for maintaining contact and providing companionship is especially important for older adults who may have limited mobility.

Once East York older adults start to use ICTs, the technology becomes incorporated into their lives for communication and information, just as it does for other age groups operating in networked societies. They use ICTs as well as telephoning and personal visits predominantly to maintain existing relationships rather than to develop new ones (see also Quan-Haase et al, 2017). With few family members living nearby, emails and telephoning become important ways to arrange personal visits. As ICTs become important in older adults' lives, learning how to use them better becomes a form of social support in itself. In particular, as ICTs expand in scope and with the constant updates to software, these older adults reach out to peers and younger family members to support their learning in mastering social media such as social networking sites and voice chat (Quan-Haase et al, 2017). Some combine newer and older technologies by putting sticky notes on their computers to remind them of passwords and commands.

Contradicting fears that ICTs are inadequate for meaningful contact (Hampton and Wellman, 2018), East York older adults see ICTs as providing real – not token – support. Those who use ICTs to communicate integrate their supportive exchanges on it with the support they exchange in person and by telephone. Moreover, variations in the nature of older adults' networks affect how they use ICTs and the resources they obtain from it.

The turn to networked individualism

The increasing digital connectivity of older Canadians is part of the transformation of much of North American society away from being enmeshed in bounded, village-like settings – or urban neighbourhoods – to being engaged in multiple, diverse social networks. Up until World War II, most people spent much of their lives surrounded by relatives, neighbours, friends, and co-workers who shared similar backgrounds and beliefs but also engaged in similar tasks and labour (Hampton and Wellman, 2018). Although the purportedly happy nature of such communities has been over-idealized in a haze of pastoralist nostalgia, the vast majority of connections were with strong ties with whom they had much in common. Along with reciprocal awareness and social support, there was mutual surveillance and social control. In these close communities, social norms were constantly reinforced and belonging often required following pre-established expectations. Similarly, families were tight-knit and often lived nearby, facilitating frequent visits and the easy exchange of social support.

Things have changed for both communities and families since the 1990s, leading toward a 'Triple Revolution' in how society operates (Rainie and Wellman, 2012, 2018):

1. The turn away from bounded groups defined by locality, ethnicity, and social class to multiple far-flung networks organized more by sociability and shared interests.

2. The proliferation of the personalized internet affording flexible communication and information exchange over great (and small) geographic distances.
3. The hyper-abundance of mobile devices that make personalized communication and information available wherever one is, as a 'third skin' (Fortunati, 2005) that is 'an extension of my hands' (Maria C. Kicevski, personal communication, 30 September 2017).

The introduction of modern ICTs affords different network structures that can transform how people form and maintain family relations as well as gain access to information and social support (Hampton, 2016; Quan-Haase et al, 2017). Technologies that facilitate contact at a distance – telephones, ships, railroads, cars, and planes – allow people to transcend tightly bounded ties of kinship, locality, occupation, gender, religion, and ethnicity. Such technologies provide opportunities to form supportive social relations in multiple contexts that do not strongly overlap: family at home; colleagues in the workplace; and friends in the neighbourhood, church, and voluntary association (Rainie and Wellman, 2012, 2018; Quan-Haase, 2016).

Thus, the Triple Revolution has created opportunities for a transition to 'networked individualism' that affects how families interact. Using ICTs, families have the potential to link lives within and across generations and over a lifetime. But they are not throwbacks to the pre-industrial village-like communities of the past. Mobility and ICTs facilitate opportunities for partial commitments to different social milieus. Moreover, each person maintains a unique individual community through email, Facebook, mobile phones, and travel. Thus, it is no wonder that older adults are embracing ICTs: they are a way to keep in touch with their siblings, children, and grandchildren – as well as their cousins by the dozens – no matter where they may live. Family members are neither isolated nor bound up in homogenous groups but are likely to have multiple involvements in networks that span kin, friends, neighbours, workmates, schoolmates, and fellow social group members.

How ICTs connect older adults with their families

Much debate has focused on how ICTs are shaping family life and how families operate in terms of the maintenance of strong bonds, the exchange of social support, the organization of get-togethers, and the sharing of news. Whether it is through email exchanges to arrange a visit or real-time video chats, families are relying on ICTs to connect and coordinate. With a specific focus on older adults, we draw on the concept of networked individualism to discuss three areas where ICTs have been integrated into family life: (1) practices of connectivity; (2) maintaining family ties near and far; and (3) feelings of connectedness.

ICTs and family practices of connectivity among older adults

ICTs are a major part of family life, shaping how families routinely connect with each other. To what extent have family routines and practices of older adults changed with ICTs, as this age group has lagged behind younger generations and may be set in longstanding ways (Schreurs et al, 2017). Yet older adults are not immune to societal change, and the move toward networked societies has had profound implications for how they maintain family ties and organize family life (Rainie and Wellman, 2012).

We found that email is by far the most frequently used ICT, utilized by the great majority (80%) of the older East Yorkers (see Figure 4.1). Email is followed in popularity by Facebook (34%) and Skype (29%). Only one-fifth use texting (20%) and Twitter use was almost non-existent (5%).

Figure 4.1 Digital communication channels used by older adults in East York for communication with all social and kin ties (*N* = 41)

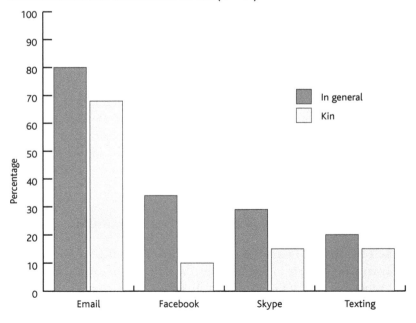

Email is widely used for keeping in touch with family. Two-thirds (68%) of our sample have integrated email into their communication repertoire with family and see it as beneficial for maintaining family ties. For example, when we interviewed Sterling, he contrasted email with the telephone, saying that email allows him to say more things, craft more articulate messages, and remember more things to say:

> 'I have two sisters, both in the US, one in South Carolina and one in Massachusetts. We communicate typically by email and usually, [Maria] and I visit once a year... I chose email because, if I'm on the phone, I never remember all the things I want to tell her. If I have a lot of information I often type my information into Word, and I go back and edit or add or clarify and then I cut and paste into an email... I initiate a couple a year, they initiate a couple a year, so probably four times, it all depends if we are starting to arrange a visit then it gets a little more frequent.' (P93, 75, M)

Email has provided routine ways of staying in touch with family, such as siblings. For many of the participants, asynchronous forms of communication such as email are perceived as a benefit, not a drawback, to sustaining meaningful contact with family members. Email exchanges not only serve to keep in touch but are particularly helpful for coordinating visits and special family events.

Facebook is the second most widely used ICT, although only 10% of our East York older adults use it for family connectivity (Figure 4.1). Facebook's role as a networking tool is unique as it provides opportunities for intergenerational exchange and creates new practices for staying in touch with children and grandchildren. In fact, Facebook is only used by one East Yorker for keeping in touch with same-generation kin; the others use it for intergenerational networking (Figure 4.2). Most older adults in our study do not report posting pictures themselves or messaging contacts but value viewing text, photo, and video updates from their children, grandchildren, and other relatives:

> 'I like Facebook because I have a lot of young cousins, who I can see what they're up to. Where they are. I just like that kind of family connection that I can get on the internet. Because they live in Alberta and I live in Ontario... Pictures,

more pictures on Facebook. I like looking at pictures of
them and their kids and their kids' kids.' (Rose, P40, 67, W)

Hence, social media can create a real sense of connectivity. Pictures
create strong bonds and provide a sense of closeness. As pictures
on Facebook are frequently updated and show a diversity of family
members, they create an expanded network of connections that can
span multiple generations.

As family members of all generations have dispersed across North
America – or remain in the home country – ICTs are particularly
relevant for supporting intergenerational networking (Figure 4.2). This
is a quite different pattern than in-person and phone interactions in
which intergenerational and intragenerational contacts are similar in
overall frequency. The pattern is similar across all ICTs, where email,
Skype, Facebook, and texting are used more frequently for keeping
in touch with intergenerational kin rather than same-generation kin.

Figure 4.2 Digital communication channels used by older adults in East York for
intergenerational and intragenerational communication with kin ties (*N* = 41)

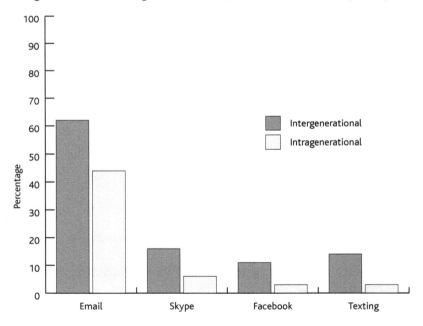

Life circumstances affect decisions around ICT use. As some older
adults' mobility becomes reduced with age and deteriorated health,
ICTs can help in reducing feelings of social loneliness and physical

isolation by complementing in-person visits. This facilitates the maintenance of multiple, often interconnected, networks both near and far.

ICTs have not only affected the routines and practices of digital older adults, even those older adults who do not use ICTs also see their practices changing (Quan-Haase et al, 2017). Most (85%) have integrated at least one type of ICT into their regular practices and see many benefits in the possibilities afforded for maintaining family ties, coordinating family events, and staying connected with diverse family ties. If they could not do it, they ask their children or grandchildren, sometimes also friends, to look something up for them online – often health information for themselves or others – or for help in contacting a geographically distant friend or relative (Quan-Haase et al, 2018a). For example, Magdalena often asks her daughters to send emails or Facebook messages to family members who were at a distance:

> 'My sister is in Arizona on vacation… It was her birthday, so I asked my daughter… to send her a message through Facebook because wherever she goes, she has it with her, and we can't reach her by phone.' (P73, 75, F)

In contrast to these older adults' enthusiasm for email's possibilities for maintaining ties, most have not embraced real-time synchronous ICTs into their routines because they see it as distracting and taking time away from more in-depth forms of interaction. While some older adults rely on Skype video chat for maintaining distant family ties, they would rather visit in person whenever possible. Moreover, older adults often avoid texting because of the small screens of mobile phones and their lack of ease in using the devices. In our sample, only 15% have texted to stay connected with their families (see Figure 4.1). Many of these older adults have deliberately maintained routines such as visiting in person and making phone calls. For example, An Dung uses his smartphone only to call people:

> 'I never use text message. I'm really clumsy, my generation we don't use this one. [The screen is] so small! Sometimes you touch the wrong bar, so it's too tricky.' (P15, 71, M)

ICTs and maintaining family ties near and far among older adults

In 1997, Frances Cairncross boldly asserted that ICTs have caused 'the death of distance'. Although distance still matters even in a technology-intensive networked society, her assertion speaks to how ICTs connect people who are geographically dispersed. ICTs have weakened, but not eliminated, the effects of distance on interpersonal relationships. For example, the *third* East York study showed that email is the most important medium for people to communicate in transoceanic relationships, helping to overcome geographic distance and time differences (Mok et al, 2010). In this, our *fourth* East York study, we find that email has been joined by Skype and Facebook. ICTs have transformed transnational family relations by enabling family members to be co-present (emotionally 'there' for each other) across distance, thereby facilitating more dynamic and multifaceted relationships in distant family life (Baldassar, 2016; Rainie and Wellman, 2012, 2018).

ICTs not only have facilitated communication among family members, they have also expanded their geographical reach. For example, a past study on older adults found that those who had more phone and email communication with their grandchildren living far away reported higher life satisfaction than those who only communicated in person (Holladay and Seipke, 2007). Toronto is a city of immigrants (National Household Survey, 2011), but the 'old country' across the Pacific or Atlantic is no longer remotely unreachable (Coughlin, 1999). Nearly three-quarters (71%) of the older adult East Yorkers report having kin living outside of Toronto, and all use the phone for maintaining these long-distance family ties. As An Dung says about his phone use:

> 'I have a brother in Montreal, a brother and relative in the US, and I have another one in Paris, France. Because long distance now is not all that expensive, my wife phones them all the time.' (P15, 71, M)

These older adults see ICTs as having a positive impact on their connections with more distant kin because of their convenience, low cost, and ease of use. Two-thirds (66%) use email, 21% use Skype, 14% use Facebook, and 10% text (Table 4.2).

Table 4.2 Digital communication channels used by older adults in East York for long-distance communication with kin (*N* = 29)

Channel used for long-distance communication with kin	Number of participants	Percentage
Email	19	66
Skype	6	21
Facebook	4	14
Texting	3	10

Skype video chat – with its co-presence – has also become important for some of our East York older adults to converse with distant family members. Although some studies have found that older adults rarely use video chat (Mok et al, 2010; Yuan et al, 2016), 21% of the older East Yorkers use Skype to contact family members living far away. Despite many being novice Skype users, they report loving the increased companionship enabled by its non-verbal cues – especially when looking at very young grandchildren or reaching out to extended kin, and connecting with friends at a distance.

> 'My new toy, with a webcam, is Skype and I enjoy it. My friend winters in the Caribbean and I Skype with her. I have a niece in the Yukon and I can Skype there. I would Skype if I know that person has a webcam… You can see that person and see how they look. Otherwise when you're talking on the phone you have no idea what's going on.' (Olga, P20, 80, W)

Facebook also opens up new opportunities for older adults to facilitate contact with geographically distant kin of all generations. For instance, Hermione was born in London, UK, and moved to Toronto when she was 21 years old. Having a lot of relatives in the UK, she actively uses Facebook to communicate with them:

> 'I'm on Facebook because I have family that is scattered; to see photographs and keep in touch with what they're doing.' (P95, 67, W, London, England)

Older adults also use the telephone and email to contact nearby family members, usually to arrange get-togethers. Despite concerns that ICTs might lead to the decrease of in-person communication, East York older adults use ICTs primarily to supplement, rather than replace, in-person interaction with kin living nearby.

Older adults make different use of ICTs for communicating with geographically distant kin. Skype is primarily used for communicating with family members living far away, both in North America and overseas. Moreover, 66% of the East Yorkers who have family members living outside of Toronto used email to communicate with them. In addition, they use the phone to connect with family members both near and far. By contrast, these older adults rely primarily on in-person communication for keeping in touch with kin living in Toronto. This is consistent with the third East York study's finding that email contact predominates for transoceanic relationships and face-to-face contact is strongly related to sociability with kin living short distances away (Mok et al, 2010).

ICTs and feelings of connectedness among older adults

Networked individuals tend to have diverse social relationships that they can actively communicate with for meaningful social contact and support of unmet needs. However, limited mobility, chronic illness, and shrinking connections are among the biggest challenges to the physical, mental, and social well-being of older adults, especially after retirement and losing a spouse (Cornwell and Waite, 2009; Dickens et al, 2011). For some, the days keep getting longer yet the time with family and close friends shortens, potentially leading to social isolation, feelings of loneliness, depression, and possibly dementia (Shankar et al, 2013; Valtorta and Hanratty, 2012). In the 2008/2009 survey on healthy ageing, 20% of older adults reported feeling lonely often or some of the time, and the proportion increases as the age group goes up (Statistics Canada, 2012).

For networked individuals, being at the autonomous centre of their personal networks can provide a sense of control, intimacy, and belonging. The benefits of ICT adoption and use are reflected in our East York data in at least three ways: (1) overcoming physical limitations for communication; (2) living alone, but feeling connected; and (3) enjoying simple pleasures through socializing.

For some older adults, constraints such as difficulty with walking and sensory loss (as in hearing and vision impairment) can affect social isolation (de Leon et al, 2003; Grenade and Boldy, 2008; Jopling, 2015; Lund et al, 2010). ICTs have been crucial for overcoming physical limitations and communication barriers in order to sustain close relationships (Erickson, 2011; Quan-Haase et al, 2017).

'The only time we get together is my birthday. Otherwise, we only speak on the phone with my cousins and a few close friends... as they are all old with walkers and canes.' (Yvonne, P45, 82, W)

For those who are hard of hearing, text-based communication channels become especially helpful (Yuan et al, 2016):

'Because I do have a hearing deficit sometimes it's difficult on the telephone for me and I've adapted to the PC more easily ... It was the first one I got used to and I find it most convenient. It's out there when I'm working in the kitchen, I can go back and forth. I get up in the morning, have my coffee with my computer, and use it to exchange email with my friends. So the PC is the most important to me.' (Catherine, P38, 73, W)

Without ICTs, older adults like Yvonne and Catherine would not have been able to maintain some of the most important relationships in their lives. Yet when they do take advantage of the social affordances of ICTs, they remain in control and can make an effort to prevent their social networks from declining despite their physical limitations.

Living alone used to be considered a factor closely associated with poor social and health outcomes for older adults (Cornwell and Waite, 2009), but studies now suggest that living alone does not necessarily deprive older adults of participating in social activities or obtaining social support (Perissinotto and Covinsky, 2014). They may not feel lonely because of the many networking opportunities that ICTs facilitate to initiate contact, seek help, or just feel connected (Cotten et al, 2013; Sum et al, 2008; Wright, 2000; Yu et al, 2016). For example, Beverley is a widow who spends a lot of time at her summer cottage that is far away from Toronto where her children and grandchildren live. Carrying a mobile phone has made her feel that she is never completely alone no matter where she is, especially when she needs to reach out to someone.

'I use my cell phone to call neighbours or if I had an emergency, I could contact a hospital or doctor because I'm up there by myself quite often.' (P2, 75, W)

But digital media is not just a boon for the constrained and isolated. Although lower levels of digital literacy can disadvantage some older adults in getting tasks done (Hargittai and Dobransky, 2017), most use ICTs to *socialize and seek help*, critical needs for networked individuals who do not live in proximity with supportive family and friends (Quan-Haase et al, 2016b; Schwenk, 2016; Wu et al, 2015). Different types of access to ICTs and levels of participation can boost self-efficacy (Czaja et al, 2006), feelings of connectedness (Cotten et al, 2013), and perceived social support among older adults (Quan-Haase et al, 2017; Yu et al, 2016).

The simple process of creating a social media account and participating in activities on social networking sites can help to bridge generational gaps (Madden, 2010). Although some older adults only post birthday wishes on social media, many of their children and grandchildren post to document significant events and precious moments in their lives (see Figure 4.2). Just being able to watch the younger generations grow up gives older adults another venue to appreciate the simple pleasures in life. For example, Dorothy has been living alone in a Toronto apartment all her life, as she never got married and has no children. She is very close to her immediate kin and talks with her brother and sister regularly by phone and email. Using Facebook to keep an eye on family photos has given her a sense of intimacy.

> 'I have a nephew in Halifax and I always find it interesting to look on his wife's Facebook because she posts things quite often and yesterday she had pictures of the boys in the backyard. So nothing major, but it's just nice that I find those small, informal things are good for keeping in touch.' (P65, 69, W)

Despite the overall positive attitude that most older adults have concerning ICTs, no ICTs can replace the richness of face-to-face interaction for them (Daft and Lengel, 1984; Quan-Haase et al, 2017). It is no surprise that the majority of older East Yorkers prefer in-person contact over the exchange of short digital snippets (see also Yuan et al, 2016), although many appreciate what video chat, email, and mobile phones can offer to facilitate communication between in-person visits. In fact, many older adults in East York regret that they have fewer of these deeper and more intimate conversations.

> 'People used to talk to one another face-to-face and now they don't. Now everything is text and short form. And it has taken away the language and that social interaction.' (Dorothy, P65, 69, W)

'I like to hear a person talk and have a conversation; and to me if you're doing it with texting, it's still not the same as a real conversation.' (Anastasia, P37, 66, W)

Many older East Yorkers use media in combination to stay connected in multiple ways with diverse social ties rather than relying on a single means (see also Greenwood et al, 2016). For example, Brian combines phone calls with frequent emails that are often jokes or titbits of information to communicate with family 330 km away. The combination of media and frequent micro communications helps him stay connected, not just socially but also emotionally – because being able to sense the tone of voice on the phone adds a real-time human touch.

'I'll call my nephew about twice a week. We're very close ... Once in a while he'll email me something ... When my brother was alive, he used to email me jokes all the time. I used to laugh every day.' (Brian, P72, 65, M)

Conclusions

Networked individualism examines the fundamental shift in the structure of society from group-based forms of interaction to socialization in multiple, loosely knit networks (Rainie and Wellman, 2012, 2018). The shift in analysis does not apply exclusively to younger generations, but can help us understand connectivity across the lifespan, including the role of family connections in the lives of older adults.

At times, the depiction of older adults is like Whistler's Mother, by no means networked but sitting alone in her chair until the end comes. Yet our research has demonstrated that most older adults in East York are engaged networked individuals. Although it has taken a long time for a majority of North American older adults (aged 65+) to start using ICTs, they are now flocking online. They are integrating a number of ICTs including now-traditional email, Skype, and Facebook to stay in touch with both near and distant family ties. ICT use is intertwined with in-person life, with these East Yorkers relying on it to coordinate in-person get-togethers, stay in touch when at a distance, and exchange brief micro communications. Whistler's Mother is now networked (Figure 4.3).

Figure 4.3 Whistler's networked mother

Source: Mashup of James McNeill Whister, Arrangement in Grey and Black No. 1, Copyright Lorain Leong (2017). Used with permission.

To an appreciable extent, it is not so much that the aged have started using ICTs, but that long-time users of ICTs have grown into older age. As is the case in all generations, ICT use is intertwined with connecting in person with the same family members. Feelings of closeness and strong family bonds drive digital connectivity. However, older adults are less likely than younger adults to use newer forms of social media such as Instagram and Snapchat. Few older adults text because they do not see its benefits, and sometimes they cannot handle the small screen and keyboards of mobile phones. Internet users continued to use ICTs as they grow older. This suggests that previous low ICT use among non-frail older adults was more a cohort effect than a true effect of old age (see also Quan-Haase et al, 2017). That is promising because in today's ageing societies, older adults face unique challenges, yet they have a lifetime of beneficial wisdom to share and continuing opportunities to engage.

In brief

1. Older adults have particularly benefited from the use of ICTs with family members because these technologies not only allow them to connect with their own generation, but also to reach out to younger generations.
2. As the family members (and friends) have spread out geographically, ICTs help their ties to persist.
3. Older adults, like most younger adults, use ICTs more to maintain existing ties than to forge new ones (Quan-Haase, 2008; Mesch et al, 2012).
4. ICTs can lessen communication barriers due to the physical limitations of oneself or others.
5. Although ICTs help to keep in touch via email, phone calls, and content sharing on social media, older adults still prefer spending time in person.

Acknowledgements

We are grateful to Christian Beermann, Brent Berry, Rhonda McEwen, Darryl Pieber, Lilia Smale, Beverly Wellman, and Isioma Elueze for their collaboration, the editors and reviewers for their comments, the Social Sciences and Humanities Research Council of Canada for their financial support, and, most importantly, the East Yorkers who invited us into their homes.

References

Anderson, M. and Perrin, A. (2017) 'Tech adoption climbs among older adults', http://assets.pewresearch.org/wp-content/uploads/sites/14/2017/05/16170850/PI_2017.05.17_Older-Americans-Tech_FINAL.pdf

Baldassar, L. (2016) 'De-demonizing distance in mobile family lives', *Global Networks*, 16(2): 145-163, http://dx.doi.org/10.1111/glob.12109

Cairncross, F. (1997) *The Death of Distance*, Boston: Harvard Business School Press.

Chayko, M. (2017) *Superconnected*, Thousand Oaks, CA: Sage.

Cornwell, E.Y. and Waite, L.J. (2009) 'Social disconnectedness, perceived isolation, and health among older adults', *Journal of Health and Social Behavior*, 50: 31-48, https://doi.org/10.1177/002214650905000103

Cotten, S. R., Anderson, W. A. and McCullough, B. M. (2013) 'Impact of internet use on loneliness and contact with others among older adults: Cross-sectional analysis', *Journal of Medical Internet Research*, 15(2): e39, https://doi.org/10.2196/jmir.2306

Coughlin, J. (1999) 'Technology needs of aging boomers', *Issues in Science and Technology*, 16(1): 53–60.

Czaja, S. J., Charness, N., Fisk, A. D., Hertzog, C., Nair, S. N., Rogers, W. A. and Sharit, J. (2006) 'Factors predicting the use of technology', *Psychology and Aging*, 21(2): 333–352, https://doi.org/10.1037/0882-7974.21.2.333

Daft, R. L. and Lengel, R. H. (1984) 'Information richness: A new approach to managerial behavior and organizational design', *Research in Organizational Behavior*, 6: 191–233.

De Leon, M. C. F., Glass, T. A. and Berkman, L. F. (2003) 'Social engagement and disability in a community population of older adults: The New Haven EPESE', *American Journal of Epidemiology*, 157(7): 633–642, https://doi.org/10.1093/aje/kwg028

Dickens, A. P., Richards, S. H., Greaves, C. J. and Campbell, J. L. (2011) 'Interventions targeting social isolation in older people', *BMC Public Health*, 11(647), https://doi.org/10.1186/1471-2458-11-647

Erickson, L. B. (2011) 'Social media, social capital, and seniors', in *Proceedings of the AMCIS*, Detroit, August, https://pdfs.semanticscholar.org/e45d/782b985c3b72a4c4174e29da0da076 0b9675.pdf

Fortunati, L. (2005) 'The mobile phone as technological artefact', in P. Glotz and S. Bertsch (eds) *Thumb Culture*, Bielefeld: Transcript Verlag, pp 149–160.

Greenwood, S., Perrin, A. and Duggan, M. (2016) 'Social media update 2016', www.pewinternet.org/2016/11/11/social-media-update-2016/

Grenade, L. and Boldy, D. (2008) 'Social isolation and loneliness among older people: Issues and future challenges in community and residential settings', *Australian Health Review*, 32(3): 468–478, https://doi.org/10.1071/AH080468

Hampton, K. N. (2016) 'Persistent and pervasive community: New communication technologies and the future of community', *American Behavioral Scientist*, 60(1): 101–124, https://doi.org/10.1177/0002764215601714

Hampton, K. N. and Wellman, B. (2018) 'All the lonely people?', forthcoming in L. A. Lievrouw and B. Loader (eds) *Handbook of Digital Media and Communication*, London: Routledge.

Hargittai, E. and Dobransky, K. (2017) 'Old dogs, new clicks', *Canadian Journal of Communication*, 42(2): 195–212, https://doi.org/10.22230/cjc.2017v42n2a3125

Heart, T. and Kalderon, E. (2013) 'Older adults', *International Journal of Medical Informatics*, 82(11), e209–e231, https://doi.org/10.1016/j.ijmedinf.2011.03.002

Holladay, S. J. and Seipke, H. L. (2007) 'Communication between grandparents and grandchildren in geographically separated relationships', *Communication Studies*, 58(3): 281–297, https://doi.org/10.1080/10510970701518371

Jopling, K. (2015) 'Promising approaches to reducing loneliness and isolation in later life', *Age UK*, www.campaigntoendloneliness.org/wp-content/uploads/Promising-approaches-to-reducing-loneliness-and-isolation-in-later-life.pdf

Lund, R., Nilsson, C. J. and Avlund, K. (2010) 'Can the higher risk of disability onset among older people who live alone be alleviated by strong social relations?', *Age and Aging*, 39: 319–326, https://doi.org/10.1093/ageing/afq020

Madden, M. (2010) 'Older adults and social media', Pew Research Center, http://pewinternet.org/Reports/2010/Older-Adults-and-Social-Media.aspx

Mesch, G., Talmud, I. and Quan-Haase, A. (2012) 'Instant messaging social networks: Individual, relational and cultural characteristics', *Journal of Social and Personal Relationships*, 29(6): 736–759, https://doi.org/10.1177/0265407512448263

Mitzner, T. L., Boron, J. B., Fausset, C. B., Adams, A. E., Charness, N., Czaja, S. J.,… Sharit, J. (2010) 'Older adults talk technology: Technology usage and attitudes', *Computers in Human Behavior*, 26(6): 1710–1721, https://doi.org/10.1016/j.chb.2010.06.020

Mok, D., Wellman, B. and Carrasco, J. A. (2010) 'Does distance matter in the age of the internet?', *Urban Studies*, 47(13): 2747–2783, https://doi.org/10.1177/0042098010377363

National Household Survey (2011) *NHS Focus on Geography Series*, Statistics Canada, http://www12.statcan.gc.ca/nhs-enm/2011/as-sa/fogs-spg/Pages/FOG.cfm?GeoCode=535&lang=E&level=3

Neves, B. B., Amaro, F. and Fonseca, J. R. S. (2013) 'Coming of (old) age in the digital age', *Sociological Research Online*, 18(2), https://doi.org/10.5153/sro.2998

Neves, B.B., Franz, R., Judges, R., Beermann, C. and Baecker, R. (2017) 'Can digital technology enhance social connectedness among older adults? A feasibility study', *Journal of Applied Gerontology*, https://doi.org/10.1177/0733464817741369

Perissinotto, C. M. and Covinsky, K. E. (2014) 'Living alone, socially isolated or lonely – What are we measuring?', *Journal of General Internal Medicine*, 29: 1429-1431, https://doi.org/10.1007/s11606-014-2977-8

Quan-Haase, A. (2008) 'University students' local and distant social ties: Using and integrating modes of communication on campus', *Information, Communication & Society*, 10(5): 671–693.

Quan-Haase, A. (2016) *Technology & Society* (2nd edn), Toronto: Oxford University Press.

Quan-Haase, A., Martin, K., Miller, M., Wellman, B. and Beermann, C. (2016a) 'Older adults networking on and off digital media', *XXXVI Sunbelt Conference*, Newport Beach, CA, 5–10 April.

Quan-Haase, A., Martin, K. and Schreurs, K. (2016b) 'Interviews with digital seniors', *Information, Communication & Society*, 19(5): 691–707, https://doi.org/10.1080/1369118X.2016.1140217

Quan-Haase, A., Mo, G. Y. and Wellman, B. (2017) 'Connected seniors', *Information, Communication & Society*, 20(7): 967–998, https://doi.org/10.1080/1369118X.2017.1305428

Quan-Haase, A., Williams, C., Kicevski, M., Elueze, I. and Wellman, B. (2018a) 'Dividing the grey divide', *American Behavioral Scientist*, forthcoming.

Quan-Haase, A., Zhang, R., Wellman, B. and Wang, H. (2018b) 'Older adults on digital media in a networked society: Enhancing and updating social connections', in M. Graham and W. H. Dutton (eds) *Society and the Internet* (2nd edn), Oxford: Oxford University Press.

Rainie, L. and Wellman, B. (2012) *Networked*, Cambridge, MA: MIT Press.

Rainie, L. and Wellman, B. (2018) 'The triple revolution in daily life', in M. Graham and W. H. Dutton (eds) *Society and the Internet* (2nd edn), London: Oxford University Press.

Schreurs, K., Quan-Haase, A. and Martin, K. (2017) 'Problematizing the digital literacy paradox in the context of older adults' ICT use: Aging, media discourse, and self-determination', *Canadian Journal of Communication*, 42(2): 359-377, https://doi.org/10.22230/cjc.2017v42n2a3130

Schwenk, T. (2016) 'A digital divide for older adults', www.jwatch.org/na42016/2016/08/09/digital-divide-older-adults

Selwyn, N., Gorard, S., Furlong, J. and Madden, L. (2003) 'Older adults' use of information and communications technology in everyday life', *Ageing and Society*, 23(05): 561-582, https://doi.org/10.1017/S0144686X03001302

Shankar, A., Hamer, M., McMunn, A. and Steptoe, A. (2013) 'Social isolation and loneliness: Relationships with cognitive function during 4 years of follow-up in the English Longitudinal Study of Ageing', *Psychosomatic Medicine*, 75: 161-170, https://doi.org/10.1097/PSY.0b013e31827f09cd

Statistics Canada (2012) 'Social participation and the health and well-being of Canadian seniors', www.statcan.gc.ca/pub/82-003-x/2012004/article/11720-eng.htm

Sum, S., Matthews, M. R., Pourghasem, M. and Hughes, I. (2008) 'Internet technology and social capital', *Journal of Computer-Mediated Communication*, 14: 202-220, https://doi.org/10.1111/j.1083-6101.2008.01437.x

Valtorta, N. and Hanratty, B. (2012) 'Loneliness, isolation and the health of older adults', *Journal of the Royal Society of Medicine*, 105: 518-522, https://doi.org/10.1258/jrsm.2012.120128

Wang, H., Zhang, A. and Wellman, B. (2018) 'How are older adults networked? Insights from East Yorkers' network structure, relational autonomy, and digital media use', *Information, Communication & Society*, 21(5): 681–696

Wright, K. (2000) 'Computer-mediated social support, older adults, and coping', *Journal of Communication*, 50: 100-118, https://doi.org/10.1111/j.1460-2466.2000.tb02855.x

Wu, Y.-H., Damnee, S., Kerherve, H., Ware, C. and Rigaud, A.-S. (2015) 'Bridging the digital divide in older adults', *Clinical Interventions in Aging*, 10: 193-201, https://doi.org/10.2147/CIA.S72399

Yu, R. P., McCammon, R. J., Ellison, N. B. and Langa, K. M. (2016) 'The relationships that matter: social network site use and social wellbeing among older adults in the United States of America', *Aging & Society*, 36: 1826-1852, https://doi.org/10.1017/S0144686X15000677

Yuan, S., Hussain, S. A., Hales, K. D. and Cotten, S. R. (2016) 'What do they like? Communication preferences and patterns of older adults in the U.S.: The role of technology', *Educational Gerontology*, 42(3): 163–174, https://doi.org/10.1080/03601277.2015.1083392

FIVE

Oversharing in the time of selfies: an aesthetics of disappearance?

Amanda du Preez

Introduction

I have recently been rebuked by my 19-year-old son for uploading selfies, as profile pics, on my Facebook page. In his view, it is not appropriate to my age or academic standing. It is an act that apparently befits attention seeking (oversharing) teenage girls, I was informed. My initial irritation apart, his reaction triggered the exploration of oversharing on social media from a life course perspective. How does oversharing differ for teenagers, young adults, mature adults and the elderly? What became clear from the research is that oversharing on social media cannot be treated as a uniform phenomenon; it is multifaceted and contextual, but may have a predominant age and perhaps even a prevalent gender.

The incident also made me aware of the linked nature of our lives and how information and communication technologies (ICTs) connect biographies across generations. Furthermore, the differences between my generation and that of my son became painfully apparent. In this case, they not only showed the different life trajectories we are pursuing currently (the different 'places' we are in our lives at this time), but also the differences between our generations. He, probably a late Millennial or early Generation Y, stands at the cusp of his manhood, barely finished with adolescence and trying to create an online persona that simultaneously shows the necessary contempt for the platform and just enough interest to upload sophisticated and cool self-depictions. On the other hand, I fall toward the end of the Baby Boomers and just within the Generation X bracket, and am simply happy if a semi-flattering photograph exists, whether a selfie or not. Clearly, my son interprets my selfies as an act of oversharing, while I think nothing incriminating was shared.

The question of oversharing requires a phenomenological hermeneutic reflection in my view. What prompts oversharing? What does it reveal about our life stages and the state of being human in an age of over-acceleration dominated by ICTs, of which social media is perhaps the most palpable platform? How do oversharing impact and speed up our embodied phenomenology? And how does it impact social interactions and relations? And familial relations. Am I indeed oversharing when I post selfies on my Facebook page?

I start my analysis by first fleshing out ideas about acceleration and the resulting aesthetics of disappearance, as put forward by philosopher and urbanist Paul Virilio. Virilio is by no means an innocent choice since he is controversial and often accused of being a technological Cassandra. Despite the controversy, as a student of Maurice Merleau-Ponty and phenomenology, Virilio provides substantial argumentation and convincing interpretations of the contemporary digital age. His work particularly asks how technologies impact on and even change what it means to be human. After introducing Virilio's notion of an aesthetics of disappearance, the discussion turns to oversharing on social media. Trends and traits of oversharing on social media are introduced. The differences in oversharing among different generations are touched upon. Finally, a comparison between Virilio's aesthetics of disappearance and oversharing is attempted.

Virilio's aesthetic of disappearance

Virilio is probably best known for his ideas on dromology or 'the science of speed', which deals with the critical engagement of the consequences of acute acceleration on culture. Dromology also refers to the intersection of speed and power, because for Virilio, 'power is accelerated movement in and over time' (Armitage, 1997, p 200). Virilio identifies the technologies of war and cinema (*vision technologies*) as the principal agents or carriers of the hastening process (Virilio, 1986, 1989, 1994). One of the main consequences of acceleration is the shrinking of geographical distances (*the end of geography*), the loss of territory (*deterritorialization*), and the negation of space. What we are left with after territory has been vanquished is a quest for time because 'the loss of material space leads to governance of nothing but time' (Virilio, 1986, p 157). It is because material space has been defeated as 'a field, as distance, as matter' that we are approaching immediacy 'since after *space-distance,* we now lack *time-distance*' (Virilio, 1986, p 150). The lack of *time-distance* refers to the implosion into immediacy, the ever-present now. Even more, increasing acceleration leads to 'time-matter disappearing and substituted by time-light' (Virilio, 1997, p 123), explaining the contemporary obsession to be instantly accessible (always on) via illuminated screens. Cronin (2011) clarifies the speeding phenomenon as follows:

> Speed (velocity) is understood literally as space (distance) mapped against time (duration), reaching its absolute limit in light, which collapses both space and time. Light, or absolute speed, dissolves the implicit dualism of embodied motion and of disembodied stimulus, anticipating a neuro-psychological event, such as an epileptic *petit mal*, manifested by momentary glitches in perception that Virilio terms as a 'picnoleptic' seizure. (Cronin, 2011, p 87)

It is this glitch or seizure, picnolepsy, that Virilio analyses in *The Aesthetics of Disappearance* (1991) to illustrate the loss of contingent reality due to increasing acceleration. Picnolepsy, or 'tiny death', refers to frequent blackouts or 'the epileptic state of consciousness produced by speed' (Virilio and Lotringer, 2007, p 48). Apparently, picnoleptics (mostly children) overcompensate for their regular loss of consciousness and lost moments by creating elaborate stories and images to cover the voids and fill in the absences. Virilio explains picnoleptics' discomfort and attempts to compensate for the loss of memory as follows:

> There is a tendency to patch up sequences, readjusting their contours to make equivalents out of what the picnoleptic has seen and what he has not been able to see, what he remembers and what, evidently, he cannot remember and that it is necessary to invent, to recreate. (Virilio, 1991, p 10)

Virilio utilizes picnolepsy as a metaphor to portray contemporary overexposure to vision technologies that not only fill in the voids but also make us see more than is visible. Here Virilio cites cinematography's ability to 'faithfully [record] the lost moments when one's senses are partitioned off', as well as 'to replicate the picnoleptic experience through special effects' (Viestenz, 2009, p 538). The cinematic technique can skip from one point in time to another, requiring the spectator to cover the gaps or make the links between sequences, and as a result vision technology, such as cinema, 'acclimatizes us to the production of continuities where there are none' (Cubitt, 1999, p 128). Not only do vision technologies provide an oversupply of reality (too much to see), they also take over the function of sight by becoming a techno-prosthesis for perception. 'They allow a kind of visual – thus physical – hallucination, which tends to strip us of our consciousness. Like the "I run for you" of automobile technology, an "I see for you" is created' (Virilio and Lotringer, 2007, p 88). In the process, we are alienated from phenomenological spatial-temporal experiences: 'You see an image of which you are not at all conscious. It imposes itself on you without your being able to detect it because it goes too fast. The prosthesis is completely alienating' (Virilio and Lotringer, 2007, p 89).

Even more, there is another paradox attached to accelerated techno-vision, namely that it traps us 'in motionless motion' (Russell, 2002, p 199). Instead of moving forward in time we are paralysed by inertia. In fact, our subjectivity is erased by absolute speed: 'the primary freedom is freedom of movement, not freedom of speed. When you go too fast, you are entirely stripped of yourself' (Virilio and Lotringer, 2007, p 76). It is herein that the aesthetics of disappearance resides for Virilio, in the substitution of embodied perception 'through the mechanical prosthesis of technology' (Cronin, 2011, p 87). The aesthetics of disappearance and the aesthetics of appearance can be distinguished as follows:

> For Virilio, the aesthetics of disappearance refers to the mediated technological effects typical of the contemporary arts. Whereas the ancient aesthetics of appearance was based on lasting material supports (wood/canvas in the case of paintings; marble in the case of statues, etc.) the present-day aesthetics of disappearance is founded on temporary immaterial supports (plastic/digital storage in the case of films, etc.). Contemporary images therefore do not so much appear (except as a function of human cognition) as continually disappear. Modern-day images thus apparently move across but actually and repeatedly vanish from the fundamentally immaterial support of the screen as part of a cinematic sequence. (Armitage, 2011, p 7)

Whereas the aesthetics of appearance thus refers to duration and unfolds in and over time and space, the aesthetics of disappearance transgresses *space-distance* and is geared towards instantaneity and the transitory: 'This shift is a significant event that places the emphasis on real time, on the live feed, instead of real space' (Virilio, 2012, p 31). The difference between the two aesthetics has significant consequences for how we perceive and experience being human. As a phenomenologist, Virilio is concerned about the loss of human or embodied perception (Armitage, 2011) that has come under pressure from a culture of speed.

Virilio (2012) refers to 'an *accelerated* reality' (p 18) that now dominates our experience of place and time. He continues by explaining that 'speed is not a phenomenon but *the relationship between phenomena*' (Virilio, 2012, p 26). This also indicates that social relationships and the interconnectedness between people are accelerated, which relates to the overall argument of oversharing in ICTs constructed here.

It is important to note that when Virilio appeals to duration and the contingent reality that unfolds over time and space, he does not argue for an unmediated or direct access to contingent reality. 'There is no continuous consciousness, there are only compositions of consciousness', Virilio and Lotringer (2007, p 49) explain, as consciousness is more akin to a 'collage, cutting and splicing'. In contrast with the 'pure vision' or total vision that vision machines create, human vision is selective and interrupted. There is always a ghostly residue left of the overspilling supplement (Featherstone, 2003, p 435), which cannot be contained. In fact, Virilio views 'the attempt to completely subdue contingency' as a destructive gesture. For Virilio, the contingent reality is an indeterminant excess that has the 'apocalyptic potential to return' (Featherstone, 2003, p 435). Localized and historical reality is therefore always excessive to totalizing vision machines that try to flatten the events onto a surface or screen. Virilio (2004, pp 38-40) is intensely aware of the violence attached to 'overexposure' (or oversharing for the sake of argument here) that offers '*the very presence of the event*' via illuminated screens to its audiences. He compares the all-encompassing drive towards pure vision and absolute speed with the petrifying stare of the Gorgon. As already indicated, it is particularly through the over-acceleration of sight machines (war and cinema) that the world's peculiarities disappear and 'render us unconscious', because 'too much speed is comparable to too much light... it is blinding' (Virilio and Lotringer, 2007, p 98). For Virilio, no life, social life included, is possible in the blinding light of complete vision and immediacy precisely because it compresses contingency via highspeed transmissions.

If we accept Virilio's hypothesis, then, namely that reality is accelerating, and as a result human interactions are accelerating and changing to adapt to the new velocity, how does this apply to communication on ICTs? Considering that the affordances these communication technologies allow 'are not in and of themselves new, their relation to one another because of networked publics creates new opportunities and challenges' (boyd, 2014, p 11). It means the technologies are not so much novel; it is the increased speed that connects them that changes human interactions. According to danah boyd (2014), the following four affordances are essential in this regard: *persistence* through the durability of online content; *visibility* in the potential audience who can bear witness; *spreadability* in the ease with which content can be shared; and finally, *searchability* that makes it easy to find content. By highlighting one aspect of communication online, namely sharing, which is enabled by all four of the affordances listed above, and particularly the impulse to overshare, how can Virilio's notion of the aesthetics of disappearance guide us in understanding the phenomenon better? Here Ben Agger's (2012) *Oversharing: Presentations of Self in the Internet Age* provides insightful pointers to explore the sociological implications of oversharing.

Oversharing and social media

In 2014 the word 'overshare' was selected as one of the words of the year, with others like 'photobomb' and 'vape'. This comes only one year after 'selfie' became the word of the year in 2013. Ben Agger (2012, preface) defines oversharing as the urge 'to divulge more… inner feelings, opinions, sexuality' than someone would 'in person, or even over the phone'. He notes that we tend to overshare when we interact with others 'through the screens of computers and smartphones' (Agger, 2012, Preface). The screen ironically creates the necessary distance to overshare, although the interaction is instantaneous. Agger (2012, p 26) makes it clear that 'Oversharing is not the same as intimacy. Intimacy is sharing based on trust'. One can switch off screen-mediated 'intimacy' whereas intimacy in the flesh requires reciprocity and commitment over time and space, and thus duration. In other words, it requires an aesthetic of appearance, in Virilio's terms.

Oversharing has more to do with 'debounding' (Agger, 2012, p, 2) or 'thin boundaries' (Agger, 2012, p 7), where the boundaries between the private and public, self and others are vacillating. Oversharing also refers to the urge to be always plugged in and available in what Agger terms 'iTime' as a pun on the invasion of the iPhone and other smartphones. Elsewhere Agger (2011, p 120) notes: 'In iTime, one can work anytime/anywhere, freeing one from the cubicle but also allowing work to seep into every nook and cranny of personal life. Upside: freedom from the job site. Downside: no downtime'. The fact that there is no longer any downtime underscores the drive 'to instantaneize' (Agger, 2012, p 1), in other words, to be instantaneously present to what is occurring online. With syndromes such as fear of missing out (FOMO) and sharing too much information (TMI), oversharing leaves nothing to chance or the imagination. As already noted, for Agger (2012, p 2) oversharing is invasive as it 'intrudes our time and place', and for that reason 'change[s] what it means to be a person' (Agger, 2012, p 1). The link with Virilio's plea for deep space-time phenomenology is glaringly obvious.

Ultimately, oversharing leads to undersharing (Agger, 2012, p 18) – just as excessive speed leads to inertia – because it deprives us of 'substantive interactions' since we never 'learn what is really important about a person'. What we are left with instead, according to Agger (2012, p 18), is 'ephemeral gossip and trivia' and thus flatness. Although this may appear counterintuitive at first, oversharing on social media is linked to low self-esteem, loneliness and is even an indicator of depression (Rashquina, 2015; Radovic et al, 2017). Oversharing can be understood as a cry for help and support online. The ever-expansive reach of communication networks globally appears to have an inverted correlation to the increasing sense of loneliness (which is why Turkle's book title, *Alone Together*, is so apt). Furthermore, if we connect oversharing and selfies, the selfie can in some instances be interpreted as an unusual manifestation of vulnerability and low self-esteem. Recent research by Sorokowska et al (2016) indicates that women tend to share selfies on social networking sites (SNSs) significantly more than men do. Although Sorokowska et al (2016, p 122) do not link low self-esteem to the number of selfies posted, but rather to extraversion and social exhibitionism, they do suggest that people with a low self-esteem may be more likely to self-promote online to raise their self-esteem. However, Kaur and Vig (2016) link excessive selfie posting, especially amongst teenagers, not only with low self-esteem but also to increasing loneliness and the development of shallow relationships with others.

Apparently, older people (adults I presume) use Facebook for updating family relationships and keeping in touch with relatives (see McAndrew and Jeong, 2012) and are not as interested in self-impression management as teenagers are. However, Christofides et al (2012) debunk this myth that adolescents disclose more and care less about privacy. In fact, it seems for both adults and teens more time spent on Facebook 'predicted increased likelihood of disclosure' (Christofides et al, 2012, p 52). In other words, the more users become comfortable with the platform, the more they tend to (over)share.

Regarding familial relations and the role of intergenerational lives, oversharing can be related to the phenomenon of helicopter parenting, where the ever-vigilant parent tries to befriend their children online to keep an eye on them. For instance, the trend of parents befriending teenagers on Facebook to monitor them would be an obvious example of linked lives, albeit a forced attempt to connect. Although this gesture is not always welcomed by teens, as Child and Westermann (2013) explain, they are not likely to decline a friend request from parents. They may change the privacy settings for the request but they will mostly accept it because of the inherent power relationship between parent and child. It is not only parents that hover online, however, as older siblings, who are often more techno-savvy than their parents step into the role of watching younger ones. The 'helicopter sibling' (Wells, 2015) then relays the information to the parents but often in a filtered manner to protect both parties. This protective intervention by older siblings is corroborated already in Ann Goetting's (1986) research on the developmental tasks fulfilled by siblings over the life cycle. The act of caring surveillance is further supported by apps such as Life360, for instance, that allow parents and older siblings to keep track of younger siblings' whereabouts.

It should therefore not come as a surprise that teenagers use 'prison code' (Agger, 2012, p 4) and 'subliminal tweeting or subtweeting' (boyd, 2014, p 69) to evade parental tracking online. These may consist of texts using acronyms and emoticons that are unfamiliar to adult readers, and apparently late nights and early mornings are best for adult-free interactions (Agger, 2012). Parental interference not only works in the direction of monitoring online activities; it now also takes the dimension of parents oversharing about their children on social media. In their research, Moser et al (2017) highlight the ethical questions involved when parents overshare by posting intrusive, compromising and embarrassing information about their children. For instance: do parents have the right to overshare their children's lives? Obviously oversharing is a complex phenomenon that requires further research, particularly as it plays out in familial relations.

I am not suggesting that all communications between parents and children via ICTs are flawed and not supportive of emotional bonding and meaningful sharing. In fact, research abounds indicating that online communication between parents and children is positive and satisfying in many ways (Madianou, 2016; Sharaievska and Stodolska, 2016; Stein et al, 2016). What most of the research does however corroborate is that meaningful sharing via ICTs mostly depends or builds on stable and strong familial ties in the first place. This means that good online communication is probably based on good face-to-face relationships nurtured by families in and over time and space. Before I turn to a comparison between oversharing and the aesthetics of disappearance a quick detour through Snapchat, an instant messaging platform that allows users to share content for a limited time can enrich and elaborate the discussion.

Snapchat and oversharing

Usually, the content shared on Snapchat is a selfie accompanied by a short text. The image disappears after the time has expired: 1 second to 10 seconds. The receiver can save the screen through screen–capture but must keep touching the screen to do so. The sender is notified when the receiver saves the message. In other words, no photo of the content can be taken. The nature of the interaction is transient and is mostly used by teenagers. The assumption that the communication will be promiscuous or revealing due to its ephemeral nature is however not correct, according to Piwek and Joinson (2016). If anything, the interaction leads to social capital in the form of bonding, as opposed to social capital gained on Facebook through bridging (Putnam, 2001).

Piwek and Joinson (2016, p 364) also describe Snapchat as allowing for more intimate and personal communication; it allows for 'more "strong emotional" ties with friends, partners and family'. Furthermore: It is possible that the narrative, conversation-like, and intimate nature of Snapchat, with an interface that affords the exchange of short impressions, becomes a preferred medium to socialize playfully in a more secluded setting than on public SNS such as Facebook. Snapchat is immersive to use because you must hold your finger on the screen to see the content, and you only have one chance to view the received content before it disappears. Therefore, you need to stay focused when receiving a message. Arguably, the combination of self-destructing images with an immersive interface that restricts the scope of user interaction with the content makes Snapchat an instant narrative vehicle that is similar to verbal story exchange (Piwek and Joinson, 2016).

Snapchat, therefore, facilitates a presence or appearance amidst the disappearance, but one must hold onto it before the content evaporates. The user is also obliged to immerse themself in the interaction; otherwise, the content may pass them by since they cannot consult it later or archive it. Amid the flow of images and messages, Snapchat focuses the attention momentarily, reminiscent of traditional storytelling when people used to huddle around a fire and listen intently. Now the screen becomes the mediator of stories that link listeners and participants. The fact that users must continue touching the screen can be interpreted as a form of 'keeping in touch'. Based on Piwek and Joinson's research, Snapchat differs from other SNS. For here is not a flow of images that bombard the viewer but instead a momentary flash that appears and when missed will not appear again. Ironically, although accelerated, Snapchat mimics real-space face-to-face interactions. And if one were to overshare, the image will soon disappear from view just like a person turning their back after a face-to-face conversation.

Oversharing: an aesthetics of disappearance?

If oversharing is a mixture of loneliness, a search for intimacy in an age of hyper-connection and an obsessive urge to be constantly in contact (FOMO), can it be linked to Virilio's notion of an aesthetics of disappearance? What can be said to disappear through oversharing? The aesthetics of disappearance come about when real space, which is the domain of the human, is overtaken by real time, which is the domain of the divine, according to Virilio and Lotringer (2007). We achieve presence or interaction in real time via technology that has 'appropriated divinity' (Virilio and Lotringer, 2007, p 230) because we no longer require the mediation of another human being to attain that interaction. For Agger (2012), oversharing should not be confused with intimacy, just as Virilio and Lotringer (2007, p 51) postulate that real time leads to 'the death of intimacy'.

In other words, perhaps oversharing (real-time presence) achieves precisely the opposite of what it intends, namely phenomenological closeness and duration, or what Virilio terms an aesthetics of appearance. Could it be that in the blinding light of instant updates, the event and the experience get lost, or disappear altogether? 'Images are all the more present when they escape, existing more through their disappearance than their appearance' (Virilio and Lotringer, 2007, p 228). Immediacy casts no shadow or veil, or even shield (as in the case of Perseus) to direct the instantaneous stare of the Gorgon. What is oversharing but a manifestation of the tripartite of 'instantaneity, ubiquity, immediacy' (Virilio and Lotringer, 2007, p 227)?

If the reader allows a further utilization of Virilio's ideas on the aesthetics of disappearance: can oversharing not be related to a form of picnolepsy? Oversharing is, after all, an impulse to share, to fill up the void with inconsequential trivia no matter what. Oversharing corresponds with picnoleptics' attempts to cover up their blackouts by creating elaborate stories and details to fill-in the blanks. Oversharing also utilizes spinning, as Agger (2012, p 5) recounts, the drive to inflate events and appearances by 'airbrushing one's flaws, telling tall tales, outright lying'. These account for the fear of being caught out not being present all the time. Ubiquitous connectivity does not allow for pauses, silences, hesitance or looking away as would occur in a face-to-face conversation in real space. Nor does it allow for holding back and not saying it all when looking at another's face. Oversharing fills in the gaps and makes all content unbearably visible without interruptions:

> It's interesting to privilege interruption on the level of chronopolitics, as opposed to geopolitics. Interruption in space was the ramparts, rules, chastity belts. Now interruption in the body is replaced by interruption in time. We plug into everyone's intimate duration. (Virilio and Lotringer, 2007, p 51)

As we plug into to others' oversharing the world shrinks because no longer do distance or territory hold any form of resistance, neither privacy nor interruptions. 'With the phenomena of instantaneous interaction that are now our lot, there has been a veritable reversal, destabilizing the relationship of human interactions, and the time reserved for reflection, in favor of the conditioned responses produced by emotion' (Virilio, 2012, p 31). Reflective responses that take time are at risk of being substituted by instantaneous emotive oversharing. Lena Durham of HBO *Girls* fame, with co-producer Jenni Konner, actively propagates such unmediated sharing in the *Lenny Newsletter* keeping readers informed about feminism, health, politics, style, friendship and everything else.

Emotion does seem to be the driver for unmitigated oversharing – not emotion in general, but the emotion that leads to activation. As Berger and Milkman (2012) reveal, emotions are not all equal when it comes to the likelihood of being shared online. While anxiety, sadness and anger are all negative emotions, anxiety and anger activate while sadness rather deactivates response. I suspect it is possible to link emotions that activate response with affects, those pre-conscious intensities that move us. Affects act as inter-personal modulators that operate outside of language, thus unmediated, and are the raw material for what becomes emotions. Virilio comments as follows on the role played by affects in online sharing:

> Because of the absolute speed of electromagnetic waves, the same feeling of terror can be felt in all corners of the world at the same time…. It creates a 'community of emotions', a communism of affects coming after the communism of the 'community of interests' shared by different social classes. There is something in the synchronization of emotion that

surpasses the power of standardization of opinion that was typical of the mass media in the second half of the 20th century. (Virilio, 2012, p 30)

As reality accelerates, our offline and online social interactions are changing accordingly. The pressure to share in real time means we are plunged into a flow of affective intensities. If we overshare in haste, it may just be because we lost our bearings in the real world.

In conclusion: the role of ICTs in also linking lives across generations is remarkable. In fact, sharing life trajectories is now possible as never before with the added benefit that the content shared is not only immediately available but can also be archived online 'forever'. In terms of the life course analysis, the concept of oversharing can be analysed from intergenerational differences, as well as how lives are closely linked. As Elder and Giele (2009, p 13) note, 'The life of a person is interwoven with the lives of significant others'. To return to the example of me uploading of selfies that disconcert my son, my online life is accordingly interweaved with that of my son. This example showed how interconnected our lives as parent and child have become as mediated by ICTs, and how my public display affects my son. Although my selfie experiment can be viewed from my perspective as an act of exerting my agency as an older female, for my son this signifies oversharing. But because our lives are interlinked, and our online activities influence each other's life courses, I will most definitely think carefully before uploading another selfie.

In brief

1. The phenomenon of oversharing as mediated via ICTs has a tendency to speed up relationships.
2. The hastened interactions online allow for an 'aesthetics of disappearance' where interactions in time and space are now replaced by instantaneous and momentary interactions in real time overcoming space-distance.
3. Oversharing is induced by the immersive familiarity with the online medium. In other words, the more familiar we become with the social media platforms, the more comfortable we become and the more likely we are to overshare.

References

Agger, B. (2011) 'iTime: Labor and life in a smartphone era', *Time and Society*, 20(1): 119–136, https://doi.org/10.1177/0961463X10380730

Agger, B. (2012) *Oversharing: Presentations of Self in the Internet Age*, New York: Routledge.

Armitage, J. (1997) 'Accelerated aesthetics: Paul Virilio's the vision machine', *Angelaki: Journal of the Theoretical Humanities*, 2(3): 199–209, https://doi.org/10.1080/09697259708571955

Armitage, J. (eds) (2011). *Virilio Now: Current Perspectives in Virilio Studies*, Cambridge: Polity.

Berger, J. and Milkman, K. (2012) 'What makes online content viral?', *Journal of Marketing Research*, 49(2): 192–205, https://doi.org/10.1509/jmr.10.0353

boyd, d. (2014) *It's Complicated. The Social Lives of Networked Teens*, New Haven, CT: Yale University Press.

Child, J. T. and Westermann, D. A. (2013) 'Let's be Facebook friends: Exploring parental Facebook friend requests from a communication privacy management (CPM) perspective', *Journal of Family Communication*, 13(1): 46–59, https://doi.org/10.1080/15267431.2012.742089

Christofides, E., Muise, A. and Desmarais, S. (2012) 'Hey Mom, what's on your Facebook? Comparing Facebook disclosure and privacy in adolescents and adults', *Social Psychological and Personality Science*, 3(1): 48–54, https://doi.org/10.1177/1948550611408619

Cronin, J. G. R. (2011) 'Excavating the future: Taking an 'archaeological' approach to technology', *Interdisciplinary Science Reviews*, 36(1): 83–89, https://doi.org/10.1179/030801811X12941390545807

Cubitt, S. (1999) 'Virilio and new media', *Theory, Culture and Society*, 16(5–6): 127–142, https://doi.org/10.1177/02632769922050908

Elder, G. H. and Giele, J. Z. (2009) *The Craft of Life Course Research*, New York: The Guilford Press.

Featherstone, M. (2003) 'The eye of war: Images of destruction in Virilio and Bataille', *Journal for Cultural Research*, 7(4): 433–447, https://doi.org/10.1080/1479758032000165066

Goetting, A. (1986) 'The development tasks of siblingship over the life cycle', *Journal of Marriage and Family*, 48(4): 703–714, https://doi.org/10.2307/352563

Kaur, S. and Vig, D. (2016) 'Selfie and mental health issues: An overview', *Indian Journal of Health and Wellbeing*, 7(12): 1149–1152.

Madianou, M. (2016) 'Ambient co-presence: Transnational family practices in polymedia environments', *Global Networks*, 16(2): 183–201.

McAndrew, F. T. and Jeong, H. S. (2012) 'Who does what on Facebook? Age, sex, and relationship status as predictors of Facebook use', *Computers in Human Behavior*, 28(6): 2359-2365, https://doi.org/10.1016/j.chb.2012.07.007

Moser, C., Chen, T. and Schoenebeck, S. (2017) 'Parents' and children's preferences about parents sharing about children on social media', in Proceedings of the ACM Conference on Human Factors in Computing Systems (CHI '17), Denver, 6-11 May, https://dx.doi.org/10.1145/3025453.3025587

Piwek, L. and Joinson, A. (2016) '"What do they snapchat about?" Patterns of use in time-limited instant messaging service', *Computers in Human Behavior*, 54: 358-367, https://doi.org/10.1016/j.chb.2015.08.026

Putnam, R. (2001) 'Social capital measurement and consequences', *Canadian Journal of Policy Research*, 2: 41-51.

Radovic, A., Gmelin, T., Stein, B. D. and Miller, E. (2017) 'Depressed adolescents' positive and negative use of social media', *Journal of Adolescence*, 55: 5-15, https://doi.org/10.1016/j.adolescence.2016.12.002

Rashquina, R. G. (2015) 'Do lonely people overshare on social media?', *The Times of India*, 23 May, https://timesofindia.indiatimes.com/life-style/relationships/love-sex/Do-lonely-people-overshare-on-social-media/articleshow/47385610.cms

Russell, C. (2002) 'Against dead time', *Time and Society*, 11(2-3): 193-208, https://doi.org/10.1177/0961463X02011002002

Sharaievska, I. and Stodolska, M. (2016) 'Family satisfaction and social networking leisure', *Leisure Studies*, 36(2): 231-243, https://doi.org/10.1080/02614367.2016.1141974

Sorokowska, A., Oleszkiewicz, A., Frackowiak, T., Pisanski, K., Chmiel, A. and Sorokowski, P. (2016) 'Selfies and personality: Who posts self-portrait photographs?', *Personality and Individual Differences*, 90: 119-123, https://doi.org/10.1016/j.paid.2015.10.037

Stein, C. H., Osborn, L. A. and Greenberg, S. (2016) 'Understanding young adults' reports of contact with their parents in a digital world: Psychological and familial relationship factors', *Journal of Child and Family Studies*, 25(6): 1802-1814, https://doi.org/10.1007/s10826-016-0366-0

Turkle, S. (2011) *Alone Together: Why We Expect More of Technology and Less of Each Other*, New York: Basic Books.

Viestenz, W. (2009) 'Cinematic ethics within the picnoleptic moment in José Luis Guerín's En construcción', *The Bulletin of Hispanic Studies*, 86(4): 537-554.

Virilio, P. (1986) *Speed and Politics: An Essay on Dromology*, New York: Semiotext(e).

Virilio, P. (1989) *War and Cinema: The Logistics of Perception*, London: Verso.

Virilio, P. (1991) *The Aesthetics of Disappearance*, New York: Semiotext(e).

Virilio, P. (1994) *The Vision Machine*, Bloomington: Indiana University Press.

Virilio, P. (1997) *Open Sky*, London: Verso.

Virilio, P. (2004) *Art and Fear*, London: Continuum.

Virilio, P. (2012) *The Administration of Fear*, Los Angeles: Semiotext(e).

Virilio, P. and Lotringer, S. (2007) *Pure War. Twenty-Five Years Later*, New York: Semiotext(e).

Wells, C. (2015) 'Big sister is watching – armed with social media they use more easily than Mom and Dad, older siblings keep an eye on younger ones', *Wall Street Journal*, Eastern edition, New York, 24 June, http://online.wsj.com/public/resources/documents/print/WSJ_-D001-20150624.pdf

SIX

The application of digital methods in a life course approach to family studies

Alexia Maddox

Introduction

The question explored in this chapter is what analytical elements of the life course approach align with the emerging field of digital methods. To do this, I consider how the emerging field of digital research methods can contribute appropriate tools and techniques relevant to the life course approach. Initially the chapter presents a working discussion of the methodological dimensions of the life course approach to family studies. It illustrates how approaches to life course research, from longitudinal cohort studies to studies of transitions and trajectories across the life course, may draw on data sources, data collection techniques and data analysis approaches that provide openings for the use of digital methods. In essence, it seeks to make the connection between existing practices and possible digital approaches. The caveat here, naturally, is that new techniques do bring the capacity for researchers to ask new questions. In a slightly non-linear way, this chapter considers how conceptual shifts in understanding of digital behaviours may be worthwhile for family studies scholars to consider. For example, literature discussing mediated sociability, computer–human interactions, computer-mediated communication (CMC) and information and communication technologies (ICTs) has been opened up through the ubiquity of networked software such as social media platforms alongside networked hardware, including mobile devices and wearable technologies. This transition of terminology leads through the internet of human things (IOHT) literature to augment methodological thinking from observational and monitoring techniques to drawing upon the agentive and self-tracking behaviours of the individual. The terminological transitions also reflect recent technological innovations (and their rapid social adoption). This movement of technological change to conceptual change has been captured through the broader notion of digital networked technologies, which incorporate everything from aware refrigerators to the Fitbit. From this veritable *Wunderkammer* of new technologies for data production, capture and analysis, we move to the considerations a researcher must undertake in order to effectively and sensitively deploy these new techniques and tools in a research study. A focus on the ethical considerations of the use of self-tracking data, for example, may highlight varying perceptions of public visibility and data privacy amongst researched populations. From ethical considerations of digital trace data analysis to the perceptions of the appropriate placements of technologies for data collection within family practice, the researcher faces a participant response minefield of both resistance due to privacy concerns and accelerated acceptance due to novelty. Consequently, the final section presents a discussion of the potential points of social resistance to the use of digital tools for data collection and analysis. The aim of this chapter, however, is not to overwhelm this discussion and consideration with all the bells, whistles and hidden permissions issues that new technologies bring. Instead, it attempts a considered gathering of the possibilities of new digital technologies for the life course approach to encourage and support an informed exploration of this new methodological terrain within family studies.

Alignments between digital methods and the life course approach

In this section, I will draw on the definitional work of Mayer and Tuma (1990), Mayer (2009) and Elder (1975) on the life course approach as a way to identify the key analytical approaches in the field. My agenda in doing this is to begin to draw out potential parallels between the life course approaches and digital methods thinking. Before focusing on the field of family studies, however, I will situate this chapter and my writing in its body of expertise. I will first consider and respond to examples of digital methods present in family studies. I then follow this up with a synopsis of digital thinking that leads to the development of three tropes through which to order and align digital approaches: the network, big data and ubiquity. From this tripartite foundation, we then leap off into an exploratory realm presenting digital propositions that speak to the key definitional work on the life course approach considered here.

As a digital methods scholar, the study of the life course and the family is not my home territory. This disconnect between the fields is also evident in the scholarly literature. A literature search on the use of digital methods for the study of families across the life course presents sparse results. The rudimentary observation of the efficacy of online surveys to reach large populations resonates with early work in the digital methods field. This early work sought to establish the advantages, limitations and authenticity of online data collection about 'offline' behaviours (Witte et al, 2000). I will touch on contemporary critiques of online–offline thinking later in this chapter, but I am compelled to respond here that this language use is a red flag within digital conceptualization which veers away from dualistic assumptions (Jurgenson, 2012). Moving on to more contemporary practices and away from this old bugbear of mine, the family studies literature does hold a few examples of recent approaches to employing digital techniques. For example, the following studies demonstrate the use of technologies within research practice, specifically as interventions in aged care (Neves et al, 2017), the creation of a digital depository as a portable life biography for youth in foster care (Gustavsson and MacEachron, 2008) and the cohort effects of information and communication technology saturation, such as millennials or Generation Y (Bolton et al, 2013; Williams et al, 2012). Regardless of these examples, it appears that within family studies using the life course approach, digital thinking is a sporadic and disconnected body of practice. Because of this, I will begin in my comfort zone by describing three prominent tropes that bring some cohesion to classifying what digital methods are. From this platform, I will then dive into the definitional thinking of two prominent scholars for the life course approach in family studies and identify alignments where digital methods could contribute an analytical lens.

The digital approach has three tropes that tend to define it: networks, big data and ubiquity. The first trope is relational and network structures (van Dijk, 1999; Wellman, 2001; Wellman et al, 2003). This trope draws together the Web 2.0 literature on social networking sites through emphasizing the structural value of relationship networks, such as friendship networks on Facebook, for analysing social engagement, participation and association. This trope focuses on social media use and highlights the analytical possibilities of the discursive structures and visual cultures accessible through social media (Tinati et al, 2014b). Information in this environment may include textual, visual, aural and kinetic components (Garcia et al, 2009). However, the predecessor to social media analysis in the literature was the rising utility of hyperlink analysis between websites (Rogers, 2009a, 2009b, 2012; Schneider and Foot, 2004). This Web 1.0-related field sought to reveal influence and association structures and issue-based clusters between websites. The second trope is the archival and volume-based qualities of 'data in the wild'. Within this trope, I specifically refer to the digital trace data that is produced through user activity online. Digital trace data of social behaviours online is one of the sources of 'big data'. The notion of big data, however, is more broadly defined through characteristics of volume, velocity, variety, veracity, value and as many 'V's as can be opportunistically fitted into this framework. In their seminal work defining the field, boyd and Crawford (2012) refer to big data as a cultural, technological and scholarly phenomenon, which incorporates the power of the algorithm to gather, order and analyse large volumes of information. In line with notions of artificial intelligence, they highlight a common perception that working with data sets analysed through automated computing processes and machine learning, rather than manual human labour, offers a higher form of intelligence.

The often implicit contention of the superiority of nonhuman analytical approaches (Ekbia et al, 2015), representing the human analyst as a cyborg, bears some of the epistemological battle scars between quantitative and qualitative practitioners (Howe, 1988). Following similar lines of argument, we see the tension created by the weighing up of representative or generalizable findings, or whole data set findings in the case of big data (Tinati et al, 2014a), against non-representative in-depth studies of an individual or group experience. These somewhat abstract methodological debates are often exacerbated by discipline agendas, normative approaches and funding imperatives. However, within the literature, response to this thinking is two-fold. Currently researchers presenting a critique of the voracious capacity of big data approaches to automate the laborious aspects of ordering and interpreting large data sets flag the continued requirement for manual coding work in order to provide valid interpretive categories. This is a limitation of working with 'data in the wild' in that it is often unstructured 'dirty data' that has not been 'designed' to support conventional styles of analysis (Nafus, 2014). Weighing up these aspects may lead the evaluating researcher to think that computational approaches are 'not so smart or quick after all'. There is also a movement within the field to counterbalance the analysis of vast volumes of digital records inherent to working with big data by complementing these analyses with small data work. Within the mixed methods approaches emerging in this area, there is a combination presented where big data analysis presents trends, social tone and visuals while small data work is used to investigate these trends from a human-centred perspective through ethnographic and other qualitative approaches.

At this stage, I will flag with the reader that digital thinking is both derivative of a wide range of fields and iterative in line with technological innovations. Consequently, the derivative and iterative nature of the field means that the digital tropes presented here are not mutually exclusive. For example, the bridge between the first trope, networks, and the second trope, big data, is traversed through the field of data visualization. Digital trace data on social media, for example, is often encoded with relational data such as followers or friendship networks. These networked or relational structures between data points are commonly used to identify and amplify key themes within social sentiment, such as studies of affect, emotion and social tone (Rill et al, 2014; Yu and Wang, 2015), to present hashtag publics, or to identify the amplification of key figures or messages within an environment (Bruns and Burgess, 2012; Bruns and Stieglitz, 2013; Bruns et al, 2013; Burgess et al, 2013; Highfield et al, 2013). The findings of these forms of analysis are commonly presented in visual formats that privilege data linkages and core-periphery data weighting as a means to visually distil and represent the viral signatures of ideas, ideologies, messages or memes. Through unpacking the close relationship between big data approaches and data visualization techniques, we can see that each trope is not mutually exclusive and that by their very nature they inform each other.

The third trope of digital methods is the ubiquitous nature of mobile technologies (Satchell, 2008; Schroeder, 2010), such as smartphones. Within this more collective and environmental trope of digital ubiquity there are further shifts that are linked to the increasing adoption of wearable technologies (Jethani, 2015), such as Fitbits, which shift digital thinking about the individual more towards the notion of digitized embodiment (Lupton, 2013, 2014, 2015, 2016). These technologies produce visual and geolocation data, giving rise to photographic cultures (Hjorth and Hendry, 2015; Iqani and Schroeder, 2016) and the spatialization of social information (Stefanidis et al, 2013). The focus on ubiquitous technologies in this third trope, also referred to as digital networked technologies (Zimmerman, 1999), also links into the more recent fields of smart homes and smart cities. Through technologies for observation and response to stimuli, these interconnected and sensor-based networks make intelligent systems that are aware. These 'smart' systems tell us about activity and consumption patterns in the home space and the city at large. With these three tropes in mind – networks, big data and ubiquity – we will now begin a tourist's view of the life course approach in family studies.

From the work of Elder (1975), understandings of family studies using the life course approach could be thought of as ways to investigate social change across successive cohorts, but also to examine, through the specific lens of ageing and the family, practices surrounding social inclusion and social mobility across a lifespan. The study of life course can be thought of as the progressive mapping and analysing of lives over time and across life stages, from early childhood or adolescence to post-retirement years. Mayer (2009) suggests that the key questions arising for life course approaches include how stable certain socioeconomic characteristics and behaviours are across the lifespan and how to best understand the dynamics of life trajectories. When this comes to the study of the family, one question to ponder is whether the researcher considers family structures and relations through their rapid change as an organizational/collective unit within society or how the relations within and beyond the family unit may articulate and recombine in response to rapid sociotechnical changes. Regardless, a life course approach to family studies will be likely to consider these two provocations for social change in a contemporary environment that is both rapid and sociotechnically augmented. Within the literature, the question as to the location of the family in the life course approach is resolved by Mayer and Tuma (1990), who situate it as a social institution in the domain of an individual life. They suggest that the life course concept refers to the way in which social institutions shape and institutionalize individual lives in the interconnected domains of education, family and work. In this way, the family and residential histories in part compose the life course. Here we can begin to see a possible overlap with the first and third tropes of digital methods that focus on the relational aspects of social relationships and on the aware nature of the home space. Defining in this discussion of family structures and their locational associations is the nature of activities, roles and relationships over time. This historical and lifespan lens raises issues for the use of digital methods in data collection, management and reporting, the current challenge here being in the capacity of these technologies to be compatible with historical and future data, software and hardware. While an analyst may use data logs to analyse historical behaviours and patterns within a family or across an individual lifespan, the use of technologies for data collection and observation of online activity cannot be assumed to remain consistent or even in use in a longitudinal sense. This is a methodological consideration that must be taken into account during the research design stage for longitudinal drawing on digital methods for data collection and analysis.

Taking a step back from the present, in his historical situation of the life course approach, Mayer (2009) notes that it draws from the work of Karl Mannheim, and in particular Mannheim's notion of the generation and, during the 1960s and 1970s, the concept of age differentiation as a form of social stratification. These two concepts were then integrated by Mannheim into the idea of the life course as a social structure and institutional pattern. Here we can see that the structural and patterning concepts within the life course approach are met with a comparative analysis between successive age cohorts. This insight suggests that network techniques and cluster analysis of comparative data approaches may have utility. Indeed, Settersten Jr and Mayer (1997) go further to suggest that while the life course can be viewed as an event history of a single individual, it can also be viewed at an aggregate level (for example, as something shared by a cohort), as a property of cultures themselves, and as something that can be compared across historical periods or between nation states. This understanding supports a concept–methodology coupling between a range of research methods that harness individual narrative at a micro scale, the meso scale of social networks and the macro scale of sources to illustrate sociocultural conditions across the life course.

From his early essay on the topic of the life course approach and social change, Elder (1975) similarly identifies some key themes that articulate methodological dimensions within the literature. Elder suggested that there were two significant thematic approaches within the literature of the time: the sociocultural perspective and the cohort-specific perspective. He described the sociocultural perspective as emphasizing the social meaning surrounding age and its contextual variations, suggesting the utility of qualitative approaches, and the cohort-historical perspective focused on age cohorts and social indicators, particularly as they relate to and illustrate cohort differentiations. From this description, however, the cohort-historical approach appeared to be more quantitatively linked. Mayer (2009) describes these quantitative approaches chronologically, suggesting that until the 1970s, cross-sectional surveys were most prevalent, only to be superseded by longitudinal studies in the 1980s. Elder additionally highlighted a range of analytical components for the dedicated scholar, including a mention of the temporal structures of family activity that were captured through time–budget studies and the role of informal networks as a collective context for family structures. This suggests that there is a spatio-temporal and dynamic aspect to the life course approach that may allow researchers to connect geolocation data with activity data to illustrate patterns and connections within and beyond family structures. Consequently, this early work reveals preliminary strands and streams of research methods and data collection approaches that may be consistent with the life course approach and the everyday practices of families as we understand them today.

While the above brief overview of methodological approaches within the literature using the life course approach to family studies cannot be considered comprehensive, the methodological dimensions that digital methods may intersect with have been increased. However, this is not sufficient to illustrate the different possibilities and uses of digital methods. These broad descriptives of the methodologies relevant to the life course approach tend to shroud the components that a researcher must consider in the design of their research. Indeed, research methodologies are constituted through several aspects beyond the method itself. In addition to the identification of method or methods to be deployed in the study design, other technical aspects the researcher considers include data sources, data collection techniques, data analysis and visualization approaches. From the literature, it is apparent that archival data sources were drawn on to illustrate changes in patterns and structures of family activity over time. This dimension suggests that the use of digital trace data and web scraping techniques (Thelwall, 2009) may also provide or produce a considerable archive of inherently timestamped information that may be drawn on. Data collection techniques may well evolve from the simple opportunities of the online survey to capture cross-sectional or longitudinal data and the recorded interview (guided by a life history timeline approach) captured on a smartphone. Where, for example, would a chronological photo essay uploaded as a digital daily diary (Harrison, 2002) fit in this spectrum of techniques for data production and collection? And once collected, the researcher may decide to incorporate geolocation information embedded in the digital images with facial recognition technologies to present a visual analysis. This analysis may visualize the tracking of both movement and association within families over time. In this way of thinking through the digital lens, we move both with and beyond the statistical representations available for cross-sectional and longitudinal data analysis to data visualization opportunities that provide shape and imagery that can enhance the cognitive literacy of the findings.

This section has covered a vast territory between digital methods and life course approaches within family studies. Table 6.1 presents a rudimentary synthesis of the relationship between the digital tropes we have explored in this chapter, the emerging field of digital methods and the analytical components of the life course approach within family studies identified above. This table cannot be considered comprehensive due to the limitation of this analysis discussed previously and the constant movement of technologies that are adopted socially and within research practice. However, when regarded as a fixed point in time, the table attempts to make the ideas presented here accessible through a visual framework.

Table 6.1 Mapping digital methods to the life course approach in family studies

Digital trope	Data source	Data collection techniques & variables	Data analysis & visualization	Life course analytical units
Network	Social media (Twitter, Facebook, Snapchat, Instagram, Tumblr, YouTube, Blogs)	• API interfaces and social media archives (https://trisma.org) • User-produced content (unstructured data)	• Hashtag communities • Visual/digital ethnography • Visual analysis	• Routines & transitions • Individual, family unit, peer group and cohort studies
	Social networks	• Relational information • Friendship networks	• Communication networks • Influence networks	• Routines & transitions • Family unit, peer group and cohort studies • Longitudinal studies
Big data	Internet (including email and other online communication technologies)	• User activity tracking • User-produced content (unstructured data) • Time-activity logging	• Thematic analysis • Activity patterns • Cluster analysis • Sentiment analysis	• Routines & transitions • Cohort studies • Longitudinal studies
	World Wide Web (websites)	• User engagement and activity tracking • Attention tracking • User-produced content (unstructured data) • Website hyperlinks	• Hyperlink analysis • Sentiment analysis (affect & emotion) • Thematic analysis • Amplification patterns	• Routines & transitions • Peer group and cohort studies • Longitudinal studies
	Institutional and commercial data repositories	• Data attributes (including metadata) • Institutionally generated classifications • Consumption and service engagement patterns • Locational information (i.e., postcodes)	• Geodemographic analysis • Cluster analysis • Lifestyle analysis	• Peer group and cohort studies • Longitudinal studies

Digital trope	Data source	Data collection techniques & variables	Data analysis & visualization	Life course analytical units
Ubiquity	Geolocational data from wearable technologies	Self-tracking data	• Socio-spatial analysis • Mobility studies • Built environment analysis	• Routines & transitions • Individual, family unit, and peer group studies • Longitudinal studies
	Activity space data from 'smart homes' and sensing environments	Tracking and sensing technologies	• Socio-spatial analysis • Mobility studies • Built environment analysis	• Routines & transitions • Individual and family unit studies • Longitudinal studies
	Smart devices, IOHT technologies	Smartphones, digital cameras and UAVs (drones)	• Socio-spatial analysis • Visual analysis • Journal analysis	• Routines & transitions • Individual, family unit, and peer group studies • Longitudinal studies

Considerations for the use of digital methods

Digital methods for data construction, collection and analysis are not a cure-all for the pervasive malaise in public engagement with research practice. For participant engagement, they may hold novelty value, rapid data collection capacity, convenience and cost effectiveness, and offer lower overt intrusion into participants' lives. In terms of data archives, they hold the attraction of performing as 'data in the wild', acting as a pseudo-bridge between the value of data archives and real-time socially produced behavioural data. Some may see the possibilities of big data as 'untainted' by the bias of the researcher, but of course the categorization and volume-based approach behind this form of digital trace information contains its own algorithmically produced biases. So, there is no one digital solution that will create the perfect storm of representative, affordable and accurate when it comes to working with research data. Moving from the ideal to the pragmatic, the digital methods literature highlights tensions raised by the use of these techniques for ethical research practice (see this discussion covered in Ackland, 2013). In my previous work considering how to work with big data to model digital communities, I raised similar ethical considerations (Maddox, 2016). In discussing how alignments across diverse data sets may identify the collective form of a digital community, I highlighted the ethical implications of using these sources to create aggregated visualization of patterns of social organization. Alongside considerations on the practicalities of achieving aggregated anonymity for research populations, I asked what could be the unintended consequences of data alignments in public access information; and how these analytical practices raise the question of participant consent. New digital techniques and tools bring their own suite of technical knowledge, but they do not exist in a social vacuum. To this end, the researcher may be well advised to consider the social perceptions relating to uses and applications of new and emerging technologies. For example, questions of privacy and surveillance are inherent to the terms and conditions through which software technologies and social media platforms are accessed. Similarly, the social adoption curve, levels of cultural capital and digital literacy required to know how to use and interpret new technologies impact upon the success with which these can be deployed amongst a participant population. Other trajectories of thinking on this topic may build out the implication of social adoption of technology and the relationship between levels of cultural capital and digital literacy upon digital technology access and engagement. During the design phase, the research practitioner must also consider the impact of how the social backlash and reputation loss that occurs for different technologies may impact upon the engagement of these populations with the proposed research. Another artefact of working in the online environment is that the somewhat unstable nature of new technologies can mean that a field site may 'disappear' overnight (Barratt and Maddox, 2016), the business model may fail or the technology or platform may fall out of fashion or favour (with the demise of Myspace being an example of this). In this sense, the researcher needs to future-proof their use of digital tools through resilient research design that takes into account these trends.

In conclusion, I will restate the argument of this chapter. The emerging field of digital methods has strong contributions to make to family studies research. The gulf in the literature between these two areas is an opportunity for intrepid researchers who are already skilled and embedded in the field. New researchers entering the field may find that crossing this gulf holds many pitfalls for the unsuspecting and naive. These pitfalls can be bridged through the development of resilient research design skills and an awareness of the many dimensions to be considered within ethical research practice. Interdisciplinary collaboration is inherent to the merging of these fields, as is the establishment of publication channels that support this emergent area. Most challenging will be the embedding of digital technologies and activities within longitudinal studies. The compatibility challenge of data collection techniques over time, and data meshing across disparate sources, is compounded by the relentless pace of the publishing landscape. While this chapter will quickly become obsolescent in its specifics, I argue that the digital tropes of network, big data and ubiquity are a guiding agenda through which to begin bridging digital methods with family studies research.

In brief
1. Digital research methods have application in the identification of data sources (such as the use of digital traces of online activity within social media), within data collection techniques (such as web scraping techniques) and through data analysis approaches, including data visualization.
2. The three tropes of digital methods introduced in this chapter are the structural aspects of social and technological networks (Trope 1: Networks), working with archival and real time digital trace data (Trope 2: Big data) and the aware nature of ubiquitous technologies (Trope 3: Ubiquity).
3. Longitudinal approaches to data collection through digital methods introduce methodological considerations of device and data compatibility, field site disruption and disappearance, and changing social receptivity towards data collection technologies over time.

References

Ackland, R. (2013) *Web Social Science: Concepts, Data and Tools for Social Scientists in the Digital Age*, Los Angeles: Sage.

Barratt, M. J. and Maddox, A. (2016) 'Active engagement with stigmatised communities through digital ethnography', *Qualitative Research*, 16(6): 701–719, https://doi.org/10.1177/1468794116648766

Bolton, R. N., Parasuraman, A., Hoefnagels, A., Migchels, N., Kabadayi, S., Gruber, T., ... Solnet, D. (2013) 'Understanding Generation Y and their use of social media: A review and research agenda', *Journal of Service Management*, 24(3): 245–267, https://doi.org/10.1108/09564231311326987

boyd, d. and Crawford, K. (2012) 'Critical questions for big data: Provocations for a cultural, technological, and scholarly phenomenon', *Information, Communication & Society*, 15(5): 662–679, https://doi.org/10.1080/1369118X.2012.678878

Bruns, A. and Burgess, J. (2012) 'Researching news discussion on Twitter', *Journalism Studies*, 13(5–6): 801–814, https://doi.org/10.1080/1461670X.2012.664428

Bruns, A., Highfield, T. and Burgess, J. (2013) 'The Arab Spring and social media audiences: English and Arabic twitter users and their networks', *American Behavioral Scientist*, 57(7): 871–898, https://doi.org/10.1177/0002764213479374

Bruns, A. and Stieglitz, S. (2013) 'Towards more systematic Twitter analysis: Metrics for tweeting activities', *International Journal of Social Research Methodology*, 16(2): 91–108, https://doi.org/10.1080/13645579.2012.756095

Burgess, J., Bruns, A. and Hjorth, L. (2013) 'Emerging methods for digital media research: An introduction', *Journal of Broadcasting & Electronic Media*, 57(1): 1–3, https://doi.org/10.1080/08838151.2012.761706

Ekbia, H., Mattioli, M., Kouper, I., Arave, G., Ghazinejad, A., Bowman, T., ... Sugimoto, C. R. (2015) 'Big data, bigger dilemmas: A critical review', *Journal of the Association for Information Science and Technology*, 66(8): 1523–1545, https://doi.org/10.1002/asi.23294

Elder, G. H. (1975) 'Age differentiation and the life course', *Annual Review of Sociology*, 1(1): 165–190, https://doi.org/10.1146/annurev.so.01.080175.001121

Garcia, A. C., Standlee, A. I., Bechkoff, J. and Yan Cui. (2009) 'Ethnographic approaches to the internet and computer-mediated communication', *Journal of Contemporary Ethnography*, 38(1): 52–84, https://doi.org/10.1177/0891241607310839

Gustavsson, N. and MacEachron, A. (2008) 'Creating foster care youth biographies: A role for the internet', *Journal of Technology in Human Services*, 26(1): 45–55, https://doi.org/10.1300/J017v26n01_03

Harrison, B. (2002) 'Photographic visions and narrative inquiry', *Narrative Inquiry*, 12(1): 87–111, https://doi.org/10.1075/ni.12.1.14har

Highfield, T., Harrington, S. and Bruns, A. (2013) 'Twitter as a technology for audiencing and fandom', *Information, Communication & Society*, 16(3): 315–339, https://doi.org/10.1080/1369118X.2012.756053

Hjorth, L. and Hendry, N. (2015) 'A snapshot of social media: Camera phone practices', *Social Media + Society*, 1(1), https://doi.org/10.1177/2056305115580478

Howe, K. R. (1988) 'Against the quantitative-qualitative incompatibility thesis or dogmas die hard', *Educational Researcher*, 17(8): 10-16, https://doi.org/10.3102/0013189X017008010

Iqani, M. and Schroeder, J. E. (2016) '#selfie: Digital self-portraits as commodity form and consumption practice', *Consumption Markets & Culture*, 19(5): 405-415, https://doi.org/10.1080/10253866.2015.1116784

Jethani, S. (2015) 'Mediating the body: Technology, politics and epistemologies of self', *Communication, Politics & Culture*, 47(3): 34-43.

Jurgenson, N. (2012) 'When atoms meet bits: Social media, the mobile web and augmented revolution', *Future Internet*, 4(1): 83-91, https://doi.org/10.3390/fi4010083

Lupton, D. (2013) 'Quantifying the body: Monitoring and measuring health in the age of mHealth technologies', *Critical Public Health*, 23(4): 393-403, https://doi.org/10.1080/09581596.2013.794931

Lupton, D. (2014) 'Critical perspectives on digital health technologies', *Sociology Compass*, 8(12): 1344-1359, https://doi.org/10.1111/soc4.12226

Lupton, D. (2015) 'Quantified sex: A critical analysis of sexual and reproductive self-tracking using apps', *Culture, Health & Sexuality*, 17(4): 440-453, https://doi.org/10.1080/13691058.2014.920528

Lupton, D. (2016) 'The diverse domains of quantified selves: Self-tracking modes and dataveillance', *Economy and Society*, 45(1): 101-122, https://doi.org/10.1080/03085147.2016.1143726

Maddox, A. (2016) 'Beyond digital dualism: Modeling digital community', in J. Daniels, K. Gregory and T. M. Cotton (eds) *Digital Sociologies*, Bristol: Policy Press, pp 9-26.

Mayer, K. U. (2009) 'New directions in life course research', *Annual Review of Sociology*, 35(1): 413-433, https://doi.org/10.1146/annurev.soc.34.040507.134619

Mayer, K. U. and Tuma, N. B. (1990) *Event History Analysis in Life Course Research*, Madison: University of Wisconsin Press.

Nafus, D. (2014) 'Stuck data, dead data, and disloyal data: The stops and starts in making numbers into social practices', *Distinktion: Scandinavian Journal of Social Theory*, 15(2): 208-222, https://doi.org/10.1080/1600910X.2014.920266

Neves, B. B., Franz, R. L., Munteanu, C. and Baecker, R. (2017) 'Adoption and feasibility of a communication app to enhance social connectedness amongst frail institutionalized oldest old: An embedded case study', *Information, Communication & Society*, 1–19, https://doi.org/10.1080/1369118X.2017.1348534

Rill, S., Reinel, D., Scheidt, J. and Zicari, R. V. (2014) 'PoliTwi: Early detection of emerging political topics on twitter and the impact on concept-level sentiment analysis', *Knowledge-Based Systems*, 69: 24–33, https://doi.org/10.1016/j.knosys.2014.05.008

Rogers, R. (2009a) *The End of the Virtual: Digital Methods*, Amsterdam: Amsterdam University Press.

Rogers, R. (2009b) 'Mapping public web space with the Issuecrawler', in C. Brossard and B. Reber (eds) *Digital Cognitive Technologies: Epistemology and Knowledge Society*, London: Wiley, pp 115–126.

Rogers, R. (2012) 'Mapping and the politics of web space', *Theory, Culture & Society*, 29(4–5): 193–219, https://doi.org/10.1177/0263276412450926

Satchell, C. (2008) 'From social butterfly to urban citizen: The evolution of mobile phone practice', in M. Foth (ed) *Handbook of Research on Urban Informatics: The Practice and Promise of the Real-Time City*, Hershey: Information Science Reference, pp 353–365.

Schneider, S. M. and Foot, K. A. (2004) 'The web as an object of study', *New Media & Society*, 6(1): 114–122, https://doi.org/10.1177/1461444804039912

Schroeder, R. (2010) 'Mobile phones and the inexorable advance of multimodal connectedness', *New Media & Society*, 12(1): 75–90, https://doi.org/10.1177/1461444809355114

Settersten Jr, R. A. and Mayer, K. U. (1997) 'The measurement of age, age structuring, and the life course', *Annual Review of Sociology*, 23(1): 233–261, https://doi.org/10.1146/annurev.soc.23.1.233

Stefanidis, A., Crooks, A. and Radzikowski, J. (2013) 'Harvesting ambient geospatial information from social media feeds', *GeoJournal*, 78(2): 319–338, https://doi.org/10.1007/s10708-011-9438-2

Thelwall, M. (2009) *Introduction to Webometrics: Quantitative Web Research for the Social Science*, San Rafael: Morgan & Claypool.

Tinati, R., Halford, S., Carr, L. and Pope, C. (2014a) 'Big data: Methodological challenges and approaches for sociological analysis', *Sociology*, 48(4): 663–681, https://doi.org/10.1177/0038038513511561

Tinati, R., Philippe, O., Pope, C., Carr, L. and Halford, S. (2014b) 'Challenging social media analytics: Web science perspectives', Paper presented at the *Proceedings of the 2014 ACM conference on Web science*, Bloomington, IN, 23–26 June, https://doi.org/10.1145/2615569.2615690

Van Dijk, J. (1999) *The Network Society: Social Aspects of New Media*, London: Sage.

Wellman, B. (2001) 'Computer networks as social network', *Science*, 293(5537): 2031–2034, https://doi.org/10.1126/science.1065547

Wellman, B., Quan Haase, A., Boase, J., Chen, W., Hampton, K., Díaz, I. and Miyata, K. (2003) 'The social affordances of the internet for networked individualism', *Journal of Computer-Mediated Communication*, 8(3), https://doi.org/10.1111/j.1083-6101.2003.tb00216.x

Williams, D. L., Crittenden, V. L., Keo, T. and McCarty, P. (2012) 'The use of social media: an exploratory study of usage among digital natives', *Journal of Public Affairs*, 12(2): 127–136, https://doi.org/10.1002/pa.1414

Witte, J. C., Amoroso, L. M. and Howard, P. E. N. (2000) 'Research methodology – Method and representation in Internet-based survey tools – Mobility, community, and cultural identity in Survey2000', *Social Science Computer Review*, 18(2): 179–195, https://doi.org/10.1177/089443930001800207

Yu, Y. and Wang, X. (2015) 'World Cup 2014 in the twitter world: A big data analysis of sentiments in U.S. sports fans' tweets', *Computers in Human Behavior*, 48(Supplement C): 392–400, https://doi.org/10.1016/j.chb.2015.01.075

Zimmerman, T. G. (1999) 'Wireless networked digital devices: A new paradigm for computing and communication', *IBM Systems Journal*, 38(4): 566–574, https://doi.org/10.1147/sj.384.0566

Cross-disciplinary research methods to study technology use, family, and life course dynamics: lessons from an action research project on social isolation and loneliness in later life

Barbara Barbosa Neves, Ron Baecker, Diana Carvalho,
and Alexandra Sanders

Introduction

As research on the relationship between digital technology and family life is emerging as an important topic for family scholars (Neves and Casimiro, 2018), what can we learn from sociotechnical research designed and conducted by social and computer scientists? What do we gain by combining cross-disciplinary methods to study technology adoption and its outcomes within family and life course contexts? What challenges do we face? This chapter considers these questions by drawing on a mixed methods project on technology and social connectedness, facilitated by a team of sociologists and human–computer interaction (HCI) researchers (Baecker et al, 2014; Neves et al, 2015, 2017a, 2017b). Informed by sociological studies of technology (MacKenzie and Wajcman, 1999), the team shared a conceptualization of technology as a sociotechnical process of interconnection between technological and human elements.

HCI, a sub-field of computer science and engineering, emerged in the early 1980s to ensure that 'humans and computers [are] interacting to perform work effectively' (Long and Dowell, 1989, p 6). Recently, a growing epistemological shift from a system-centred to a human-centred approach has moved the discipline 'from evaluation of interfaces through design of systems and into general sense-making of our world' (Bannon, 2011, p 50). This 'human-centred informatics' lens has relocated some HCI work from laboratories to the field, aligning with a sociological quest to understand the complex interplay of social and technological dimensions in everyday life. As such, we posit that both disciplines gain from combining methods and collaboratively studying sociotechnical systems, including how digital technology affects family dynamics and vice versa.

The cross-disciplinary work presented here is based on an *action research project* that evaluated a new digital technology to tackle social isolation and loneliness in later life. As action research projects are focused on addressing practical issues through involving researchers and participants as co-collaborators (Berg, 2004), this strategy enabled systematic action to both solve a problem and advance scientific knowledge in a critical area. Furthermore, action research projects follow a pragmatist epistemology, allowing use of multiple methods (Ivankova, 2014). Although action research projects are employed in both HCI and sociology, cross-disciplinary and mixed methods approaches remain scant, particularly in the study of interventions to tackle social isolation and loneliness among older adults (Franz et al, 2015; Neves et al, 2017b).

Social isolation and loneliness amongst older adults (aged 65+) correspond to a higher likelihood of social disengagement, depression, functional decline, and premature mortality (Cornwell and Waite, 2009; Perissinotto et al, 2012; Steptoe et al, 2013). Loneliness is a subjective feeling of a lack of companionship, whereas social isolation is a scarcity of quality social connections, of social support, and of social participation (Cornwell and Waite, 2009; Perissinotto et al, 2012). While loneliness and social isolation are related, they can be experienced independently of each other: we can be socially isolated but not feel lonely, or feel lonely despite an active social network (group of social ties). Both have similar negative effects on health and social inclusion.

Frail older adults living in institutions (care homes, long-term care, complex continuing care) seem especially vulnerable to these issues (Prieto-Flores et al, 2011). Transitions to care homes (institutionalization) and associated changes in social connections can also contribute to experiences of loneliness and social isolation (Bradshaw et al, 2012; Prieto-Flores et al, 2011). We used a life course perspective to conceptualize these experiences, framing them within life course dynamics that connect the five paradigmatic principles of life course theory – life-span development, human agency, historical time and place, timing, and linked lives (Elder et al, 2003). Of particular importance was the principle of linked lives, which highlights social connections and refers to 'connections [that] extend across generations and across people's lives through convoys of friends and relatives' (Elder, 2000, pp 1617–1618). Additionally, institutionalization was understood as a critical life transition in which individuals experience changes to their personal/social state, role, and identity (Elder et al, 2003).

Literature on social isolation and loneliness suggests that new communication technologies can lessen the risks of both in later life by enhancing opportunities for social connectedness (Findlay, 2003; Masi et al, 2011). Social connectedness is fostered by strengthening ties between 'linked lives' through meaningful interactions with close relatives and friends; it is the quality and not the quantity of social interactions that minimizes the risks of loneliness and social isolation (Cooney et al, 2014; Gierveld et al, 2015). Older adults, however – particularly those who are frail and require aged care support – are less likely to adopt new technologies, more likely to discontinue usage with age, and are significantly affected by lack of technology accessibility and digital literacy (Neves et al, 2013, 2015; Berkowsky et al, 2015). Even among those who used digital technologies before entering residential care, active use is affected by life course-related socioeconomic factors, including access, frailty, and reduced social participation (Berkowsky et al, 2015; Neves et al, 2017a, 2017b). While research has shown that institutionalized or frail older adults want to maintain connections with family and friends through different media (Tsai et al, 2015; Sayago et al, 2011), they are limited by the aforementioned factors.

To address the complex needs and aspirations of this group of older adults, we co-created an accessible, Android- and iPad-based communication app (Baecker et al, 2014; Neves et al, 2015). This technology was designed with and for older adults who are potentially frail, institutionalized, concerned with maintaining social connectedness with loved ones, or experiencing difficulties with standard technologies because of motor issues or digital skills. The app enables users to send audio, images, and videos created on their tablet, and also has a 'wave' (text) feature that forwards a pre-set message to recipients (see Figure 7.1). Media is sent to recipients' devices as an email attachment to which they can respond. Users' contacts are displayed as a list through which they can swipe, much like a digital photo-frame (Figure 7.1). During exploratory design studies, users expressed a clear preference for regulating when they sent and received communication, not wanting a real-time device comparable to the telephone. The app is therefore asynchronous. To accommodate users with motor or visual limitations, the interface features large, non-textual touch icons that respond to swipes and taps but do not require typing. To develop and test this app, we used principles of participatory research design (Ehn, 2008) and a 'social shaping of technology' approach, which considers the multitude of social, cultural, economic, and symbolic elements that affect the design, implementation, and effects of technology (MacKenzie and Wajcman, 1999). The app was deployed in two Canadian care homes to evaluate adoption and use of the technology, and its feasibility as a means of enhancing social connectedness for frail residents.

Figure 7.1 The contact list interface showing one contact (top), the message options interface with four options (middle), the new message notification interface (bottom)

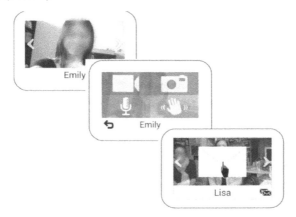

Combining methods: computer science and sociological approaches

Deployment and feasibility design

Our action research project combined a deployment and a feasibility study. A deployment is a common type of field study in HCI that trials a novel technology or prototype with its target users in situ. Deployments aim to assess the adoption and impact of new technologies within the intended 'everyday practice' context of usage (Siek et al, 2014). A feasibility study tests a previously unexamined intervention with a population about whom we lack in-depth knowledge in a real-life/constrained setting rather than an ideal experimental environment (Bowen et al, 2009). Both employ mixed methods. As such, these two approaches complemented each other in the pursuit of our research aims: the deployment helped analyse how participants adopted and used the app within their daily contexts, while the feasibility study allowed evaluation of both *acceptability* (adoption and appropriate use of the technology) and *efficacy* (the results of that usage) (Bowen et al, 2009).

To examine the feasibility of the app to enhance user-perceived social connectedness, we conducted a two-month app deployment (2014) in a long-term care facility and a three-month deployment (2015) in a multi-care retirement community. The sites were located in Toronto, Canada. To explore sociotechnical factors of adoption and use (acceptability) as well as the potential of the technology to enhance social connectedness within a specific setting (efficacy), we combined different social research techniques: semi-structured interviews, psychometric scales (Duke Social Support Index and the UCLA Three-Item Loneliness Scale), and field (participant) observations. But we also aimed to test and improve the technology's functions and interface, as at the core of a deployment study is understanding how the user experience and the technology can be redesigned and enriched iteratively (Siek et al, 2014). As such, we included three techniques commonly used in HCI: usability testing, accessibility testing, and log data and analysis.

Usability testing asks users to perform representative tasks on a technology to help researchers refine its quality by finding key flaws (Lazar et al, 2010). Mostly, these tests are conducted to evaluate the ease of use and learnability of a technology's interface (Franz and Neves, 2018). Although typical usability testing requires participants to execute a set of tasks (to assess speed of task performance and type/rate of errors by users), specific types of usability techniques – such as the *Think Aloud* protocol and its variants – facilitate insight into the participant's mental model of the system (Franz et al, 2018). This protocol requests participants to verbalize their thoughts while performing tasks (Lewis, 1982). Our usability testing included a list of tasks and the Think Aloud approach when possible (depending on participants' impairments).

As accessibility issues can be strong inhibitors of technology use – especially among frail, institutionalized older adults – accessibility testing is another valuable technique (Sayago et al, 2011). Though the most prevalent method used to determine whether a system meets accessible design standards is an assessment by experts (Franz et al, 2018), we utilized an accessibility evaluation with our participants due to its documented benefits over expert evaluation, which include the capacity to observe the severity of accessibility issues in practice (Web Accessibility Initiative, 2010). These tests included inspecting if accessibility standards were met and ranking elements such as colour contrast, font size, and auditory and weight factors.

Lastly, log data and analysis were used to measure frequency of use and types of messages sent and received (audio, video, text, or picture). Logs are actions recorded by a device or computerized service while it is being used, ranging from clicks to shared content (Dumais et al, 2004). Logs have the advantage of capturing actions and not perceptions of actions; instead of relying on participant-reported frequency of use, we measure how many times the technology is being used. Nonetheless, we were not interested in replacing participants' perceptions with 'real' traces of use; rather, we aimed to compare both to find patterns and differences. Additionally, logs have to be combined with other data as they show 'what' action was performed, not 'how', 'why', or its impact.

Stages and procedures

Our studies featured pre-, mid-, and post-deployment stages. These stages changed slightly from the first to the second study, as we learnt from the original deployment (see Table 7.1). Despite the changes, the results were consistent across the two studies. Yet refining procedures allowed us to gather more in-depth data to contextualize our findings. At pre-deployment, participants and a study partner (one relative, caregiver, or friend) received individual training in the use of the app and tablet (which only had our app installed). The training showed participants how to use the technology, having them send and receive different types of messages. Researchers privately administered a social support and loneliness scale with each participant, and created a baseline profile to record their social network composition, social interaction levels, and sociodemographics. Participants were then provided with the tablet with our app for use as they saw fit over a period of two to three months. In the second study, we also interviewed study partners at the pre-deployment stage to ascertain their perception of participants' social interaction levels, engagement, and relationships.

The mid-deployment phase occurred four to six weeks after pre-deployment. Here, we re-administered the aforementioned scales and conducted accessibility and usability tests that included questions and tasks related to app use. In the second study, accessibility and usability tests were conducted post-deployment to give participants enough time to engage with the device, as we concluded from the first deployment that users needed time to become familiar with, and critical of, the technology.

At post-deployment, we repeated the scales and conducted semi-structured interviews with participants and study partners. Over the course of the study, we visited participants weekly to collect field observations and answer questions.

We applied two scales: Wardian et al's (2012) Abbreviated Duke Social Support Index, which includes social interaction and satisfaction rating subscales, and Hughes et al's (2004) Short Revised UCLA Loneliness Scale, which comprises yes/no questions about feeling left out or isolated and lacking companionship. The semi-structured interviews, which lasted approximately 40 minutes, were used to explore participants' experiences with the app and to understand their use and non-use, communication with relatives, and social engagement. Study partners were also interviewed to gather their feedback on use, preferences, challenges, and opportunities with the app. The usability and accessibility tests lasted an average of 40 minutes and consisted of tasks (including sending and accessing different types of messages) and questions about features, weight, colour, font, and volume. In the first study, we tried the Think Aloud technique and used Likert-type scales (1 to 5, from Strongly agree to Strongly disagree) but found that participants struggled with both (Neves et al, 2015). In the second, questions were open-closed and based on a qualitative and comparative approach (Franz et al, 2018). Both usability and accessibility tests were video-recorded; we filmed how participants' hands interacted with the technology to improve usability. Observations used an unstructured format, allowing note-taking when appropriate – these notes described interactions and reactions, how participants used the app, the context, and activities. The app recorded logs measuring time, frequency, and type of use; message content, however, was not recorded. Participants were aware of what was being recorded.

Table 7.1 Deployment stages and data collection

Deployment stage	First study (2014, *n* = 4)	Second study (2015, *n* = 12)
Pre	• Individual training session • Psychometric scales • Baseline profiles	• Individual training session • Psychometric scales • Semi-structured interviews • Semi-structured interviews with study partners
Mid	• Psychometric scales • Usability tests • Accessibility tests • Log data & analysis	• Psychometric scales • Semi-structured interviews • Log data & analysis
Post	• Psychometric scales • Semi-structured interviews • Semi-structured interviews with study partners • Log data & analysis	• Psychometric scales • Semi-structured interviews • Semi-structured interviews with study partners • Usability tests • Accessibility tests • Log data & analysis
← Participant Observation (throughout the study) →		

Data analysis

Interviews and usability and accessibility tests were analysed with qualitative profiling and thematic analysis. Field notes complemented the interviews and contributed to the qualitative profiling, which allowed us to craft profiles for and contextualize each participant (Seidman, 2006). Thematic analysis was employed to detect themes within and across cases, which were both identified in the data and using a priori categories (namely technology-related codes) (King and Horrocks, 2010). At least two researchers coded independently, then collectively to test for convergence. A third ensured basic inter-rater reliability (Patton, 1990) of half of the data by manually counting discrepancies in assignment of codes and themes, reaching over 90% for all interviews and tests. Usability and accessibility tests were also analysed with descriptive and correlational statistics to measure speed of task performance, type and rate of issues encountered, and number of tasks successfully completed (Franz et al, 2018).

Scales were analysed descriptively and with Friedman and Sign tests, which are nonparametric techniques suiting our sampling. This analysis aimed to measure differences over time (from pre- to post-deployment). We adopted a liberal criterion regarding our small sample size (*n* = 16), as health practitioners also use these scales to assess individual patients and gather baseline information (Neves et al, 2017a). However, advanced statistical analysis was not feasible. Logs were analysed with descriptive statistics and confidence intervals, as analysis of variance significance testing is not as useful in log analysis since we look for both effect size and its practical significance (Dumais et al, 2004).

Participants

The first study included five frail 'oldest old' people (aged 80+) living in a long-term care facility and five relatives. The second comprised 13 older adults living in a multi-care retirement community and their study partners (relatives or friends). One participant withdrew in the first study due to health decline, and one participant in the second due to lack of interest. As such, our data relates to 16 participants.

Recruitment challenges of institutionalized and frail older adults include their declining health, compressed life expectancy, and ethical concerns (Hall et al, 2009), which affects timeframes of longitudinal studies. Participant recruitment was facilitated by care home staff, and older adults with cognitive impairments that restricted capacity to provide consent were not enrolled. The project was approved by the University of Toronto Research Ethics Board (REB) and all participants gave verbal and written informed consent.

Participants' ages ranged from 74 to 95 (M = 83.9; SD = 5.5); ten identified as female and six as male. Participants in the first study were Chinese Canadians. Data were collected in their native languages with the assistance of staff and a Cantonese-speaking researcher. All except one participant were digitally illiterate (had never used a digital device) and had to learn touchscreen gestures (tapping/swiping). In the second study, the sample included Canadians, British Canadians, American Canadians, Latin American Canadians, Italian Canadians, and Japanese Canadians; all participants were fluent in English and had higher levels of education. Four of the 12 were digitally illiterate; eight had used a computer before, but only had a basic or medium-level understanding of the system (struggling with some functions). Eight participants joined the study with relatives, and four with friends. All participants had health limitations (from motor impairments to Parkinson's) and were considered frail by the staff.

Lessons learned

General findings: acceptability and efficacy of the app

Combining studies allowed observation of differences in uptake and use, even within the small sample (Neves et al, 2015, 2017a, 2017b). Eleven participants used the app weekly (average two days per week), whereas five were occasional users (once every two weeks). At post-deployment, two of the occasional users stopped using the app: one did not get messages from his only contact in the app (his son); the other was 'more interested' in knitting and cooking. The most reported motivation to use the tool was to connect/reconnect with grandchildren, 'the digital generation'. Participants shared that by using a digital tool they hoped to feel closer to their grandchildren, particularly since moving to a care home. Adoption of the tool was influenced by different sociotechnical factors (from attitudes to usability of the technology), including life course dimensions such as life history (past experiences with technology, life transitions, socioeconomic and educational experiences), linked lives (social networks, family support), age-related roles (grandparenting), agency (choices and actions), and place (living settings).

Some participants were active users, enjoying sending and receiving messages, while others were more passive, preferring receiving messages. One participant noted: 'I just like to get pictures and see my grandchildren dancing and acting in China... the dog chasing my grandchildren and they laughing out loud'. Overall participants had a clear preference for types of messages, preferring to receive text and send audio. Yet these preferences were in contrast with the communication patterns of relatives and friends, who mostly sent picture and video messages. Other divergent intergenerational practices, norms, and expectations were found in both studies regarding reply time and (a)synchronicity. Reply time issues included our participants not replying quickly to messages, sometimes taking one or two days. Relatives, particularly grandchildren, found this delay 'annoying'. Our grandparents thought this reply time was appropriate as they need to 'think before reply'. So while our participants praised the asynchronous nature of the app, as they could control time and type of interactions, relatives had a preference for synchronous (real-time) communication. Relatives' preference for a synchronous tool led most participants to question their choices or feel 'discouraged' by family.

All participants, even those who were digitally illiterate at the study's commencement, reported high perceived usefulness of the app for social interaction due to its simplicity and options. But not having at least one tie actively involved in the project meant that for two participants the app had no use and was potentially detrimental. One confided that, 'if he [son] doesn't answer then I don't need this... I am just here waiting'. The app therefore had the potential to make participants more aware of family tensions and their own loneliness and/or social isolation. Nevertheless, it increased the sense of social interaction (communication frequency and type) with family and friends for 13 participants. However, only six reported high perceived social connectedness at post-deployment – those with relatives living abroad or far away. These participants used the app to reconnect, communicate more frequently, and deepen relationships with those relatives.

We concluded that, to facilitate the adoption of the app and its feasibility to enhance social connectedness and tackle both social isolation and loneliness, participants needed *adjustment periods* to learn to use the app and to *manage different intergenerational preferences, norms, and expectations.* Furthermore, *having geographically distant relatives* amplified the app's feasibility to contribute to higher levels of social connectedness. Although the app is a promising tool to address social isolation and loneliness, it is also limited by the aforementioned sociotechnical factors (see also Neves et al, 2015, 2017a, 2017b).

Cross-disciplinary insights

By combining social and HCI research methods, we were able to strengthen our data collection and analysis, uncovering a richer understanding of technology adoption and its impacts on older adults and their linked lives with family and friends. Our cross-disciplinary approach also shed light on the interplay of sociotechnical context(s) (technology, residential settings), structure (sociodemographic and socioeconomic factors, such as social class, age, gender, social norms), and agentic elements (attitudes, meanings, experiences).

Our social research methods, namely semi-structured interviews, psychometric scales, and participant observation, helped contextualize long-term app use, providing insights into adoption, appropriation, use, and perceived effects. Importantly, they showed how people are affected by their life experiences in adopting technology and how people shape their use to suit interests, social dynamics and roles, needs, aspirations, and constraints in their everyday lives. Having pre- and post-interviews with different users (participants and study partners) added to our understanding of the app from multiple angles and 'end users'.

This combination of methods is advantageous for sociologists and for HCI researchers interested in a 'human-centred informatics' framework. For example, it allowed us to refine HCI usability and accessibility testing: our observations and analyses of the results helped identify that the Likert-type scales were not the most appropriate instrument for our participants, who would tell a story instead of selecting a score or ask us if their story matched any of the scores (Neves et al, 2015). We could also visibly note impression management efforts (Goffman, 1956) – the need to make a good impression on the researcher and be positive about the app – during the usability and accessibility sessions of the first study. Two participants who only had use of one of their arms indicated that the device was easy to lift and carry, although we could see them struggling; additionally, all participants reported not having difficulties with the app, while we saw them struggling with some functions throughout the study. These tests were set up as informal activities, but the feeling of being tested or evaluated did not seem to subside. These findings led to adjusting the test procedures for the second study, as we:

- opted for task-based questions, that is, asking participants to 'lift the device' before answering about its weight. We saw answers changing in the first study: two participants reported that the device was easy to lift during the sessions, but when asked later to perform it, both acknowledged that it was not that easy when only having use of one hand;
- emphasized that their role was to find issues with the app so we could improve it;
- used comparative questions to assess different features and their preference (swiping vs. tapping); and
- asked about how other older adults would perceive or assess that technology.

This adjusted approach gave us a better grasp of their mental models of the system and helped reduce impression management efforts, as participants became more critical as testers.

Sociologists also experienced a threefold gain from adding usability and accessibility tests to their toolbox. Firstly, exploring how people simultaneously use, adapt, and perceive functions (and their models of technology) deepens our understanding of sociotechnical systems and the practices and embodied performances surrounding them. Secondly, the sessions and their video recordings uncovered new strategies of use. When the app was not responding as our participants intended, they would try different gestures, including gestures not taught during the study. For instance, when tapping was ineffective, they would try tracing the icon with their fingers. These strategies helped further deconstruct ideas about learning processes in later life, often perceived as passive. Thirdly, the sessions highlighted the impression management of researchers: we continued to use 'correct' terms, such as tapping and swiping, while most participants would use other terms (touching, punching, caressing, among others). This language disconnection was particularly noticeable in the usability and accessibility tests: we never adopted their terminology and they did not adopt ours. These tests gave a new view into our position in the field and its implications, contributing to researchers' reflexivity.

The use of logging data, however, fell short of its promise. Due to problems with Wi-Fi connection in some areas of the care homes, functions and timestamps were not recorded consistently over time. There were also several 'missing events' (events not logged), 'dropped data' (gaps in logs as data were aggregated when logs grew in size), and 'misplaced semantics' (meanings of logs changing as events were encoded with tags and data) (Dumais et al, 2004). From this, we learnt that a more precise definition of metrics and a continuous curation of logs (cleaning data errors, distortions, and keeping semantics consistent) should have been a core concern during fieldwork. Despite these issues, the general picture of use recorded by logs seemed to match perceptions of usage by participants and study partners. Nevertheless, a more accurate dataset would have allowed us to explore the relationship between 'actual use' and 'perceived use'.

Despite these limitations, our mixed methods design strengthened our research. Although this approach allows for data triangulation, we were interested in moving beyond this by having methods 'talking to each other' to uncover data patterns and inconsistencies. By embracing the messiness of deployment, mixed methods, and cross-disciplinary studies, we were able to capture and analyse the complexity of technology adoption and use and its relationship to social, technology, and family dynamics.

Challenges and opportunities for technology, families and life course studies

These methodological reflections help identify the challenges and opportunities of cross-disciplinary and mixed methods research to study technologies, families, and the life course. With regard to challenges, agreeing on ethical conducts in terms of procedure and practice can be complex – particularly in the era of big data and 'public' massive data collection of human behaviour (or its traces). For instance, our team had to discuss the benefits and perils of recording and accessing the content of messages sent and received through our app. We decided not to log that data, but it had to be negotiated with all team members. Informed consent, participant incentives, and risk management strategies were also actively discussed, as standards varied. Beyond axiology, our HCI researchers were focused on 'real use', while the sociologists focused on contrasting 'real use' and perceptions over time. Sociologists were also more interested in a life course perspective, particularly in terms of life transitions and linked lives. These interests – related to different epistemologies and ontologies – had to be properly accommodated. In addition, potential limitations of a pragmatic epistemology, such as short-sighted practicality, can be more challenging in cross-disciplinary teams studying the digital as a tool and a method, that is, a system allowing for both social life and sociological analysis. Other aspects included subjectivity and intra-comparability issues when refining (and de-standardizing) instruments throughout the research process. Finally, adjusting translation processes was essential: team members had to learn to be open to different expertise and to communicate effectively; knowledge transfer and mobilization had to be based on disseminating complex cross-disciplinary work in a cohesive, accessible, and targeted manner.

Regarding opportunities, our study showed that a more complete understanding of use of digital communication technologies can enhance knowledge of shared family meanings and social practices, in both structural and agentic terms. For instance, examining technology adoption/use and its context(s) allowed observation of dimensions that directly shape the life course, including family praxis, intergenerational roles, and age and gendered performances (Hagestad and Dykstra, 2016). We argue that technology, as a sociotechnical system, is also one of these dimensions. The growing pervasiveness, embeddedness, and role of digital technology in Western societies means that, increasingly, these technologies should be recognized as a part of trajectories/ transitions rather than as an external element. The experiences of one of our participants illustrates how technology can be a central dimension in key turning points: Jen, a librarian, retired when the computerized library system changed from one she was familiar with to one so different that it caused her constant anxiety. Her decision was, in part, motivated by technology. By situating technology in its social context, we can investigate how it shapes society and how, in turn, society shapes it (MacKenzie and Wajcman, 1999). Moreover, social scientists gain from participating in the process of technology development: by being part of the 'black box' of technology (Latour, 1999), they can further sociotechnical knowledge of – and contribute to – the design, implementation, and use of technologies.

Combining disciplinary perspectives and techniques also affords several methodological benefits to family and life course research. For instance, cross-disciplinary methods can help bridge micro and macro polarizations within family and life course research, enabling better access to their interplay and to the meso level. Furthermore, the combination of methods can assist in mapping family and life transitions 'in action'. Though the use of data from multiple time points underpins life course studies, these inquiry types are often based on retrospective methods that capture data before and after participants' experiences of the phenomena under study (Bengtson and Allen, 1993). Deployment studies instead promote continuous study of these phenomena, and the repetition of methods and/or stages facilitates flexibility and self-correction over a study's course without affecting inter-comparability. Moreover, the diverse methods presented here provided access to both 'recorded and observed' life moments and histories (Hagestad and Dykstra, 2016, p 68). Employing methods from unusual academic partners in life course work can foster creative and innovative approaches to research, and encourage examination of atypical or underexplored angles.

In brief

1. Combining social and human-computer interaction methodologies strengthened a mixed methods research project that evaluated the adoption, use, acceptability, and efficacy of a digital communication tool to address issues of social isolation and loneliness in later life.
2. Main challenges included the management of diverse research perspectives, interests, expertise, and ethical considerations.
3. Cross-disciplinary mixed methods approaches can enhance family and life course studies by: highlighting the micro/macro interplay in individual lives, capturing the immediacy of life transitions, facilitating access to observed and recorded life moments and histories, and identifying underexplored angles.

Acknowledgements

We would like to thank the participants and staff of the retirement communities we have worked with. We are also grateful to Rachel Franz, Christian Beermann, Rebecca Judges, Mags Ngo, Nadia Nassar, Cosmin Munteanu, Annette Mayer, Chris Arnold, Hubert Hu, Steve Tsourounis, Benjamin Rabishaw, Sarah Crosskey, Kate Sellen, and all former TAGlab members who contributed to the InTouch project.

References

Baecker, R., Sellen, K., Crosskey, S., Boscart, V. and Neves, B. B. (2014) 'Technology to reduce social isolation and loneliness', in *Proceedings of the 16th International ACM SIGACCESS Conference on Computers & Accessibility*, New York: ACM, pp 27-34, https://doi.org/10.1145/2661334.2661375

Bannon, L. (2011) 'Reimagining HCI: Toward a more human-centered perspective', *Interactions*, 18(4): 50-57, https://doi.org/10.1145/1978822.1978833

Bengtson, V. L. and Allen, K. R. (1993) 'The life course perspective applied to families over time', in P. Boss, W. J. Doherty, R. LaRossa, W. R. Schumm and S. K. Steinmetz (eds) *Sourcebook of Family Theories and Methods*, New York: Springer, pp 469-504.

Berg, B. L. (2004) *Qualitative Research Methods for the Social Sciences*, Boston: Pearson.

Berkowsky, R. W., Rikard, R. V and Cotten, S. R. (2015) 'Signing off: Predicting discontinued ICT usage among older adults in assisted and independent living', in J. Zhou & G. Salvendy (eds) *Human Aspects of IT for the Aged Population*, NY: Springer, pp 389-398.

Bowen, D. J., Kreuter, M., Spring, B., Cofta-Woerpel, L., Linney, L., Weiner, D.,… Fernandez, M. (2009) 'How we design feasibility studies', *American Journal of Preventive Medicine*, 36(5): 452–457, https://doi.org/10.1016/j.amepre.2009.02.002

Bradshaw, S. A., Playford, E. D. and Riazi, A. (2012) 'Living well in care homes: A systematic review of qualitative studies', *Age and Ageing*, 41(4): 429-440, https://doi.org/10.1093/ageing/afs069

Cooney, A., Dowling, M., Gannon, M. E., Dempsey, L. and Murphy, K. (2014) 'Exploration of the meaning of connectedness for older people in long-term care in context of their quality of life', *International Journal of Older People Nursing*, 9(3): 192-199, https://doi.org/10.1111/opn.12017

Cornwell, E. Y. and Waite, L. J. (2009) 'Social disconnectedness, perceived isolation, and health among older adults', *Journal of Health and Social Behavior*, 50(1): 31-48, https://doi.org/10.1177/002214650905000103

Dumais, S., Cutrell, E., Sarin, R. and Horvitz, E. (2004) 'Implicit queries (IQ) for contextualized search', in *Proceedings of the 27th Annual International ACM SIGIR Conference on Research and Development in Information Retrieval*, New York: ACM, pp 594–594.

Ehn, P. (2008) 'Participation in design things', in *Proceedings of the Tenth Anniversary Conference on Participatory Design 2008*, Bloomington: Indiana University, pp 92–101.

Elder, G. H. (2000) 'The life course', in E. F. Borgatta and R. J. V. Montgomery (eds) *The Encyclopedia of Sociology: Second edition, Volume 3*, South Yarra: Macmillan Reference USA, pp 1614–1622.

Elder, G. H., Johnson, M. K. and Crosnoe, R. (2003) 'The emergence and development of the life course', in J. T. Mortimer and M. J. Shanahan (eds) *Handbook of the Life Course*, New York: Plenum Press, pp 3–19.

Findlay, R. A. (2003) 'Interventions to reduce social isolation amongst older people: Where is the evidence?', *Ageing and Society*, 23(5): 647–658, https://doi.org/10.1017/S0144686X03001296.

Franz, R. and Neves, B. B. (2018) 'Usability is ageless: Conducting usability tests with older adults', in B. B. Neves and F. Vetere (eds) *Ageing and Digital Technology: Designing and Evaluating Emerging Technologies for Older Adults* (forthcoming). New York: Springer.

Franz, R. L., Munteanu, C., Neves, B. B. and Baecker, R. (2015) 'Time to retire old methodologies? Reflecting on conducting usability evaluations with older adults', in *Proceedings of the 17th International Conference on Human–Computer Interaction with Mobile Devices and Services Adjunct*, New York: ACM, pp 912–915.

Franz, R., Neves, B. B., Epp, C. D. and Baecker, R. (2018) 'Investigating best practices for usability and accessibility testing with older adults: Connecting fieldwork and insights from experts in the human–computer interaction community', forthcoming.

Gierveld, J. D. J., Van der Pas, S. and Keating, N. (2015) 'Loneliness of older immigrant groups in Canada: Effects of ethnic–cultural background', *Journal of Cross-Cultural Gerontology*, 30(3): 251–268, https://doi.org/10.1007/s10823-015-9265-x

Goffman, E. (1956) *The Presentation of Self in Everyday Life*, New York: Random House.

Hagestad, G. O. and Dykstra, P. A. (2016) 'Structuration of the life course: Some neglected aspects', in J. T. Mortimer and M. J. Shanahan (eds) *Handbook of the Life Course*, New York: Springer, pp. 131–157.

Hall, S., Longhurst, S. and Higginson, I. J. (2009) 'Challenges to conducting research with older people living in nursing homes', *BMC Geriatrics*, 9(1), 38, https://doi.org/10.1186/1471-2318-9-38

Hughes, M. E., Waite, L. J., Hawkley, L. C. and Cacioppo, J. T. (2004) 'A short scale for measuring loneliness in large surveys: Results from two population-based studies', *Research on Aging*, 26(6): 655–672, https://doi.org/10.1177/0164027504268574

Ivankova, N. V. (2014) *Mixed Methods Applications in Action Research: From Methods to Community Action*, Thousand Oaks: Sage.

King, N. and Horrocks, C. (2010) *Interviews in Qualitative Research*, Thousand Oaks, CA: Sage.

Latour, B. (1999) *Pandora's Hope: Essays on the Reality of Science Studies*, Cambridge, MA: Harvard University Press.

Lazar, J., Feng, J. and Hochheiser, H. (2010) *Research Methods in Human–Computer Interaction*, Chichester: John Wiley & Sons.

Lewis, C. (1982) *Using the 'Thinking Aloud' Method in Cognitive Interface Design*, New York: Watson Research Center.

Long, J. and Dowell, J. (1989) 'Conceptions of the discipline of HCI: Craft, applied science, and engineering', in *People and Computers V: Proceedings of the Fifth Conference of the British Computer Society*, Cambridge: Cambridge University Press, vol. 5, p 9.

MacKenzie, D. and Wajcman, J. (1999) *The Social Shaping of Technology*, London: Open University Press.

Masi, C., Chen, H. Y., Hawkley L., Cacioppo, J. T. (2011) 'A meta-analysis of interventions to reduce loneliness', *Personality and Social Psychology Review*, 15(3): 219-266, https://doi.org/10.1177/1088868310377394

Neves, B. B. and Casimiro, C. (2018). 'Connecting families? An introduction', in B. B. Neves and C. Casimiro (eds) *Connecting Families?*, Bristol: Policy Press.

Neves, B. B., Amaro, F. and Fonseca, J. R. (2013) 'Coming of (old) age in the digital age: ICT usage and non-usage among older adults', *Sociological Research Online*, 18(2): 6, https://doi.org/10.5153/sro.2998

Neves, B. B., Franz, R., Munteanu, C., Baecker, R. and Ngo, M. (2015) '"My hand doesn't listen to me!": Adoption and evaluation of a communication technology for the "oldest old"', in *Proceedings of the 33rd Annual ACM Conference on Human Factors in Computing Systems*, New York: ACM, pp 1593-1602.

Neves, B. B., Franz, R., Judges, R., Beermann, C. and Baecker, R. (2017a) 'Can digital technology enhance social connectedness among older adults? A feasibility study', *Journal of Applied Gerontology*, https://doi.org/10.1177/0733464817741369

Neves, B. B., Franz, R. L., Munteanu, C. and Baecker, R. (2017b) 'Adoption and feasibility of a communication app to enhance social connectedness amongst frail institutionalized oldest old: An embedded case study', *Information Communication & Society*, https://doi.org/10.1080/1369118X.2017.1348534

Patton, M. Q. (1990) *Qualitative Evaluation and Research Methods*, Thousand Oaks, CA: Sage.

Perissinotto, C. M., Cenzer, I. S. and Covinsky, K. E. (2012) 'Loneliness in older persons: A predictor of functional decline and death', *Archives of Internal Medicine*, 172(14): 1078–1084, https://doi.org/10.1001/archinternmed.2012.1993

Prieto-Flores, M. E., Forjaz, M. J., Fernandez-Mayoralas, G., Rojo-Perez, F. and Martinez-Martin, P. (2011) 'Factors associated with loneliness of noninstitutionalized and institutionalized older adults', *Journal of Aging and Health*, 23(1): 177–194, https://doi.org/10.1177/0898264310382658

Sayago, S., Sloan, D. and Blat, J. (2011) 'Everyday use of computer-mediated communication tools and its evolution over time: An ethnographical study with older people', *Interacting with Computers*, 23(5): 543–554, https://doi.org/10.1016/j.intcom.2011.06.001

Seidman, I. (2006) *Interviewing as Qualitative Research: A Guide for Researchers in Education and the Social Sciences*, New York: Teachers College Press.

Siek, K. A., Hayes, G. R., Newman, M. W. and Tang, J. C. (2014) 'Field deployments: Knowing from using in context', in *Ways of Knowing in HCI*, New York: Springer, pp 119–142.

Steptoe, A., Shankar, A., Demakakos, P. and Wardle, J. (2013) 'Social isolation, loneliness, and all-cause mortality in older men and women', *Proceedings of the National Academy of Sciences*, 110(15): 5797–5801, https://doi.org/10.1073/pnas.1219686110

Tsai, H. Y. S., Shillair, R. and Cotten, S. R. (2015) 'Getting grandma online: Are tablets the answer for increasing digital inclusion for older adults in the US?', *Educational Gerontology*, 41(10): 695–709, https://doi.org/10.1080/03601277.2015.1048165

Wardian, J., Robbins, D., Wolfersteig, W., Johnson, T. and Dustman, P. (2012) 'Validation of the DSSI-10 to measure social support in a general population', *Research on Social Work Practice*, 23: 100–106, https://doi.org/10.1177/1049731512464582

Web Accessibility Initiative (2010) *Involving Users in Evaluating Web Accessibility*, www.w3.org/WAI/eval/users.html

From object to instrument: technologies as tools for family relations and family research

Cláudia Casimiro and Magda Nico

Introduction

Over the past two decades, we have witnessed major revolutions in technology: broadband connections, mobile connectivity, and the rise of social media and social networking (Pew Research Center, 2014; Rainie and Wellman, 2012). These revolutions have spread and expanded rapidly, especially in Western societies, making the internet both faster and more accessible, and changing the way people develop their activities of daily living and create and maintain relationships across various levels: professional and personal (family, friends, and even strangers). In fact, 'Humankind is now almost entirely connected, albeit with great levels of inequality in the bandwidth as well as in the efficiency and price of the service' (Castells, 2013, p 132).

As recent North American and European data show, the usage of information and communication technologies (ICTs) such as the internet, mobile phones, tablets, and computers, constitutes a reality for millions of individuals and families, and their usage continues to grow. The percentage of EU–28 households with internet access reached 85% in 2016. In under a decade, from 2007 to 2016, this number rose by 30% (EUROSTAT, 2017) and today almost 50% 'of the world's population is connected online and an estimated 8.4 billion connected things are in use worldwide' (Rainie and Anderson, 2017, p 2).

With the increasing usage of electronic technologies, today seems to be the era of e-society, e-government, e-democracy, e-commerce, e-learning, e-health, e-participation, and of course also e-romance and e-dating. ICTs (gradually more accessible, affordable, and portable) and the lives of children, young people, and adults, have become inextricably intertwined (Carvalho et al, 2015, 2016).

In this new digital landscape, as Coyne et al (2012) maintain, the dependence that many individuals demonstrate regarding these technologies seems, at times, paradoxical:

> In a recent survey (Popkin, 2011), for example, 3,000 British adults said the top five things they could not 'live without' were sunshine, the Internet, clean drinking water, refrigerators, and Facebook. Flushing toilets came in ninth. 'Brits are obsessed by the weather, so it's not surprising sunshine was rated as the top thing we couldn't live without,' said the pollster. 'But to say you can't live without material things over drinking water is crazy.' (Coyne et al, 2012, p 359)

This ubiquitous penetration of communication technologies in households and the daily lives of families generates major impacts on the wired family (Meszaros, 2004) that may be difficult to measure as they seem to bring both opportunities and challenges. However, this relationship between family and technology is a two-way street over the life course. Not only is technology a factor positively and/ or negatively affecting family formation and dynamics, but it also represents an important tool for providing the analytical coherence and comparability that family research, more specifically family histories, deserve and crave.

Technologies as an object of family research

As the development of technologies and digital devices advances, and their penetration into the present-day activities of individuals and families becomes more intense, so do studies proliferate and diversify. The literature on the interplay between family life and ICTs contains four main sociological objects: intimate couple life; intergenerational relationships; transnational or migrant families; and the life course.

Intimate couple life

Relationships, including intimate couple life, vary across the lifespan: they 'are dynamic and change over time, at the very least on the scale of a lifetime' (Palchykov et al, 2012, p 1). Being married at the age of 25, without children, is not the same as being married at 65, with children (and living through, for example, the so-called 'empty nest' stage), or at 80, with children, grandchildren, and great-grandchildren.

And the effect of technology on family life seems dependent on the timing of the life under question. Nevertheless, much of the research treats relationships as static and focuses on some of their specific moments and aspects. The most frequent subjects approached are the making and breaking of relationships – for example, online dating, infidelity, marital dissolution, and divorce (Casimiro, 2015; Dutton et al, 2008; Stevenson and Wolfers, 2007; Whitty et al, 2007; Young, 2006) – the daily lives of couples (Hertlein and Blumer, 2014), long-distance relationships (Dargie et al, 2015), and also work-family balance (Chesley and Johnson, 2010).

Intergenerational relationships

Studies on how these ICTs impact intergenerational relationships, in turn, focus on two core fields: parent/child relationships and multigenerational ties. Furthermore, within these two fields the research studies numerous themes.

In recent decades, Western societies have experienced a marked turndown in their birth rates, which makes infants highly esteemed. Concurrently, 'new values concerning childhood and children and families' educational mobilization in all social milieus have strongly influenced the social demand for ICT' (Almeida et al, 2011, p 221). In the quest to 'support school work and promote academic success' (Almeida et al, 2011, p 221), allied to a consumer society, parents give their children and teenagers a range of technological gadgets and paraphernalia. The surveillance and monitoring of young people's usage of ICTs hence feature among the challenges posed to modern-day parenting (Anderson, 2016; Livingstone and Helsper, 2008) – what Lim (2016, p 21) calls 'the practice of 'transcendent parenting' which goes beyond traditional, physical concepts of parenting, to incorporate virtual and online parenting and how these all intersect'. Technologies have also been studied as tools that allow for the exercise of parenting or co-parenting (Blum-Ross and Livingstone, 2017; Ganong et al, 2012).

Contrary to what the most pessimistic views about recent family transformations have proclaimed in heralding a loss of importance of family bonds, intergenerational ties are actually becoming increasingly significant and diverse (Bengtson, 2001). In this scenario, ICTs seem to play an important role in helping to create and maintain connections and ties within and across generations (Harwood, 2000; Neves and Amaro, 2012; Neves et al, 2013; Quan-Haase et al, 2017), whether living in the same or in different geographical contexts as happens with transnational families.

Transnational or migrant families

In a globalized world that encourages and sometimes forces migration, digital technologies offer new avenues for transnational family communication (Gonzalez et al, 2012), facilitating family solidarity and intergenerational support (Cuban, 2017), and strengthening cultural values (Benítez, 2012). As Baldassar (2016, p 159) argues,

> the transformations in distant care brought about by ICTs begin to stretch the limits of our distinctions between proximate and distant family life, in particular through transformations in co-presence (the feeling of 'being there'), which challenge the epistemology of intersubjectivity.

Life course

The concept of 'life course' has received several different uses and may correspondingly thus assume different meanings: '(a) life course as time or age, (b) life course as life stages, (c) life course as events, transitions, and trajectories, (d) life course as life-span human development, and (e) life course as early life influences (and their accumulation) on later adult outcomes' (Alwin, 2012, p 206). Regardless of the multiple significances of the term, there still remains a gap in the literature focusing on the intersection between family life and the use of information and communication technologies whether from a life course perspective, over the life course, or taking a longitudinal approach. The same does not necessarily hold true for family research, which is highly connected with the tradition and methods of the life course perspective (Billari, 2009).

Although there is a growing interest in the context of family life and ICTs, most studies restrict their attention to childhood, adolescence, and older adults while a few focus on transitions – for example, transition to parenthood (Bartholomew et al, 2012). However, a life course framework that emphasizes a continuum of social events and transitions over time, in different contexts, and not a particular life stage or age group is crucial for understanding how ICTs are applied and integrated into family dynamics, and what opportunities and challenges arise from such usage (Jo et al, 2014).

The weight and intensity of social contacts, such as personal and social networks, change across the life course with age, labour market entry, marriage, parenting – that is, across several life events (David-Barrett et al, 2016; Kalmijn, 2012). ICTs are now essential tools in the activation, creation, and maintenance of these networks, which, in turn, are created or shaped by ICTs (Licoppe and Smoreda, 2005). Hence the need for more studies to help understand not only how individuals use information technologies in their various life stages but also how this usage changes according to their trajectories, across life course and in various contexts.

Virtues and/or risks of ICT usage in family life

In the studies examining the articulation of ICTs with such complex sociological objects, such as intimate partnerships, intergenerational relationships, transnational families, and life courses, scholars report both positive and negative social effects from usage of these technologies: 'whatever their limits in scope, many of the innovations' impacts on family life are decidedly mixed' (Aponte, 2009, p 577).

Regarding children and the transition to adult life, technologies appear to be a double-edged sword. A thorough examination of all the impact ICTs may have in different stages of the life course is beyond the scope of this review, but a few can be outlined. According to research, digital technologies improve cognitive thinking, enhance creativity, and stimulate prosocial behaviour (Greitemeyer, 2011) and learning capacities (Danoso et al, 2009; Livingstone et al, 2011) – though the latter claim 'in contrast to conventional beliefs' (Arukaroon and Krairit, 2017, p 21), still lacks ample supporting evidence (Livingstone, 2012). ICTs also seem to facilitate family communication (Rudi et al, 2014), and help to occupy leisure time (Cardoso et al, 2009). Simultaneously, they can entail disadvantages and risks that are distressing for parents and families. For instance, ICTs may hinder family communication (Hughes and Hans, 2001); produce family quarrels and tensions regarding teenagers' autonomy and parental authority (Cardoso et al, 2013; Mesch, 2006); create addiction (Gentile et al, 2013); affect academic performance through distraction (Jacobsen and Forste, 2011); and lead to the disclosure of unintended personal information, and to the occurrence of potentially dangerous encounters (Berson and Berson, 2005), cyberbullying, and cyber-harassment (Mishna et al, 2009; Pereira et al, 2016). This multifaceted impact is also visible within couples using technology: 'A portion of them quarrel over its use and have had hurtful experiences… at the same time, some couples find that digital tools facilitate communication and support' (Lenhart and Duggan, 2014, p 2). As previously mentioned, the effect ICTs have on family dynamics and family functioning varies according to the life courses of families and the uses given to such technologies by individuals. However, regardless of family life course, much of the research has either studied whether their influences are beneficial and advantageous, or highlighted their harmful consequences and destructive repercussions.

Several studies conclude that technologies maintain and create (new) intimacies, strengthen family bonds and family ties, develop social cohesion, increase offline family relationships, and promote well-being and relationship quality (Chesley and Fox, 2012; Hirdman, 2010; Jamieson, 2013; Jiang et al, 2011; Ling, 2008; Neves, 2015; Valentine, 2006; Williams and Merten, 2011). As Wen et al (2011, p 251) argue, regarding social networking games such as QQ Farm, these 'can improve the communication among family members locally, and enhance the connectedness between family members remotely'. Families have come to enjoy the sense of a 'new connectedness', boosted by several electronic devices, in particular by mobile phone interactions and communal internet experiences that enable 'shared moments with family members both near and far' (Wellman et al, 2008, p 16). Advantages include the easier coordination of family activities and the connectedness with relational partners – text messaging, for example, 'is an important relational tool' (Pettigrew, 2009, p 711) – that becomes possible as the 'mobile phone dissolves the boundaries that separate work and home' and continuously mediates 'interactions... known as "constant touch", "perpetual contact" or "connected relationships"' (Wajcman et al, 2008, pp 635-636).

Although a significant proportion of the research highlights the positive impact new technologies and the internet have on social lives and family relationships (Amichai-Hamburger and Hayat, 2011), there is also a considerable body of research challenging these optimistic assumptions. Many studies also approach the downsides to the pervasiveness of ICT usage, and question 'the forms of "sociability" that we want to develop among our human community' (Sicard, 2001, p 429). Some of the risks and drawbacks more commonly reported by studies include family tensions and conflicts (Huisman et al, 2012; Mesch, 2006); compulsion and problematic internet usage, or internet addiction disorder (Kerkhof et al, 2011; Ng and Wiemer-Hastings, 2005; Weinstein et al, 2014), and privacy, security, or vigilance issues (Kanter et al, 2012). Neither the utopian nor the dystopian views of the internet's influence on social and family life (Katz and Rice, 2002) are able to accurately describe the changes brought about by digital technologies to contemporary societies. In fact, 'The Internet represents an extension of broader social roles and interests in the "offline" world' (Colley and Maltby, 2008, p 2005). Thus, for more precise interpretations of the impact of the internet and related ICTs on the family, as will be later stressed in this chapter, we must consider the different socioeconomic circumstances in which it takes place and how this may change over historical and individual time.

Technologies as tools for family research within the life course perspective

This chapter draws on the aforementioned research to explore another dimension of ICTs and families: technology as a research method. Technology is not only shaping family processes, dynamics, and transformations, but it is also affecting the research process: the analytical process. Technologies do indeed provide new opportunities to family research. Computer assisted qualitative data analysis software emerges as a tool capable of tackling problems of comparability and the triangulation of qualitative and quantitative data that are not exclusive to family studies even if significantly experienced by this field. Lessons learned from family research, especially as dealing with the multiple – and equally legitimate – players and narrators of family life, dynamics, and trajectories, can clearly be applied to other research fields.

The example described in this chapter concerns a project based on the life course approach across two 'entry points' (macro and micro), and a family-centred methodology as the privileged unit of analysis. This correspondingly seeks to deepen knowledge about the processes of social mobility in Portugal over recent decades. Qualitative data based on biographical interviews, life history calendars, and socio-genealogical trees on ten families serve to identify social mobility strategies, experiences, dissonances, and reproductions across different generations of these same families.[1]

This research functions here as an example of technology as a fundamental instrument for the successful triangulation of different family data. One of the main project goals aims to contribute to our understanding of how different strategies and trajectories over the life course get configured and interlinked as well as to characterize their coexistence within the same family unit. The development of the qualitative component of this project – based on family histories – encountered at least two challenges, as illustrated below. The MaxQda® CAQDAS 'technology' contributed significantly to overcoming these challenges, each arising out of an analytical problem and a life course perspective theoretical principle. Next we share these challenges and our exploratory practices to overcome them.

Triangulation of data and the 'timing of lives' principle

On the subject of family social mobility studies, Paul Thomson (2004) eloquently said that:

> On the one hand, there are well-funded survey researchers who manipulate their statistics as 'facts', interpreting them often with the insights of little more than common sense hunches. On the other hand, there are lone researchers who never have sufficiently large numbers of interviews, or have drawn those interviews from insufficiently representative samples, to substantiate any of the hypotheses they may generate from the in-depth interviews which they carry out themselves, and which – in part reflecting a sense of impotence – often abandon any intention of interpreting society 'as it really is', instead shifting to post-modern or narrative approaches, in which the interview text replaces society as the focus of study. These two camps are reinforced by self-recruiting networks, and by occasional outbursts of mutual hostility. (Thomson, 2004, p 238)

There are many who, like Thompson (2004), advocate an approach with both eyes open for a mixed approach to the study of family histories (on social mobility or any other topic), and for interlinking life course and life story (Cohler and Hostetler, 2002). Even when there is the will and knowledge to carry out such endeavours, the results often encapsulate the mixing of methods within a rhetorical logic – that is, mixing methods for a close-up illustration of a bigger picture, or for background which is fairly 'easy to do', 'but does not take you very far' (Mason, 2006, p 4). Even for those not opposed to either the qualitative or the quantitative traditions,[2] the attempts to triangulate and to combine quantitative and qualitative data sometimes results in a simple post hoc addition of the qualitative data as 'illustrative'. The fact remains that without using a common analytical instrument to 'ask distinctive but intersecting questions' in a 'multidimensional logic' (Mason, 2006, p 4), this alleged sum of results will never amount to more than two partial and weakly linked conclusions. The simple accumulation of results ends up not really being 'more than the sum of the parts' or any true triangulation of family data through the combination of two points of view (Flick, 2006).

In principle, however, some would argue there is such an instrument that can operate as a common denominator. In Miller's *Researching Life*

Stories and Family Histories (2000), the author states that the mobility tables generated from the (qualitative) family history chart provide *the* instrument for combining the results of family histories. However, there are two problems with this instrument for the combination of qualitative and quantitative family research.

First, these tables are 2 × 2 matrixes. In this sense, they apply only two moments in time: parents' class when the individual was 15 years old (line) and at a later age (column) – usually the time of the survey/inquiry. This ends up disrespecting the view of life as a process, as a trajectory, as a sequence, as a 'course', and ultimately undermining the importance of the life course theory. 'Life' (or social mobility across generations of the same family for that matter) cannot be understood only as 'origin' and 'destination'. Family research must reach further than connecting (two) dots.

Second, the subjective, qualitative, and comprehensive explanation expressed by the interviewees gets irreversibly lost in this quantification of the trajectory, or applied merely with an unfair secondary status, serving only as 'illustrative of those social processes that have affected families over a long span of time' (Miller, 2000, p 61). 'Bringing life back into life course research' in family studies must represent a priority (Nico, 2016). Albeit persistent recommendations, life course methodology debates remain vigorous but chiefly focused on a complex descriptive analysis of sequences and statistical procedures that themselves analyse the timing predictors of such events. Furthermore, it has already been argued that there is a need to put the 'course' back into life course research, embracing complex descriptions of the orders and sequences of events (Aisenbrey and Fasang, 2010). Nevertheless, this argument needs to be taken further. Taking 'life' into consideration in the analysis of the life course inevitably requires the inclusion of qualitative data, ideally at different stages in the research, combining three biographical approaches: realistic, neo-positivist, and narrative (Miller, 2000), and across two levels of analysis (the family and the individual).

New technologies, features and uses for some of the content analysis software now available may contribute significantly to overcoming these two problems, in particular by jointly analysing family histories, on the one hand, and family and individual stories, on the other hand. One means of achieving this involves applying the life calendar and the biographical interview to various members of the same family, and then having them fill out and comment on their factual trajectory. In the example set out here, we are dealing with occupational and/or class trajectory, but the analytical procedures may be adjusted and applied to reproductive trajectories, housing careers, attachment development, family stress and turning points, among other family-related topics.

The two problems raised above may be jointly tackled in a multi-step MaxQda® procedure. Concerning data organization, each person interviewed in the family results in two documents apiece: one is the life calendar, fully filled out, with statuses on the trajectory under analysis; the other is the translated conversation held around those statuses, changes in statutes as well as the overall trajectory. While the life calendar statuses can be automatically coded,[3] the answers provided are subject to regular content analysis (thematic or holistic). At a later stage, there are different outputs that qualitatively and quantitatively mix the family timing of lives:

- Holistic form analysis (Cohler and Hostetler, 2002): taking as its main source the life calendars of all the interviewees, this analysis focuses on the structure of life rather than the narrative content. This provides for the clustering of the heterogeneity and the transmissibility of social trajectories by family type. The 'document comparison charts', the 'codelines' and the 'similarity analysis' (available in Maxqda®) are extremely helpful in this regard.
- Biographical-interpretative method (Wengraf, 2000): this technique arose of applying a complex structure of categories that simultaneously incorporates the status (demographic, love-related, occupational, or other) of the family member at any given point in time, to the biographical and subjective accounts made of those statuses and trajectories. This takes two material sources into consideration: the 'life lived' (calendar) and the 'life told' (interview) (Wengraf, 2000). A typology of the match and mismatch between the discourses and the actual trajectories within a given family may help in disentangling the typologies both of family and of class identity.
- Similarity analysis of (i) the social and family trajectories, between or within families (through the 'document comparison chart' in Maxqda®); and (ii) between social trajectories, between or within families, from the same or different generations (through 'similarity analysis' in MaxQda®) both in quantitative and qualitative terms (life calendars and interviews, respectively) may also be applied.

Comparability of cases and the 'linked lives' principle

The second issue concerns the comparability of cases (families) and the linked lives principle. Taking the triangulation of family research data

– in particular, family histories – onto the next step implies addressing the 'linked lives' life course principle. According to this principle:

> Each generation is bound to fateful decisions and events in the other's life course. (Elder, 1994, p 6)

> Individual lives are always *linked lives* (Elder, 1985); one person's resources, resource deficits, successes, failures, chronic strains and (expected or unexpected) transitions can become focal conditions, event turning points, in the lives of others, especially other family members. (Moen and Hernandez, 2009, p 259)

This principle of 'linked lives', considered by Elder (1985, 1994; Elder et al, 2002; Elder and Giele, 2009) as the most important factor, emphasizes how any individual event holds meaningful consequences, both trans- and intergenerational, for the life courses of others. These spillover effects are methodologically difficult to identify and measure, especially because they imply applying methods other than those hegemonically applied in life course research, such as sequence analysis or, especially, event history analysis.

The issue of linked lives is simultaneously sociologically relevant and socially important. There is sociological relevance to understanding at a micro level how people's lives and the events embedded in them interfere positively and negatively with other lives, especially those with whom they share a household or family; and, furthermore, to understanding at a macro level how the accumulation and interaction of the ways people's lives and the events embedded in them interfere positively and negatively with other lives, especially within the family.

Interviewing and analysing individuals out of their family context is not consistent with the family research tradition merely because 'individuals are much easier (and cheaper) to survey than families, groups, networks, or organizations' (Moen and Hernandez, 2009, p 258). However, the 'ongoing relationships of two or more people over time' have not provided the main subject of family research analysis. The couple-level or network-level research are fairly common but 'household'-level data almost exclusively occurs in quantitative formats, especially through numerous official statistical data sets, such as the European Community Household Panels, European Union Statistics on Income and Living Conditions, or the Household Budget Survey, to mention just a few. Qualitative family histories are, on the other hand, quite common in the analysis of social mobility and the social transmission of poverty, among other topics of analysis (Bertaux, 1974; Bertaux and Thompson, 1997; Bertaux and Bertaux-Wiame, 1980; Bertaux and Delcroix, 2000). However, these types of research also incorporate two different premises that limit and restrict the study of how lives are linked: the premises that one spokesperson per generation is sufficient for tackling social change; and that the influence and transmission of an objective and subjective social positioning predominantly constitutes a one-way street, that is, from the older to the younger generations.

As such, the family histories usually applied in sociology depart from a temporal causal matrix, in which the direction of the effects of certain lives onto other lives is generationally marked – that is, the lives of older family members influence the trajectories of their younger counterparts (Breen, 2000; Fergunsson et al, 2008; Raitano, 2015). And while this remains true, there are two aspects that fall outside the scope of this kind of analysis: (1) the generational order through which lives interlink is not only unidirectional; (2) the effects (their nature, direction, impact, etc.) of that transmission oscillate significantly across time.

Once again, new technology, its features and the applications of some of the content analysis software now available may help overcome these two problems, especially by ensuring more comprehensive analysis of how the lives of family members are interlinked, through:

- providing an additional coding of the material gathered: this coding strategy takes into account how the co-occurrence of events coded in the life calendars and in the text become visible in the 'code relation browser' feature. The idea here involves coding the pairs of event cause (in one individual) and event effect (in more than one individual) to provide the analytical material for subsequent analysis;
- generating a typology of these linkages: analysis of the co-occurrences leads to the identification of the predominant pairs of events. Analysis of these pairs, per family, may lead to the construction of a typology reflecting the density, type, and temporal lag of these events; and as well as the spheres, generations, and social backgrounds involved in those same events.

Conclusion

In this chapter, we aimed to convey not only the dual but also, and more importantly, the reciprocal relationship between technology and family research over the life course or whenever applying life course principles.

On the one hand, a plethora of sociological studies have focused on the intersection between information and communication technologies and intimate lives of couples, intergenerational relationships, transnational or migrant families, and the usage and impact of these ICTs throughout the life course. The focus has fallen on the study of these subjects across their various dimensions, such as family formation (starting, making, and breaking relationships), family time, work-life family balance, family communication, autonomy, intimacy and bonding, family roles, routines and rituals, and family conflicts. The proportion and intensity of the multiple changes brought about by digital technologies, such as the internet, to social and family life in contemporary societies may be difficult to accurately interpret and measure. One way of overcoming such difficulties involves framing the understanding of the impact or effects of ICTs on family life through taking into consideration the various socioeconomic contexts in which this same impact takes place, and how this then evolves over historical and individual time.

The contemporary family is progressively a networked family, adopting a variety of digital technologies to coordinate their lives, to be connected throughout the day, and to bond and share moments online. Technology thus complexifies the very object of family over the life course while also opening up new research avenues based on social change itself.

On the other hand, attention also must focus on how new analytical technologies, particularly computer-assisted qualitative data analysis software and its new outputs and possibilities, are able to shed new light on important family research issues. Software such as MaxQda® is able to make two major contributions to family research – especially through family histories – and life course research. Escaping the temptation to fall into binary choices of methodology represents one dimension to this contribution. The software allows us to develop a mixed method approach to objective and subjective family trajectories (over time). It achieves this by applying common categories of analysis to code both the statutes in the life calendar and the respective biographical accounts. Avoiding using spokespersons in family research, and instead tackling family histories and data from different informants, provides the other contribution. This provides new insights into family research by encouraging theoretical and analytical frameworks in which the family does in fact constitute the primary unit of analysis. The leading topics, in these cases, incorporate the links, the dynamics, and the transmissions between members of the same family, and not the members per se.

In brief

1. The relationship between families and technology is twofold: technology as a sociological object and technology as an instrument for family and life course research.

2. The literature review on the interplay of family life and technologies identifies four main sociological objects: intimate couple life; intergenerational relationships; transnational or migrant families; and life course.

3. The main impact of ICTs (both positive and negative) on family dynamics has been described. Social contexts and a life course approach (especially the historical and cultural location, and the timing of lives) require consideration for a more precise understanding of the repercussions of ICTs for individual and family lives.

4. New uses and features of content analysis software may significantly contribute to the triangulation of quantitative and qualitative data gathered through family histories.

5. The idea of taking the family or the households as the unit of analysis par excellence in family research can be enabled and achieved through new and creative uses of CAQDAS.

Notes

[1] The 'Family Portraits of Contemporary Portugal: Generations, Life Courses and Social Mobility' project was funded by the 'Fundação para a Ciência e Tecnologia' [reference: SFRH/BPD/76580/2011].

[2] Presenting studies such as Lewis' *Children of Sanchez* (1970) as rivals to those illustrated by Erikson and Goldthorpe's intergenerational social mobility studies (Erikson and Goldthorpe, 2009).

[3] Analysis, Lexical Search, New, Write status, Run search, Code with new code.

References

Aisenbrey, S. and Fasang, A. E. (2010) 'New life for old ideas: The "second wave" of sequence analysis bringing the "course" back into the life course', *Sociological Methods & Research*, 38(3): 420–462, https://doi.org/10.1177/0049124109357532

Almeida, A. N. de, Alves, N. de A., Delicado, A. and Carvalho, T. (2011) 'Children and digital diversity: From "unguided rookies" to "self-reliant cybernauts"', *Childhood*, 19(2): 219–234, https://doi.org/10.1177/0907568211410897

Alwin, D. F. (2012) 'Integrating varieties of life course concepts', *The Journals of Gerontology, Series B: Psychological Sciences and Social Sciences*, 67(2): 206–220, https://doi.org/10.1093/geronb/gbr146

Amichai-Hamburger, Y. and Hayat, Z. (2011) 'The impact of the internet on the social lives of users: A representative sample from 13 countries', *Computers in Human Behavior*, 27: 585–589, https://doi.org/10.1016/j.chb.2010.10.009

Anderson, M. (2016) 'Parents, teens and digital monitoring', Pew Research Center, www.pewinternet.org/files/2016/01/PI_2016-01-07_Parents-Teens-Digital-Monitoring_FINAL.pdf

Aponte, R. (2009) 'The communications revolution and its impact on the family: Significant, growing, but skewed and limited in scope', *Marriage & Family Review*, 45(6-8): 576–586, https://doi.org/10.1080/01494920903396778

Arukaroon, B. and Krairit, D. (2017) 'Impact of ICT usage in primary-school students' learning in the case of Thailand', *International Journal of Web-Based Learning and Teaching Technologies (IJWLTT)*, 12(2): 21-42, https://doi.org/10.4018/IJWLTT.2017040102

Baldassar, L. (2016) 'De-demonizing distance in mobile family lives: Co-presence, care circulation and polymedia as vibrant matter', *Global Networks*, 16(2): 145–163, https://doi.org/10.1111/glob.12109

Bartholomew, M. H., Schoppe-Sullivan, S. J., Glassman, M., Dush, C. M. K. and Sullivan, J. M. (2012) 'New parents' facebook use at the transition to parenthood', *Family Relations*, 61(3): 455–469, https://doi.org/10.1111/j.1741-3729.2012.00708.x

Bengtson, V. L. (2001) 'Beyond the nuclear family: The increasing importance of multigenerational bonds', *Journal of Marriage and Family*, 63(1): 1–16, https://doi.org/10.1111/j.1741-3737.2001.00001.x

Benítez, J. L. (2012) 'Salvadoran transnational families: ICT and communication practices in the network society', *Journal of Ethnic and Migration Studies*, 38(9): 1439-1449, https://doi.org/10.1080/1369183X.2012.698214

Berson, I. R. and Berson, M. J. (2005) 'Challenging online behaviors of youth: Findings from a comparative analysis of young people in the United States and New Zealand', *Social Science Computer Review*, 23(1): 29-38, https://doi.org/10.1177/0894439304271532

Bertaux, D. (1974) 'Mobilité sociale biographique une critique de l'approche transversal', *Revue Française de Sociologie*, 15(3): 319-362, https://doi.org/10.2307/3320160

Bertaux, D. and Bertaux-Wiame, I. (1980) *Une enquete sur la boulangerie artisanale. Par l'approche biographique*, Subvention C.O.R.D.E.S. n 43/76 Rapport Final, vol. I C.N.R.S., Paris, http://docplayer.fr/777880-Une-enquete-sur-la-boulangerie-artisanale.html#show_full_text

Bertaux, D. and Delcroix, C. (2000) 'Case histories of families and social processes: enriching sociology', in P. Chamberlayne, J. Bornat and T. Wengraft (eds), *The Turn to Biographical Methods in Social Science. Comparative Issues and Examples*, London: Routledge, pp 71–89.

Bertaux, D. and Thompson, P. (1997) *Pathways to Social Class: A Qualitative Approach to Social Mobility*, Oxford: Clarendon Press.

Billari, F. C. (2009) 'The life course is coming of age' (Editorial), *Advances in Life Course Research*, 14(3): 83–86, https://doi.org/10.1016/j.alcr.2009.10.001

Blum-Ross, A. and Livingstone, S. (2017) '"Sharenting", parent blogging, and the boundaries of the digital self', *Popular Communication*, 15(2): 110–125, https://doi.org/10.1080/15405702.2016.1223300

Breen, R. (2000) Class Inequality and Social Mobility in Northern Ireland, 1973 to 1996, *American Sociological Review, 65*(3), 392–406, https://doi.org/10.2307/2657463

Cardoso, G., Espanha, R., Lapa, T. and Araújo, V. (2009) *E-Generation 2008: Os Usos de Media por Crianças e Jovens em Portugal*, Lisboa: OBERCOM, https://obercom.pt/wp-content/uploads/2016/06/E-Generation-2008-Os-Usos-de-Media-pelas-Crian%C3%A7as-e-Jovens-em-Portugal-%E2%80%93-Mar2009.pdf

Cardoso, G., Espanha, R. and Lapa, T. (2013) 'Dinâmicas familiares e mediação: crianças, autonomia e controlo', in G. Cardoso (ed), *A Sociedade dos Ecrãs*, Lisboa: Edição Tinta da China, pp 123–155.

Carvalho, J., Francisco, R. and Relvas, A. (2015) 'Family functioning and information and communication technologies: How do they relate? A literature review', *Computers in Human Behavior*, 45: 99–108, https://doi.org/10.1016/j.chb.2014.11.037

Carvalho, J., Fonseca G., Francisco R., Bacigalupe, G. and Relvas, A. P. (2016) 'Information and communication technologies and family: Patterns of use, life cycle and family dynamics', *Journal of Psychology & Psychotherapy*, 6(240): 1–3, http://dx.doi.org/10.4172/2161-0487.1000240

Casimiro, C. (2015) 'Self-presentation in the Portuguese online dating scene: Does gender matter?', in I. A. Degim, J. Johnson and T. Fu (eds), *Online Courtship – Interpersonal Interactions Across Borders*, Amsterdam: Institute of Network Cultures, University of Amsterdam, pp 71–95, http://networkcultures.org/blog/publication/no-16-online-courtship-interpersonal-interactions-across-borders/

Castells, M. (2013) 'The impact of the internet on society: A global perspective', in Chairman's Advisory, BBVA (ed) *19 Key Essays on How Internet Is Changing Our Lives*, Spain: BBVA, pp 127–147, www.bbvaopenmind.com/wp-content/uploads/2014/03/BBVA-OpenMind-Technology-Innovation-Internet-Francisco-Gonzalez-Knowledge-Banking-for-a-Hyperconnected-Society.pdf

Chesley, N. and Fox, B. (2012) 'E-mail's use and perceived effect on family relationship quality: Variations by gender and race/ethnicity', *Sociological Focus*, 45: 63–84, https://doi.org/10.1080/00380237.2012.630906

Chesley, N. and Johnson, B. E. (2010) 'Information and communication technology, work, and family', in S. Sweet and J. Casey (eds) *Work and family encyclopedia*, Chestnut Hill, MA: Sloan Work and Family Research Network, https://workfamily.sas.upenn.edu/wfrn-repo/object/ej08hr00at6ew6q3

Cohler, B. J. and Hostetler, A. (2002) 'Linking life course and life story. Social change and the narrative study of lives over time', in J. Mortimer and M. J. Shanahan (eds) *Handbook of the Life Course*, New York: Kluwer Academic Publications, pp 555–576.

Colley, A. and Maltby, J. (2008) 'Impact of the internet on our lives: Male and female personal perspectives', *Computers in Human Behavior*, 24(5): 2005–2013, https://doi.org/10.1016/j.chb.2007.09.002

Coyne, S. M., Bushman, B. J. and Nathanson, A.I. (2012) 'Media and the family: A note from the guest editors', *Family Relations*, 61(3): 359–362, https://doi.org/10.1111/j.1741-3729.2012.00713.x

Cuban, S. (2017) *Transnational Family Communication: Immigrants and ICTs*, New York: Palgrave Macmillan.

Danoso, V., Ólafsson, K. and Broddason, T. (2009) 'What we know, what we do not know', in S. Livingstone and L. Haddon (eds) *Kids Online: Opportunities and Risks for Children*, Bristol: Polity Press, pp 19–29.

Dargie, E., Blair, K. L., Goldfinger, C. and Pukall, C. F. (2015) 'Go long! Predictors of positive relationship outcomes in long-distance dating relationships', *Journal of Sex & Marital Therapy*, 41(2): 181–202, https://doi.org/10.1080/0092623X.2013.864367

David-Barrett, T., Kertesz, J., Rotkirch, A., Ghosh, A., Bhattacharya, K., Monsivais, D. and Kaski, K. (2016) 'Communication with family and friends across the life course', *PLoS ONE*, 11(11): e0165687, https://doi.org/10.1371/journal.pone.0165687

Dutton, W. H., Helsper, E. J., Whitty, M. T., Buckwalter, G. and Lee, E. (2008) 'Mate selection in the network society: The role of the internet in reconfiguring marriages in Australia, the United Kingdom and United States', Available at SSRN https://ssrn.com/abstract=1275810

Elder, G. H. (1985) 'Perspectives on the life course', in G. H. Elder Jr. (ed) *Life Course Dynamics. Trajectories and Transitions*, London: Cornell University Press, pp 23-49.

Elder, G. H. (1994) 'Time, human agency, and social change: Perspectives on the life course', *Social Psychology* Quarterly, 57(1): 4-15, www.jstor.org/stable/2786971

Elder, G. H. and Giele, J. Z. (2009) 'Life course studies: An evolving field', in G. H. Elder and J. Z. Giele (eds) *The Craft of the Life Course Research*, New York: The Guilford Press, pp 1-24.

Elder, G. H., Johnson, M. K. and Crosnoe, R. (2002) 'The emergence and development of life course theory', in J. T. Mortimer and M. J. Shanahan (eds) *Handbook of the Life Course*, New York: Kluwer Academic Publications, pp 3-19.

Erikson, R. and Goldthorpe, J. H. (2009) *Income and Class Mobility between Generations in Great Britain: The Problem of Divergent Findings from the Data-sets of British Birth Cohort Studies*, Stockholm: Swedish Institute for Social Research, www.sofi.su.se/polopoly_fs/1.64980.1323949612!/WP09no4.pdf

EUROSTAT (2017) *Digital Economy and Society Statistics – Households and Individuals*, http://ec.europa.eu/eurostat/statistics-explained/index.php/Digital_economy_and_society_statistics_-_households_and_individuals#Internet_usage

Fergunsson, D. M., L., Horwood, J. and Boden, J. M. (2008) 'The transmission of social inequality: Examination of the linkages between family socioeconomic status in childhood and educational achievement in young adulthood', *Research in Social Stratification and Mobility*, 26: 277–295, https://doi.org/10.1016/j.rssm.2008.05.001

Flick, U. (2006) 'Triangulation', in V. Jupp (ed) *The Sage Dictionary of Social Research Methods*, London: Sage, http://methods.sagepub.com/reference/the-sage-dictionary-of-social-research-methods/n211.xml

Ganong, L. H., Coleman, M., Feistman, R., Jamison, T. and Markham, M. S. (2012) 'Communication technology and postdivorce coparenting', *Family Relations*, 61(3): 397-409, https://doi.org/10.1111/j.1741-3729.2012.00706.x

Gentile, D. A., Coyne, S. M. and Bricolo, F. (2013) 'Pathological technology addictions: A review of the literature and a diagnosis paradigm', in K. Dill (ed) *The Oxford Handbook of Media Psychology*, New York: Oxford University Press, pp 382-402.

Gonzalez, V. M., Jomhari, N. and Kurniawan, S. H. (2012) 'Photo-based narratives as communication mediators between grandparents and their children and grandchildren living abroad', *Journal Universal Access in the Information Society*, 11(1): 67-84, https://doi.org/10.1007/s10209-011-0234-z

Greitemeyer, T. (2011) 'Effects of prosocial media on social behavior: When and why does media exposure affect helping and aggression?', *Current Directions in Psychological Science*, 20(4): 251-255, https://doi.org/10.1177/0963721411415229

Harwood, J. (2000) 'Communication media use in the grandparent-grandchild relationship', *Journal of Communication*, 50(4): 56–78, https://doi.org/10.1111/j.1460-2466.2000.tb02863.x

Hertlein, K. M. and Blumer, M. L. C. (2014) *The Couple and Family Technology Framework: Intimate Relationships in a Digital Age*, New York: Routledge.

Hirdman, A. (2010) 'Vision and intimacy: Gendered communication online', *Nordicom Review*, 31(1): 3-13, http://urn.kb.se/resolve?urn=urn:nbn:se:su:diva-38939

Hughes Jr, R. and Hans, J. D. (2001) 'Computers, the internet, and families: A review of the role new technology plays in family life', *Journal of Family Issues*, 22(6): 776-790, https://doi.org/10.1177/019251301022006006

Huisman, S., Edwards, A. and Catapano, S. (2012) 'The impact of technology on families', *International Journal of Education and Psychology in the Community*, 2(1): 44-62, www.ceeol.com/search/article-detail?id=217876

Jacobsen, W. C. and Forste, R. (2011) 'The wired generation: Academic and social outcomes of electronic media use among university students', *Cyberpsychology, Behavior, and Social Networking*, 14(5): 275-280, https://doi.org/10.1089/cyber.2010.0135

Jamieson, L. (2013) 'Personal relationships, intimacy and the self in a mediated and global digital age', in K. Orton-Johnson and N. Prior (eds) *Digital Sociology: Critical Perspectives*, London: Palgrave Macmillan, pp 13-33.

Jiang, L. C., Bazarova, N. and Hancock, J. T. (2011) 'The disclosure–intimacy link in computer-mediated communication: An attributional extension of the hyperpersonal model', *Human Communication Research*, 37(1): 58-77, https://doi.org/10.1111/j.1468-2958.2010.01393.x

Jo, H.-H., Saramaki, J., Dunbar, R. I. M. and Kaski, K. (2014) 'Spatial patterns of close relationships across the lifespan', *Scientific Reports*, 4(6988): 1-7, https://doi.org/10.1038/srep06988

Kalmijn, M. (2012) 'Longitudinal analyses of the effects of age, marriage, and parenthood on social contacts and support', *Advances in Life Course Research*, 17(4): 177-190, https://doi.org/10.1016/j.alcr.2012.08.002

Kanter, M., Afifi, T. and Robbins, S. (2012) 'The impact of parents "friending" their young adult child on facebook on perceptions of parental privacy invasions and parent–child relationship quality', *Journal of Communication*, 62(5): 900–197, https://doi.org/10.1111/j.1460-2466.2012.01669.x

Katz, J. E. and Rice, R. E. (2002) *Social Consequences of Internet Use: Access, Involvement and Expression*, Cambridge, MA: MIT Press.

Kerkhof, P., Finkenauer, C. and Muusses, L. D. (2011) 'Relational consequences of compulsive internet use: A longitudinal study among newlyweds', *Human Communication Research*, 37(2): 147–173, https://doi.org/10.1111/j.1468-2958.2010.01397.x

Lenhart, A. and Duggan, M. (2014) *Couples, the Internet, and Social Media*, Pew Research Center, www.pewinternet.org/2014/02/11/couples-the-internet-and-social-media/

Lewis, Ó. (1970) *Os filhos de Sanchez*, Lisboa: Moraes Editores.

Licoppe, C. and Smoreda, Z. (2005) 'Are social networks technologically embedded? How networks are changing today with changes in communication technology', *Social Networks*, 27(4): 317-335, https://doi.org/10.1016/j.socnet.2004.11.001

Lim, S. S. (2016) 'Through the tablet glass: Transcendent parenting in an era of mobile media and cloud computing', *Journal of Children and Media*, 10(1): 21-29, https://doi.org/10.1080/17482798.2015.1121896

Ling, R. (2008) *New Tech, New Ties: How Mobile Communication is Reshaping Social Cohesion*, Cambridge, MA: MIT Press.

Livingstone, S. (2012) 'Critical reflections on the benefits of ICT in education', *Oxford Review of Education*, 38(1): 9-24, https://doi.org/10.1080/03054985.2011.577938

Livingstone, S. and Helsper, E. J. (2008) 'Parental mediation of children's internet use', *Journal of Broadcasting & Electronic Media*, 52(4): 581-599, https://doi.org/10.1080/08838150802437396

Livingstone, S., Haddon, L., Görzig, A. and Ólafsson, K. (2011) *Risks and Safety on the Internet: The Perspectives of European Children*, London: EU Kids Online, www.lse.ac.uk/media@lse/research/EUKidsOnline/EU%20Kids%20II%20%282009-11%29/EUKidsOnlineIIReports/D4FullFindings.pdf

Mason J. (2006) 'Six strategies for mixing methods and linking data in social science research', NCRM Working Paper Series, 4/2006, http://eprints.ncrm.ac.uk/482/1/0406_six%2520strategies%2520for%2520mixing%2520methods.pdf

Mesch, G. S. (2006) 'Family relations and the internet: Exploring a family boundaries approach', *Journal of Family Communication*, 6, 119–138, https://doi.org/10.1207/s15327698jfc0602_2

Meszaros, P. S. (2004) 'The wired family. Living digitally in the postinformation age', *American Behavioral Scientist*, 48(3): 377–390, https://doi.org/10.1177/0002764204270276

Miller, R. L. (2000) *Researching Life Stories and Family Histories*, Sage: London.

Mishna, F., Saini, M. and Solomon, S. (2009) 'Ongoing and online: Children and youth's perceptions of cyber bullying', *Children and Youth Services Review*, 31(12): 1222-1228, https://doi.org/10.1016/j.childyouth.2009.05.004

Moen, P. and Hernandez, E. (2009) 'Social convoys, studying linked lives in time, context and motion', in G. H. Elder and J. Z. Giele (eds) *The Craft of Life Course Research*, New York: The Guilford Press, pp 258-279.

Neves, B. B. (2015) 'Does the internet matter for strong ties? Bonding social capital, Internet use, and age-based inequality', *International Review of Sociology*, 25(3): 415-433, https://doi.org/10.1080/03906701.2015.1050307

Neves, B. B. and Amaro, F. (2012) 'Too old for technology? How the elderly of Lisbon use and perceive ICT', *The Journal of Community Informatics*, 8(1), http://ci-journal.net/index.php/ciej/article/view/800/904

Neves, B. B., Amaro, F. and Fonseca, J. R. (2013) 'Coming of (old) age in the digital age: ICT usage and non-usage among older adults', *Sociological Research Online*, 18(2): 6, www.socresonline.org.uk/18/2/6.html

Ng, B. D. and Wiemer-Hastings, P. (2005) 'Addiction to the internet and online gaming', *Cyberpyschology and Behavior*, 8(2): 110-113, https://doi.org/10.1089/cpb.2005.8.110

Nico, M. (2016) 'Bringing life 'back into life course research': Using the life grid as a research instrument for qualitative data collection and analysis', *Quality and Quantity*, 50(5): 2107-2120, https://doi.org/10.1007/s11135-015-0253-6

Palchykov, V., Kaski, K., Kertész, J., Barabási, A. and Dunbar, R. I. M. (2012) 'Sex differences in intimate relationships', *Scientific Reports*, 370, Epub 2012/04/21, https://doi.org/10.1038/srep00370

Pereira, F., Spitzberg, B. H. and Matos, M. (2016) 'Cyber-harassment victimization in Portugal: Prevalence, fear and help-seeking among adolescents', *Computers in Human Behavior*, 62 (Supplement C): 136-146, https://doi.org/10.1016/j.chb.2016.03.039

Pettigrew, J. (2009) 'Text messaging and connectedness within close interpersonal relationships', *Marriage & Family Review*, 45(6-8): 697-716, https://doi.org/10.1080/01494920903224269

Pew Research Centre (2014) *Three Technology Revolutions*, Pew Internet & American Life Project, www.pewinternet.org/three-technology-revolutions/

Quan-Haase, A., Mo, G. Y. and Wellman, B. (2017) 'Connected seniors: How older adults in East York exchange social support online and offline', *Information, Communication & Society*, 20(7): 967-983, https://doi.org/10.1080/1369118X.2017.1305428

Rainie, L. and Anderson, J. (2017) *The Internet of Things Connectivity Binge: What Are the Implications?* Pew Research Center, www.pewinternet.org/2017/06/06/the-internet-of-things-connectivity-binge-what-are-the-implications/

Rainie, L. and Wellman, B. (2012) *Networked: The New Social Operating System*, London: MIT Press.

Raitano, M. (2015) 'Intergenerational transmission of inequalities in Southern European countries in comparative perspective: evidence from EU-SILC 2011', *European Journal of Social Security*, 7(2): 292–314, http://journals.sagepub.com/doi/pdf/10.1177/138826271501700208

Rudi, J., Dworkin, J., Walker, S. and Doty, J. (2014) 'Parents' use of information and communications technologies for family communication: Differences by age of children', *Information, Communication & Society*, 18(1): 78-93, https://doi.org/10.1080/1369118X.2014.934390

Sicard, M.-N. (2001) 'Nouvelles technologies et communication', *L'année sociologique*, 51(2): 429-437, https://doi.org/10.3917/anso.012.0429

Stevenson, B. and Wolfers, J. (2007) 'Marriage and divorce: Changes and their driving forces', *The Journal of Economic Perspectives*, 21(2): 27-52, www.nber.org/papers/w12944.pdf

Thompson, P. (2004) 'Researching family and social mobility with two eyes: Some experiences of the interaction between qualitative and quantitative data', *International Journal of Social Research Methodology*, 7(3): 237-257, https://doi.org/10.1080/1364557021000024785

Valentine, G. (2006) 'Globalizing intimacy: The role of information and communication technologies in maintaining and creating relationships', *Women's Studies Quarterly*, 34(1/2): 365–393, www.jstor.org/stable/40004765

Wajcman, J., Bittman, M. and Brown, J. E. (2008) 'Families without borders: Mobile phones, connectedness and work-home divisions', *Sociology*, 42(4): 635–652, https://doi.org/10.1177/0038038508091620

Weinstein, A., Feder, L. C., Rosenberg K. P. and Dannon P. (2014) 'Internet addiction disorder: Overview and controversies', in K. P. Rosenberg and L. C. Feder (eds), *Behavioral Addictions: Criteria, Evidence, and Treatment*, London: Academic Press, 99-117.

Wellman, B., Smith, A., Wells, A. and Kennedy, T. (2008) *Networked Families*, Pew Research Center, www.pewinternet.org/2008/10/19/networked-families/

Wen, J., Kow, Y. M. and Chen, Y. (2011) 'Online games and family ties: Influences of social networking game on family relationship', in P. Campos, N. Graham, J. Jorge, N. Nunes, P. Palanque and M. Winckler (eds) *Human–Computer Interaction – INTERACT 2011. INTERACT 2011. Lecture Notes in Computer Science*, vol. 6948, Springer, pp 250–264. https://link.springer.com/content/pdf/10.1007%2F978-3-642-23765-2_18.pdf

Wengraf, T. (2000) 'Uncovering the general from within the particular: From contingencies to typologies in the understanding of cases', in P. Chamberlayne, J. Bornat, T. Wengraft (eds) *The Turn to Biographical Methods in Social Science: Comparative Issues and Examples*, London: Routledge, pp 140-164.

Whitty, M. T., Baker, A. and Inman, J. A. (2007) *Online Matchmaking*, Basingstoke: Palgrave Macmillan.

Williams, A. L. and Merten, M. J. (2011) 'iFamily: Internet and social media technology in the family context', *Family & Consumer Sciences*, 40(1): 150–170, https://doi.org/10.1111/j.1552-3934.2011.02101.x

Young, K. S. (2006) 'Online infidelity', *Journal of Couple & Relationship Therapy*, 5(2): 43-56, https://doi.org/10.1300/J398v05n02_03

PART II

Empirical approaches

Use of communication technology to maintain intergenerational contact: toward an understanding of 'digital solidarity'

Siyun Peng, Merril Silverstein, J. Jill Suitor, Megan Gilligan, Woosang Hwang, Sangbo Nam, and Brianna Routh

Introduction

For more than half a century, gerontologists and family scholars have been concerned with describing and explaining patterns of contact between parents and their adult children – a dimension of intergenerational relations that is often referred to as *associational solidarity* (Silverstein and Bengtson, 1997; Silverstein and Giarrusso, 2010). It is not surprising that associational solidarity has been a central focus of studies of later-life families, because such contact is essential in the exchange of both expressive and instrumental support between the generations (Hank, 2007; Swartz, 2009). In this paper, we extend the study of associational solidarity by considering older mothers' use of technology to maintain contact with adult children – what we refer to as 'digital solidarity'.

The role of digital solidarity in the study of intergenerational solidarity

The intergenerational solidarity paradigm (Bengtson and Roberts, 1991; Silverstein and Bengtson, 1997) incorporates six interrelated components of family solidarity: (a) affectional (emotional closeness); (b) associational (frequency of contact); (c) normative (norms of obligation); (d) consensus (agreement about values); (e) structural (geographical proximity); and (f) functional (exchange of support). We propose that digital solidarity adds a new dimension to the concepts of both associational solidarity and functional solidarity by augmenting face-to-face and telephone communication, and enabling the provision of expressive and, in some contexts, instrumental forms of support. Our development of the concept of digital solidarity rests on it being a form of communication that is instant and virtual (and, after purchase of the required device, inexpensive). As such, it serves to enhance intergenerational cohesion in ways that both complement and supplement more traditional forms of communication that require greater investments of time and efforts of coordination. Digital communication can be more frequent, while still being perceived as less intrusive than phone or face-to-face contact, and consequently may be particularly valuable to help frail older parents stay in regular contact with their adult children.

In this chapter, we focus on the role of communication technology (CT) in associational solidarity. Although we propose that digital solidarity is an important dimension of functional solidarity as well, our data do not provide details on the type of content of the emails and texts exchanged between mothers and their adult children necessary to study this dimension.

The role of digital solidarity in older adults' use of CT has been demonstrated by the finding that older adults who use the internet are most likely to do so as a means of engaging with family and friends to socialize and exchange support (Thayer and Ray, 2006). This suggests that understanding patterns of older mothers' use of CT with their adult children may provide valuable information that can be used to create interventions designed to increase internet use by women in later life. Such increased use would be beneficial across a wide array of contexts beyond the family, including managing finances, healthcare, and recreation, all of which contribute to older adults' independence and quality of life (Khosravi et al, 2016; Vuori and Holmlund-Rytkönen, 2005).

Despite the potential benefit of technology use by older adults, recent national surveys have reported that only 64% of adults 65 and older use the internet, compared with 87% of adults aged 50-64 (Pew Research Center, 2017). Such a pattern of adoption of new technologies by age is not surprising, but it is troubling, considering that use of the internet has the potential to play an increasingly important role in individuals' social lives and well-being as they age. In particular, older adults who adopt CT expand their opportunities for such interactions at a time when their opportunities for in-person interactions may decline due to changes in mobility and access to driving.

It is commonly believed that skill deficits and high costs account for older adults' lower use of CT, but some studies have found that low motivation and interest are the key factors that deter older adults from using CT (Lee et al, 2011; Melenhorst et al, 2006). Given that most CT use by older adults involves communication with family members, we suggest that a good starting point for understanding these processes is to compare older adopters and non-adopters who are especially likely to be motivated to interact with family members – specifically, older mothers with adult children. Studies have shown consistently that older mothers are highly invested in their adult children and have high rates of contact and exchanges of emotional support with them (Suitor et al, 2015). Thus, older mothers provide an excellent opportunity for understanding why some older individuals adopt CT whereas others do not.

The data we use to address this question were collected as part of the Longitudinal Study of Generations (LSOG) and the Within-Family Differences Study (WFDS), studies that provide extensive information on mothers and their offspring, allowing us to examine the ways in which the combination of demographic and socioemotional factors shape older adults' use of CT. Further, because the data for these two studies were collected several years apart (WFDS in 2008; LSOG in 2016), we can also take cohort effects into consideration by examining changes in the rates of emailing and text messaging as the availability of smart phones and tablets became more widespread.

Explaining older mothers' use of CT with their adult children

Theoretical and empirical scholarship has emphasized the combination of cohort membership, demographic characteristics, and socioemotional factors in understanding associational solidarity (Treas and Gubernskaya, 2012; Ward et al, 2013). Given that we conceive of digital solidarity as a new dimension of associational solidarity, we propose that the same set of factors will play a role in digital solidarity as in traditional dimensions of associational solidarity (Silverstein et al, 2012; Suitor et al, 2015). However, as we will discuss below, in some cases we suggest that factors that may shape traditional face-to-face and telephone contact may reduce use of CT between mothers and their adult offspring.

Because the literature has shown that characteristics of parents and children influence these processes, we will consider characteristics of mothers and offspring separately. Given that we are studying which mothers use CT with offspring and not whether they use CT with particular offspring, we consider aggregate, rather than individual-level, characteristics of adult children.

Mothers' characteristics

Cohort membership and older mothers' CT use with adult children

One of the tenets of theories of intergenerational solidarity (Bengtson and Roberts, 1991) and the life course (Elder, 1985; Riley et al, 1994; Settersten, 2003) is the salient role of cohort membership. A cohort refers to a group of individuals who share a defining characteristic (typically people who experienced a common event in a selected time period).

The history of the development of the communication technologies we are investigating makes mothers' cohort membership a crucial characteristic to take into consideration when predicting which mothers use CT to interact with their adult children. The mothers who participated in the WFDS and LSOG represent cohorts that differ markedly by the point at which CT – particularly emailing and texting – became common. The mothers who participated in the WFDS were born, on average, in the early 1930s, whereas the mothers who participated in the LSOG were born between the mid-1940s and mid-1950s. Although neither of these two groups of women were exposed to communication technology prior to adulthood, CT became widely available at earlier stage of lives of the LSOG cohort. Further, the introduction of the iPhone in 2007 and iPad in 2010 increased the ease of emailing and texting for mothers in the LSOG (interviewed in 2016) compared to mothers in the WFDS (interviewed in 2008), thus further increasing the likelihood that LSOG mothers would use CT with their adult offspring. These differences in exposure to computer-related technologies led us to hypothesize that members of the LSOG cohort would be substantially more likely than members of the WFDS cohort to report that they used CT to interact with their adult children.

Demographic characteristics of mothers

Education. Studies have shown that better educated mothers have less contact with children, probably because friends rather than relatives may be more important in the social networks of the more highly educated (Fischer, 1982; Grundy and Shelton, 2001; Tomassini et al, 2004). However, a recent Pew study revealed that 65% of older adults who have a college degree reported owning a smartphone compared to only 27% of those with a high school diploma or below in 2016 (Anderson and Perrin, 2017). Further, occupations requiring higher levels of education often require employees to adapt to technology use

(Fairlie, 2004). Operational skills, openness to change, and supportive learning environments are motivators for technology adoption among older adults (Hill et al, 2008). These motivators may be more relevant among families with higher educational backgrounds and occupations requiring more education. Thus, we hypothesized that education would be a positive predictor of mothers' use of CT with adult children.

Age. Mothers' need for support increases with age, which could be expected to fuel greater contact (Suitor et al, 2015). However, studies of technology have found that internet use decreases with age (Elliot et al, 2014; Gell et al, 2015), suggesting that age may be negatively associated with contact in the case of mothers' use of CT with their children. However, these studies did not differentiate cohort effects from age. In fact, older adults make up the fastest growing consumer segment of the internet (Hart et al, 2008). This implies that age itself is not a barrier to CT and that many older adults are eager to adopt CT use (Neves et al, 2013). The difference of CT use in age mainly reflects the cohort effects of age on exposures to CT.

As a result of these competing arguments, we do not propose a specific single hypothesis regarding mothers' age, when health and cohort are controlled for. Given the collinearity between cohort and age, it is important to emphasize that the analytic approach we take allows us to explore the role of age within two contiguous cohorts – in other words, net of cohort effects.

Race. The preponderance of studies over the past two decades has shown greater cohesion in non-White than White families (Kaufman and Uhlenberg, 1998; Sechrist et al, 2007; Silverstein and Bengtson, 1997; Suitor et al, 2015). However, this greater cohesion does not necessarily translate into higher levels of contact and, in fact, has yielded mixed findings in this regard (Ajrouch et al, 2001; Krause, 2006).

The literature on race and CT shows a much more consistent picture, with much higher rates of internet usage among Whites compared to other racial and ethnic groups (Gell et al, 2015). This may be due to limited access to technology throughout the life course, as well as educational and occupational differences for low-income minority populations (US Census Bureau, 2012). For example, a study of older adults found that non-technology users were more likely to be low-income and Black/Latino (Choi and DiNitto, 2013). Although the socioeconomic digital divide is decreasing among younger generations,

White youth are nevertheless still more likely to have greater breadth and depth of experiences using technology than are their Black/Latino counterparts (Warschauer and Matuchniak, 2010). Thus, we hypothesized that Whites would be more likely to use CT with their children than would non-Whites.

Marital status. Studies have found that older adults who are married are more likely to use CT in general (Elliot et al, 2014; Gell et al, 2015). The literature on parent–adult child contact does not provide a consistent basis for arguing that older mothers' use of CT with their offspring will or will not conform to this pattern (Suitor et al, 2015). Thus, in the absence of clear findings, we offer a tentative expectation that married mothers will be more likely to engage in CT communication with their adult children than unmarried mothers.

Mothers' health. Health is a characteristic of mothers that may differentially impact on traditional forms of communication and use of CT. Typically, contact between mothers and adult children increases when mothers experience health declines (Hank, 2007; Suitor et al, 2015). However, such health declines are likely to present obstacles to mothers' initial or continued use of CT to communicate with their children. The broader literature on technology use has shown that older adults in worse health are less likely to use CT (Elliot et al, 2014; Gell et al, 2015). This is particularly the case when poor health reduces vision and manual dexterity. Further, poor health may not only deter people from learning CT but can also force users to stop using CT. Thus, we propose that older mothers in poor health will be less likely to use CT with their adult children.

Characteristics of adult children

Gender. Classic and contemporary theories of gender role development argue that girls and women are socialized to be the kin-keepers in the family (Coser, 1991; Gilligan, 1982; Rossi and Rossi, 1990). Consistent with this argument, empirical research has found that mothers have closer and more active ties with their daughters than their sons throughout the life course in both childhood and adulthood (Suitor et al, 2015). Additionally, although the gender divide in technology usage often favours men for many forms of technology, women are more likely than men to use technology to communicate (Kimbrough et al, 2013). Thus, we propose that mothers with a greater proportion of daughters in their families will be more likely to use CT with their adult offspring.

Relationship quality. As individuals age, they increasingly perceive that their life expectancy is finite and emphasize socioemotional dimensions of their lives (Carstensen, 1993). This theory can be used to suggest that older mothers would be likely to interact more with adult children with whom they have closer relationships and interact less with offspring with whom they have conflictual relationships. In fact, empirical evidence regarding relationship quality and contact between older mothers and their adult children is consistent with this argument (Lawton et al, 1994; Silverstein et al, 1995). However, these studies considered 'traditional' telephone and face-to-face contact. In the case of CT, it is not clear how relationship quality would affect contact – further, because closeness and tension are conceptually different dimensions of relationship quality, rather than simply opposite points on a continuum (Suitor et al, 2011, 2015), closeness and tension may have different effects on CT use. We propose that mothers who report higher average levels of emotional closeness to their offspring will be more likely to use CT with their adult children. However, we do not propose specific hypotheses regarding mothers' average tension with their offspring and CT use. On one hand, mothers who have higher average tension may be less likely to use CT with their children, consistent with a general trend to seek less contact with these offspring. However, it is possible that mothers with high average tension with their offspring are more likely to use CT as a way of maintaining normative levels of contact without having to engage in direct telephone or face-to-face contact.

Geographic proximity. Living further from adult children has been found to substantially decrease face-to-face and phone contact (Hank, 2007; Kalmijn, 2006). However, the broader literature on communication has found that individuals separated by distance are more likely to use communication technologies (Hampton and Wellman, 2003; Treas and Gubernskaya, 2012). If use of CT is compensatory for geographic distance, we expect mothers whose children, on average, live further away, will use CT more than those whose offspring live closer.

Summary

In summary, we hypothesize that CT use will be more likely among mothers born in the later cohort, as well as mothers who are better educated, White, married, and in better health. Further, we hypothesize that CT use will be more prevalent among mothers who have a greater proportion of daughters, and who overall feel closer to, and live farther away from, their adult children. We also explore the roles of mothers' age and level of mother–child tension on CT use with children.

Methods

Longitudinal Study of Generations (LSOG)

Data for this investigation derive from the LSOG, a multigenerational and multi-panel study of 418 three-generation families that began in 1971 and has continued for eight additional waves up to 2016. The original sample of three-generation families was identified by randomly selecting grandfathers from the membership of a large health maintenance organization in Southern California. For the current analysis, we rely on data from the 2016 survey which was administered to 684 members of the third generation, for an effective follow-up rate of 73.2%. The large majority (79.8%) of this sample responded via a web survey with the remainder responding with a mail-back paper survey. We selected 669 respondents who were 60–72 years of age at the time of the survey, corresponding to early and middle waves of the baby-boom generation.

The analytic sample for this study included 241 older mothers who reported on 708 adult children. The sample was restricted to respondents (a) who were female, (b) who had at least two children. We restricted the number of children to match the WFDS dataset, which only included older adults who had at least two children. Using these criteria, 366 respondents were excluded. Further, 57 respondents were omitted because they were missing data on the dependent variable. We compared people with missing data on the dependent variable with those who did not have missing data on the dependent variable and found no substantial demographic differences, with one exception: people with higher education were more likely to be missing data for the dependent variable. Five cases were excluded using listwise deletion to handle missing data on the independent variables, because there were fewer than 1% missing on any variable in the analysis

(Allison, 2010). Mothers' and children's demographic characteristics are presented in Table 9.1.

Within-Family Differences Study (WFDS)

The data for this study were collected as part of the WFDS, which involved selecting a sample of mothers 65–75 years of age with at least two living adult children from Massachusetts City and town lists (for a more detailed description of the WFDS, see Suitor et al, 2013). The first wave of interviews took place with 566 women between 2001 and 2003; the second wave of data collection was from 2008 to 2011. At the second wave, 420 mothers were interviewed, representing 86% of mothers who were living at T2.

The analytic sample for this study includes 325 older mothers who reported on 1,196 adult children. Thirty-eight respondents were omitted because they were missing data on the dependent variable. We compared people with missing data on the dependent variable with those who did not have missing data on the dependent variable

Table 9.1 Demographics on mothers and adult children

	Data Source	
	LSOG	WFDS
Mothers	N = 241	N = 325
Using CT with children (in %)	95.4	31.1
Married (in %)	81.8	39.7
Ethnicity (in %)		
Non-White	3.3	27.4
White	96.7	72.6
Education (in %)		
Less than high school	1.7	17.2
High school graduate	13.3	35.4
Post-high school	7.1	7.4
Some college	34.9	14.8
College graduate	17.4	12.9
Graduate school	25.7	12.3
Age (SD)	64.0 (2.7)	77.7 (3.1)
Number of children (SD)	2.9 (1.3)	3.7 (1.6)
Subjective health (SD)	3.1 (0.8)	3.2 (1.1)
Adult children	N = 708	N = 1,196
Characteristics (in %)		
Daughters	50.4	55.1
Married	75.3	69.5
Closeness (SD)	4.3 (1.5)	6.2 (1.2)
Tension (SD)	1.7 (1.1)	2.1 (1.5)
Distance to mother (SD)	4.5 (2.0)	4.5 (1.8)

and found no substantial demographic difference, with one exception: people with lower education were more likely to be missing data on the dependent variable. Fifty-seven cases were excluded using listwise deletion to handle missing data on the independent variables, because there were fewer than 5% missing on any variable in the analysis (Allison, 2010). Mothers' and children's demographic characteristics are presented in Table 9.1.

Combined data sets

In order to combine the two datasets, we transformed education, subjective health, closeness, tension, and distance variables to make them consistent across the datasets.

Measures

Dependent variables

In the LSOG data, *older mothers' use of CT with children* was measured by combining mothers' email contact with a child and mothers' contact with a child via texting. Mothers' email contact with a child was measured by asking the respondents the following question regarding each of their children: 'During the past year, how often have you had contact with this child by email?' Similarly, mothers' contact with a child via texting was measured by asking: 'During the past year, how often have you had contact with this child by texting?' We coded mothers' use of CT with children as 0 if mothers had not used email/texting to communicate with any of their children in the past year or 1 if mothers had used email/texting with at least one child.

In the WFDS data, *older mothers' use of CT with children* was measured by asking the respondents the following question regarding each of their children: 'Have you emailed or instant messaged with your child in the past year?' We coded mothers' use of CT with children as 0 if mothers had not used CT to communicate with any of their children in the past year or 1 if mothers had used CT with at least one child. Results show that 31.1% of the 325 mothers used CT with at least one adult child in the WFDS, whereas 95.4% of the 241 mothers used CT with at least one adult child in the LSOG (see Table 9.1).

Mothers' characteristics

Race was coded as 0 = non-White or 1= White. *Family size* was measured using the number of living adult children in the family. We controlled for family size because mothers' opportunities to use CT with children increase with the number of offspring. *Marital status* was coded as 0 = not married or 1 = married. *Age* was a continuous variable ranging from 60 to 72. *Subjective health* was recoded as 1= poor, 2 = fair, 3 = good, or 4 = excellent. *Mothers' educational attainment* was recoded as 1 = less than high school, 2 = high school or vocational school graduate, 3 = post-high school training not college, 4 = some college (1-3 years), 5 = college graduate, 6 = graduate or professional school.

Aggregate children's characteristics

Because we are concerned with mothers' likelihood of using CT to communicate with any of their adult children, rather than with a particular child, we consider aggregate demographic and relational characteristics of children in each family.

Gender was coded as 0 = son; 1 = daughter. *Marital status* was coded as 0 = not married or 1 = married. *Mothers' closeness with children* was transformed to range from 1 (not at all close) to 6 (extremely close). *Mothers' tension with children* was transformed to range from 1 (no tension at all) to 6 (a great deal). *Mothers' residential distance to children* was transformed into 1 = same house, 2 = same neighbourhood, 3 = within an hour, 4 = 1-2 hours, 5 = more than 2 hours away.

Children's characteristics were transformed either into family averages (percentages or means). In the case of variables that were dichotomous prior to transformation (child's gender and marital status) aggregate percentages could range from 0 to 100; in the case of ordinal or interval variables (closeness, tension, and distance), the mean of the aggregated variables was used.

Analytic plan

We present the multivariate analyses using only the combined dataset because separate analyses using the WFDS and the LSOG datasets produced consistent results. In the combined data set, we created a variable called *data source* (0 = LSOG, 1 = WFDS) to serve as an indicator of cohort membership. We conducted the analyses using logistic regression with STATA 14.

Table 9.2 Logistic regression model predicting mothers' use of CT with adult children (N = 566 mothers who have at least 2 children; combined data: age = 60-83)

Predictors	Model 1		Model 2	
	OR	95% CI	OR	95% CI
Data Source				
Data source (0 = LSOG; 1=WFDS)	0.08**	0.02-0.31	0.75	0.07-8.11
Mother Characteristics				
Race (0 = non-White; 1 = White)	2.76**	1.30-5.84	2.90**	1.36-6.22
Family size	1.05	0.90-1.23	1.04	0.89-1.22
Age	0.92	0.85-1.00	0.92	0.85-1.00
Married	1.04	0.61-1.78	1.04	0.60-1.78
Education	1.43**	1.22-1.68	1.43**	1.20-1.69
Self-rated health	1.93**	1.34-2.78	3.60**	1.82-7.14
Average Children Characteristics				
Percentage of daughter	0.81	0.34-1.94	0.85	0.36-2.01
Percentage of married children	0.84	0.33-2.13	0.78	0.31-1.96
Tension with children	1.12	0.84-1.51	1.12	0.84-1.49
Emotional closeness with children	1.20	0.85-1.69	1.21	0.85-1.72
Distance to children	1.54*	1.09-2.17	1.56*	1.11-2.18
Interaction				
Data source X Self-rated health			0.44*	0.20-0.97
Model Statistics				
BIC	497.873		500.35	
AIC	441.471		439.61	

*p < .05. **p < .01.

Results

Table 9.2 presents the results of the logistic regression models predicting older mothers' use of CT with children. As shown in Model 1, mothers in better health ($OR = 1.93$; $p < 0.01$), with higher education ($OR = 1.43$; $p < 0.01$), and who were White ($OR = 2.76$; $p < 0.01$) were more likely to use CT than their counterparts. Mothers were also more likely to use CT with adult children when, on average, their adult children lived further away ($OR = 1.54$; $p < 0.05$). Mothers who were members of the earlier cohort (WFDS) were much less likely to use CT with children than were mothers who were members of the more recent cohort (LSOG) ($OR = 0.08$; $p < 0.01$).

Next, we conducted a series of interaction tests to assess whether the associations between data source and older mothers' use of CT were moderated by other factors. As shown in Model 2, we found that the interaction term of data source and health was statistically significant ($OR = 0.44$; $p < 0.05$), indicating that mothers' health played a more important role in CT use among members of the more recent cohort (LSOG) than the earlier cohort (WFDS). We further illuminate this pattern in Figure 9.1, which shows that the slope of the effect of health on mothers' CT use is steeper in the LSOG than in the WFDS. There is no statistically significant difference in probability of using CT between the two data-sets when mothers were in poor health. We will discuss the implications of these findings in the discussion.

Figure 9.1 Interaction plot of data source and self-reported health

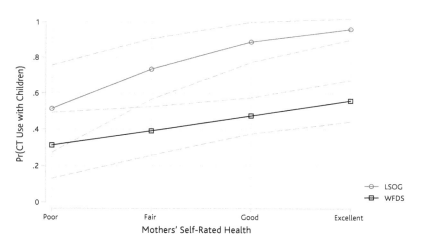

Discussion

Our goals in this paper were threefold. Our first goal was to introduce the concept of digital solidarity as an extension of the classic intergenerational solidarity paradigm. Our second was to document older mothers' use of email and texting for communicating with their adult children. Our final goal was to explore the roles of cohort, demographic characteristics, and socioemotional factors in older mothers' use of digital communication. To address these questions, we used data from the Longitudinal Study of Generations and the Within-Family Differences Study.

We proposed that digital solidarity is a new aspect of associational solidarity with implications for functional solidarity, two key components of the solidarity model (Bengtson and Roberts, 1991; Silverstein and Bengtson, 1997), the conceptual framework that has guided the study of intergenerational relations for nearly half a century. We consider this an important extension because it expands the applicability of solidarity as a conceptual tool into the twenty-first century, when digital communication has increasingly become a primary mode of contact and support provision for adults (Treas and Gubernskaya, 2012). Evidence that digital solidarity represents a unique construct was found in its distinctive relationship with social advantage of various forms. The well-known digital divide, although not desirable, has consequences for how families maintain contact, and calls attention to the different strategies that older parents and adult children use to stay in touch.

We found that use of CT to communicate with adult children was shaped by cohort membership, with more recent cohorts of older mothers being substantially more likely to use this technology with their children – 95.4% ages 60-72 in 2016 (LSOG) vs 31.1% of mothers aged 73-83 in 2008 (WFDS). This difference was confirmed using logistic regression analysis in which we controlled for other factors that predicted mothers' use of CT. In fact, mothers interviewed in 2008 (WFDS) had 92% less likelihood of using CT with children than mothers who were interviewed in 2016 (LSOG) ($OR = 0.08$; $p < 0.01$). Although it would be tempting to attribute this pattern to age, the analysis showed that age did not affect CT use beyond effects of cohort membership. Thus, we suggest the pattern greatly reflects the timing of the introduction of smartphones and tablets around 2010. Cohort and mothers' health interact to further shape CT use, with the effect of cohort disappearing among mothers with poor health. This suggests that despite CT development between 2008 and 2016, CT use among older mothers in the worst health did not increase. Thus, poor health presents a persistent barrier to the use of digital communication precisely when older adults may need the most support from family.

Drawing from the literature on intergenerational relations, we considered several demographic variables as potential predictors of mothers' CT use with adult children. Consistent with our hypotheses, we found that education and race predicted mothers' CT use; better educated and White mothers were more likely to use CT with their offspring than their counterparts who were less educated or were non-White, respectively. Thus, these patterns also mirror those found in studies of CT use outside of the intergenerational context (Elliot et al, 2014; Gell et al, 2015). However, marital status and age did not.

Finally, we proposed that several socioemotional and relational characteristics of children would shape their mothers' use of CT. Because we were concerned with whether mothers used CT with any of their offspring, rather than which specific children mothers used CT with, it was necessary to aggregate these characteristics. Contrary to our hypotheses, neither the proportion of daughters nor average parent–child closeness or tension predict CT use. However, as expected, mothers whose children, on average, lived further from them were more likely to use CT to communicate. This suggests that CT can potentially compensate for barriers to contact imposed by geographic dispersion of the multigenerational family.

Taken together, we found that mothers' characteristics played a larger role in CT use than did aggregate characteristics of their offspring. We find the absence of effects for aggregate demographic and relational characteristics surprising, given that such factors have been found to play a role in other aspects of patterns and consequences of mother–child relations (Pillemer et al, 2017; Suitor et al, 2007). We speculate that aggregate measures may not fully capture nuanced variation in CT use at the relationship level.

Future directions

The present analyses provided new insights into patterns and predictors of older mothers' use of emailing and texting with their adult offspring. However, we hope that many questions beyond the scope of this chapter will be pursued in future research.

First, neither the LSOG nor WFDS collected data on CT in earlier waves, thus limiting our ability to explore the trajectory of CT use by older mothers. Such panel data we would allow us to further examine cohort effects due to the introduction of smartphones and tablets. Moreover, panel data would allow us to differentiate between two pathways of barriers to CT use: whether poor health acts as a barrier to CT by stopping non-users from adopting CT or by forcing users to quit using CT.

As noted above, children's aggregate demographic characteristics and relationship quality did not predict mothers' CT use with them. Perhaps these factors would prove more fruitful when studying which particular children mothers engage in CT with. Given the important role of adult children's CT use in their mothers' adoption of this technology, knowing which children mothers are most likely to communicate with using CT may shed light that could be used in developing interventions designed to increase mothers' use of CT in other contexts.

We also hope that future research will explore more fully the role of race in CT. Given that older Black women are more likely to have chronic conditions that would limit their mobility (Fuller-Thomson et al, 2009), and thus their in-person interaction, adopting CT with their offspring to facilitate meeting health care needs may be especially important.

Finally, we focused only on mothers. However, older men who are unmarried have been found to be at greater risk of social isolation and unmet need for care than their female counterparts. Thus, priority should be given to studying CT use of men with the goal of finding ways to increase their access to and use of these technologies.

Implications

Lower use of CT among mothers who were in poorer health, non-White, and less educated suggest disparities in the use of CT and unequal distribution of its benefits. Beyond the interpersonal benefits mothers may receive from using CT with adult children, learning new technologies can enhance cognitive functioning and physical well-being (Chan et al, 2016; Schulz et al, 2015). Given that our findings suggest that CT may not be equally accessible, adjustment should be made to the accessibility of technologies to older adults (Neves et al, 2017). For example, although studies have shown that older adults with some impairments, such as pain and difficulties with breathing, use CT to improve their communication and reduce health-related tasks (Gell et al, 2015), our study suggests that those in poor health have the lowest rate of CT usage, and this rate did not increase following the introduction of smartphones and tablets. This suggests that intervention studies are needed to understand how redesigning devices and applications may make CT more accessible to older adults whose health prevents them from adopting current CT technologies. Such increased access could enhance their social connection to family members, allow greater monitoring of vulnerabilities by their offspring, and give them opportunities for securing digital assistance with their health conditions.

In brief

1. In this paper, we extend the study of associational solidarity by considering older mothers' use of technology to maintain contact with adult children – what we refer to as 'digital solidarity'. Digital solidarity may be the key to facilitating older adults' CT use and to increase their wellbeing.
2. The introduction of smartphones and tablets around 2010 may have dramatically increased the proportion of older mothers using communication technology (CT) with their adult children from 31.1% in 2009 to 95.4% in 2016.
3. Mothers who are least likely to use CT with their adult children are those who are in an older cohort, have worse health, less education, live closer to children, and are non-White. This suggests that a select group of families may benefit from CT.
4. Our study suggests that women in poor health have the lowest rate of CT use, and this rate did not change after the introduction of smartphones and tablets.

References

Ajrouch, K. J., Antonucci, T. C. and Janevic, M. R. (2001) 'Social networks among Blacks and Whites: The interaction between race and age', *The Journals of Gerontology Series B: Psychological Sciences and Social Sciences,* 56(2): S112–S118, https://doi.org/10.1093/geronb/56.2.S112

Allison, P. D. (2010) 'Missing data', in J. Wright and P. Marsden (eds) *Handbook of Survey Research*, Bingley: Emerald Group Limited, pp 631–658.

Anderson, M. and Perrin, A. (2017) 'Technology use among seniors', Pew Research Center, www.pewinternet.org/2017/2005/2017/technology-use-among-seniors/

Bengtson, V. L. and Roberts, R. E. L. (1991) 'Intergenerational solidarity in aging families: An example of formal theory construction', *Journal of Marriage and the Family*, 53(4): 856–870, https://doi.org/10.2307/352993

Carstensen, L. L. (1993) 'Motivation for social contact across the life span', in J. E. Jacobs (ed) *Developmental Perspectives on Motivation*, Lincoln: University of Nebraska Press, pp 209–254.

Chan, M. Y., Haber, S., Drew, L. M. and Park, D. C. (2016) 'Training older adults to use tablet computers: Does it enhance cognitive function?', *The Gerontologist*, 56(3): 475–484, https://doi.org/10.1093/geront/gnu057

Choi, N. G. and DiNitto, D. M. (2013) 'The digital divide among low-income homebound older adults: Internet use patterns, eHealth literacy, and attitudes toward computer/internet use', *Journal of Medical Internet Research*, 15(5): e93, https://doi.org/10.2196/jmir.2645

Coser, R. L. (1991) *In Defense of Modernity: Role Complexity and Individual Autonomy*, Redwood City, CA: Stanford University Press.

Elder, G. H. (1985) 'Perspectives on the life course', in G. H. Elder (ed) *Life Course Dynamics: Trajectories and Transitions, 1968–1980*, Ithaca, NY: Cornell University Press, pp 23–49.

Elliot, A. J., Mooney, C. J., Douthit, K. Z. and Lynch, M. F. (2014) 'Predictors of older adults' technology use and its relationship to depressive symptoms and well-being', *The Journals of Gerontology Series B: Psychological Sciences and Social Sciences*, 69(5): 667–677, https://doi.org/10.1093/geronb/gbt109

Fairlie, R. W. (2004) 'Race and the digital divide', *Contributions in Economic Analysis & Policy*, 3(1), article 15, https://doi.org/10.2202/1538-0645.1263

Fischer, C. S. (1982) *To Dwell among Friends: Personal Networks in Town and City*, Chicago: University of Chicago Press.

Fuller-Thomson, E., Nuru-Jeter, A., Minkler, M. and Guralnik, J. M. (2009) 'Black-White disparities in disability among older Americans', *Journal of Aging and Health*, 21(5): 677–698, https://doi.org/10.1177/0898264309338296

Gell, N. M., Rosenberg, D. E., Demiris, G., LaCroix, A. Z. and Patel, K. V. (2015) 'Patterns of technology use among older adults with and without disabilities', *The Gerontologist*, 55(3): 412–421, https://doi.org/10.1093/geront/gnt166

Gilligan, C. (1982) *In a Different Voice: Psychological Theory and Women's Development*, Cambridge, MA: Harvard University Press.

Grundy, E. and Shelton, N. (2001) 'Contact between adult children and their parents in Great Britain 1986–99', *Environment and Planning A*, 33(4): 685–697, https://doi.org/10.1068/a33165

Hampton, K. and Wellman, B. (2003) 'Neighboring in netville: How the internet supports community and social capital in a wired suburb', *City & Community*, 2(4): 277–311, https://doi.org/10.1046/j.1535-6841.2003.00057.x

Hank, K. (2007) 'Proximity and contacts between older parents and their children: A European comparison', *Journal of Marriage and Family*, 69(1): 157–173, https://doi.org/10.1111/j.1741-3737.2006.00351.x

Hart, T. A., Chaparro, B. S. and Halcomb, C. G. (2008) 'Evaluating websites for older adults: Adherence to 'senior-friendly' guidelines and end-user performance', *Behaviour & Information Technology*, 27(3): 191-199, https://doi.org/10.1080/01449290600802031

Hill, R., Beynon-Davies, P. and Williams, M. D. (2008) 'Older people and internet engagement: Acknowledging social moderators of internet adoption, access and use', *Information Technology and People*, 21(3): 244-266, https://doi.org/10.1108/09593840810896019

Kalmijn, M. (2006) 'Educational inequality and family relationships: Influences on contact and proximity', *European Sociological Review*, 22(1): 1-16, https://doi.org/10.1093/esr/jci036

Kaufman, G. and Uhlenberg, P. (1998) 'Effects of life course transitions on the quality of relationships between adult children and their parents', *Journal of Marriage and Family*, 60(4): 924-938, https://doi.org/10.2307/353635

Khosravi, P., Rezvani, A. and Wiewiora, A. (2016) 'The impact of technology on older adults' social isolation', *Computers in Human Behavior*, 63, 594-603, https://doi.org/10.1016/j.chb.2016.05.092

Kimbrough, A. M., Guadagno, R. E., Muscanell, N. L. and Dill, J. (2013) 'Gender differences in mediated communication: Women connect more than do men', *Computers in Human Behavior*, 29(3): 896-900, https://doi.org/10.1016/j.chb.2012.12.005

Krause, N. (2006) 'Social relationships in late life', in R. Binstock, L. George, S. Cutler, J. Hendricks and J. Schulz (eds) *Handbook of Aging and the Social Sciences* (6th edn), Cambridge: Academic Press, pp 181-200.

Lawton, L., Silverstein, M. and Bengtson, V. L. (1994) 'Affection, social contact, and geographic distance between adult children and their parents', *Journal of Marriage and Family*, 56(1): 57-68, https://doi.org/10.2307/352701

Lee, B., Chen, Y. and Hewitt, L. (2011) 'Age differences in constraints encountered by seniors in their use of computers and the internet', *Computers in Human Behavior*, 27(3): 1231-1237, https://doi.org/10.1016/j.chb.2011.01.003

Melenhorst, A.-S., Rogers, W. A. and Bouwhuis, D. G. (2006) 'Older adults' motivated choice for technological innovation: Evidence for benefit-driven selectivity', *Psychology and Aging*, 21(1): 190-195, https://doi.org/10.1037/0882-7974.21.1.190

Neves, B. B., Amaro, F. and Fonseca, J. (2013) 'Coming of (old) age in the digital age: ICT usage and non-usage among older adults', *Sociological Research Online*, 18(2): 6, https://doi.org/10.5153/sro.2998

Neves, B. B., Franz, R., Judges, R., Beermann, C. and Baecker, R. (2017) 'Can digital technology enhance social connectedness among older adults? A feasibility study', *Journal of Applied Gerontology*, https://doi.org/10.1177/0733464817741369

Pew Research Center. (2017) 'Internet/broadband fact sheet', www.pewinternet.org/fact-sheet/internet-broadband/

Pillemer, K., Suitor, J. J., Riffin, C. and Gilligan, M. (2017) 'Adult children's problems and mothers' well-being', *Research on Aging*, 39(3): 375–395, https://doi.org/10.1177/0164027515611464

Riley, M. W. E., Kahn, R. L. E., Foner, A. E. and Mack, K. A. (1994) *Age and Structural Lag: Society's Failure to Provide Meaningful Opportunities in Work, Family, and Leisure*, Hoboken: John Wiley & Sons.

Rossi, A. S. and Rossi, P. H. (1990) *Of Human Bonding: Parent–Child Relations across the Life Course*, Piscataway, NJ: Transaction Publishers.

Schulz, R., Wahl, H.-W., Matthews, J. T., De Vito Dabbs, A., Beach, S. R. and Czaja, S. J. (2015) 'Advancing the aging and technology agenda in gerontology', *The Gerontologist,* 55(5): 724–734, https://doi.org/10.1093/geront/gnu071

Sechrist, J., Suitor, J. J., Henderson, A., Cline, K. and Steinhour, M. (2007) 'Regional differences in parent–adult child relations', *Journals of Gerontology Series B: Psychological Sciences and Social Sciences*, 62(6): 388–391, https://doi.org/10.1093/geronb/62.6.S388

Settersten, R. A. (2003) 'Propositions and controversies in life-course scholarship', in R. A. Settersten (ed) *Invitation to the Life Course: Toward New Understandings of Later Life*, Amityville, NY: Baywood, pp 15–45.

Silverstein, M. and Bengtson, V. L. (1997) 'Intergenerational solidarity and the structure of adult child–parent relationships in American families', *American Journal of Sociology*, 103(2): 429–460, https://doi.org/10.1086/231213

Silverstein, M. and Giarrusso, R. (2010) 'Aging and family life: A decade review', *Journal of Marriage and Family*, 72(5): 1039–1058, https://doi.org/10.1111/j.1741-3737.2010.00749.x

Silverstein, M., Conroy, S. J. and Gans, D. (2012) 'Beyond solidarity, reciprocity and altruism: Moral capital as a unifying concept in intergenerational support for older people', *Ageing and Society*, 32(7): 1246–1262, https://doi.org/10.1017/S0144686X1200058X

Silverstein, M., Parrott, T. M. and Bengtson, V. L. (1995) 'Factors that predispose middle-aged sons and daughters to provide social support to older parents', *Journal of Marriage and Family*, 57(2): 465–475, https://doi.org/10.2307/353699

Suitor, J. J., Gilligan, M. and Pillemer, K. (2013) 'Continuity and change in mothers' favoritism toward offspring in adulthood', *Journal of Marriage and Family*, 75(5): 1229-1247, https://doi.org/10.1111/jomf.12067

Suitor, J. J., Gilligan, M. and Pillemer, K. (2015) 'Stability, change, and complexity in later life families', in L. George and K. Ferraro (eds) *Handbook of Aging and the Social Sciences* (8th ed), Cambridge: Academic Press, pp 206-226.

Suitor, J. J., Sechrist, J., Gilligan, M. and Pillemer, K. (2011) 'Intergenerational relations in later-life families', in A. R. Settersten and L. J. Angel (eds) *Handbook of Sociology of Aging*, New York: Springer, pp 161-178.

Suitor, J. J., Sechrist, J. and Pillemer, K. (2007) 'When mothers have favorites: Conditions under which mothers differentiate among their adult children', *Canadian Journal on Aging*, 26(2): 85-99, https://doi.org/10.3138/cja.26.2.085

Swartz, T. T. (2009) 'Intergenerational family relations in adulthood: Patterns, variations, and implications in the contemporary United States', *Annual Review of Sociology*, 35(1): 191-212, https://doi.org/10.1146/annurev.soc.34.040507.134615

Thayer, S. E. and Ray, S. (2006) 'Online communication preferences across age, gender, and duration of Internet use', *Cyberpsychology & Behavior*, 9(4): 432-440, https://doi.org/10.1089/cpb.2006.9.432

Tomassini, C., Kalogirou, S., Grundy, E., Fokkema, T., Martikainen, P., Broese van Groenou, M. and Karisto, A. (2004) 'Contacts between elderly parents and their children in four European countries: Current patterns and future prospects', *European Journal of Ageing*, 1(1): 54-63, https://doi.org/10.1007/s10433-004-0003-4

Treas, J. and Gubernskaya, Z. (2012) 'Farewell to moms? Maternal contact for seven countries in 1986 and 2001', *Journal of Marriage and Family*, 74(2): 297-311, https://doi.org/10.1111/j.1741-3737.2012.00956.x

US Census Bureau. (2012) *Statistical Abstract of the United States: 2012*, Washington, DC: US Government Printing Office.

Vuori, S. and Holmlund-Rytkönen, M. (2005) '55+ people as internet users', *Marketing Intelligence & Planning*, 23(1): 58-76, https://doi.org/10.1108/02634500510577474

Ward, R., Deane, G. and Spitze, G. (2013) 'Life-course changes and parent–adult child contact', *Research on Aging*, 36(5): 568-602, https://doi.org/10.1177/0164027513510325

Warschauer, M. and Matuchniak, T. (2010) 'New technology and digital worlds: Analyzing evidence of equity in access, use, and outcomes', *Review of Research in Education*, 34(1): 179-225, https://doi.org/10.3102/0091732X09349791

Careful families and care as 'kinwork': an intergenerational study of families and digital media use in Melbourne, Australia

Jolynna Sinanan and Larissa Hjorth

Introduction

Jessica Chan is 19 years old and lives in the outer suburbs of Melbourne with her mother and father. She is first generation Australian, her Singaporean Chinese mother and her Malaysian Chinese father immigrated to Australia in 1989. She is baking vegetarian curry puffs, while her mother Nancy is stir-frying some chicken for their relatives who are coming over for Sunday dinner. While sharing the kitchen, they are debating whether Jessica should get the latest iPhone 7 as she is leaving for a university exchange to New York for six months, a few weeks later. The conversation is not what one would usually expect: Jessica, the teenage daughter is not asking her mother to buy her the newest iPhone. Nancy is insisting that she is going to buy it for her and she should download Facebook, Skype and WhatsApp for when she is away from home. Nancy's mother has no intention of checking up on Jessica constantly, but she does want *to feel as though* she is updated with what she is doing and that she can easily contact her when she wants to.

   In her studies of three generations of Italian Australians, migration scholar Loretta Baldassar (2016) has observed that in the mid-twentieth century, Italians leaving home would experience a social death – that is, they would be disconnected from their family networks due to the distance of migration. In the early twenty-first century, however, leaving Italy no longer means experiencing a kind of social death, it means that the family of the person emigrating would purchase a new computer. Similarly, Jessica's exchanges, highlighting transnational forms of intimacy and intergenerational mobility, involve culturally and generationally specific forms of care in and through media practice. These practices are more than just 'social surveillance' (Marwick, 2012), instead illustrating the complex and paradoxical weave of power and care involved in what can be called 'friendly' surveillance (Hjorth et al, 2016).

This chapter empirically explores the ways in which intimacy, surveillance and care are interwoven with and through digital media practices in Melbourne. While much of the initial discussion around surveillance focused upon corporate and governmental dimensions (Farman, 2013; Andrejevic, 2006) overlooking the informal, micro and social forms (Marwick, 2012), more recently literature has started to focus upon mundane, emergent practices around maintaining intimacy and care-at-distance in families (Clark, 2012; Sengupta, 2012; Leaver, 2017; Burrows, 2017). We know very little about the ways digital media practices relating to care and intimacy are being played out in everyday familial contexts.

As such, we argue that the 'doing family' practices – the ways that family members maintain co-presence through routines and everyday tasks (Nedelcu and Wyss, 2016) – playing out across intergenerational and cross-cultural relationships reveal textures of intimacy and boundary work that entangle with the mundane to create new types of social surveillance and disappearance. These new forms of surveillance are also intertwined with expressions of 'caring about', that is having affection and concern for family members and working on maintaining bonds of relationships (see McKay, 2007; Yeates, 2004; Lynch and McLaughlin, 1995). For transnational and families separated by distance, family members 'do family' through everyday activities that extend beyond the home including through digital media (Madianou, 2016, 2017; Morgan, 1996; Wajcman et al, 2008).

This examination of surveillance as care, locative media and intergenerational families draws on ethnographic research conducted in Melbourne with 13 households across 2015-2016 as part of a larger, cross-cultural study of locative media and intergenerational families in Melbourne, Shanghai and Tokyo.[1] The study contributes to research on locative media (Wilken and Goggin, 2015; Wilken, 2012) that refers to the capacities of mobile devices that are utilized by applications such as Facebook Places; they can provide users information about their surroundings but also provide others with information on where the user is located.

Melbourne provides a rich context for studying the diverse meanings of families as there are a significant number of migrants for whom social media is essential for maintaining transnational relationships.

For instance, 42% of Melbourne's population was born overseas and, following English, the second most common language spoken is Mandarin (City of Melbourne, 2013). Half of our participants were born overseas and the sample also included single parents and families without children. Their experiences demonstrate changing definitions of family in multicultural, urban areas such as Melbourne. Further, our attention to Lesbian, Gay, Bisexual, and Transgender (LGBT) households (four) emphasizes those working to define and redefine the meanings of kinship in Australia.

This chapter is indebted to two key ideas from recent mobile media scholarship and migration scholarship. The first is 'friendly' surveillance mentioned above, theorized by Hjorth et al (2016). 'Friendly' surveillance advances the literatures on types of social surveillance (Marwick, 2012) or what Leaver (2017) calls 'intimate surveillance' to highlight the complex entanglements of power and care in different familial relationships. The second is 'kinwork', which explores the work of kinship that is mostly enacted by women, posed by di Leonardo (1987) and investigated in depth in relation to Italian migrants to Australia by Baldassar (2016, 2007a, 2007b). We aim to advance these areas of scholarship by locating our argument in the notion of 'digital kinship', which has emerged from the wider, cross-cultural study (Hjorth et al, forthcoming). The chapter is therefore structured as follows: firstly, digital kinship is established within debates in scholarship that consider what it means to be 'family' in an age of networked media (Clark, 2012; Horst, 2012), the asymmetries that occur between family roles regarding who does the 'work' of the family (Baldassar, 2007a, 2007b; Wilding, 2007) and the influences of digital media.

We then explore the relationship between 'friendly' surveillance as an expression of care as part of digital kinship. This section highlights how discussions of digital media in relation to families often emphasize the collective noun 'the family' (Wilding, 2017). Instead, the notion of digital kinship attempts to critically engage with different family roles and their implications within intergenerational families. This perspective takes into account the gender and power dimensions that are inherent in relationships between family members such as between couples or between mother and daughter, for example.

The more abstract ideas we present are then illustrated through ethnographic case studies from our fieldwork in Melbourne before concluding with some of the implications of locative media practices relating to care and intimacy within intergenerational familial contexts. The ways kinship intersects with digital practices and how such a perspective has implications for intimacy, co-presence and publicness are the starting point for this chapter.

Digital kinship: an intergenerational perspective on uses of digital media

As the traditional focus of anthropology, kinship has remained central to understandings of culture. Here, kinship is summarized as family kin group that is determined by structure and biological relatedness, family relationships that are created and maintained (see Carsten, 2003) and the multiple meanings, tensions and negotiations that occur within different categories of family relationships.

Initially, British social anthropology viewed kinship as an organizing, political and governing structure and not only a set of relationships between people. There were clear modes of conduct between related members within the hierarchy of the family. Yet contemporary kinship studies have also extended the role of choice within relationships, where family as structure became secondary to everyday experiences, contradictions and ambivalence in nuclear, extended and separated families (Godelier, 2012; Peletz, 1995). Carsten (2000, 2003, 2007) has most notably revisited kinship, emphasizing how kinship is largely influenced by behaviour and draws attention to how kinship can be made by caring and nurturing within a relationship, whether those involved are related by blood, or not.

Ethnographic studies in migration have made significant contributions to the role of digital media in transnational family relationships and the transforming meanings of kinship. Madianou and Miller (2012) coined the term polymedia from their extensive research with Filipina mothers working in England as maids and their 'left-behind' families in the Philippines. A key aspect of the study was absent mothering and how the women 'mothered' using new media, thus approaching kinship considering how new media contributed to impacting upon behaviour and maintaining familial relationships.

In the aforementioned study by Baldassar (2016), she notes how more recent waves of migration alongside the sheer availability of digital media also transform previous understandings of cultural inflections of kinship. Previously, through letter-writing, family members were able to fulfil their expected role as a category – that is, a son abroad could portray himself as an ideal son and emphasize working and missing home, whereas digital media, and social media in particular, create a constant feeling of co-presence, where the son who has left home is more similar to the actual, individual person. As we discuss further, the sense of co-presence and constant contact afforded by social media platforms such as Facebook and WhatsApp, might also contribute to alleviating migrants' feelings of guilt at not visiting relatives in their country of origin. Prior to social media, other migration scholars have noted the importance of visiting for ritual occasions and highlight the complex range of emotions that accompany attendance and non-attendance (Conradson and McKay, 2007).

Considering the 'digital' in relation to kinship captures some of these tensions and complexities and draws on these approaches, offering a perspective that reveals how kinship moves in and out of 'online' and 'offline' spaces (Hjorth et al, forthcoming). Further, digital kinship draws attention to how these spaces contain their own histories, connections and memories.

Digital media as 'friendly' surveillance and kinwork at a distance

Digital media has also influenced how some of the 'work' of the family is done. 'Work' includes micro-coordination of everyday tasks, but also showing care and acknowledgement of family relationships. As a domestic technology, the mobile phone draws attention to locality and place and redefines public and private space (Hjorth, 2008). The mobile phone also transforms meanings of publicness, experiences of intimacy and invites new forms of presence and proximity (Hjorth, 2007; Prøitz, 2007). Further, locative media invites rethinking privacy (Gazzard, 2011; Farman, 2013; de Souza e Silva and Frith, 2012). Rather than approaching privacy as something that is possessed or not, for example, Dourish and Anderson (2006) highlight that privacy is something we constantly do and define through practice. As we illustrate shortly, privacy and surveillance within different kinds of family relationships are often navigated with concern for others in mind as well as acting out of individual interest and autonomy. The effort and concern invested in considering the feelings of others is only one aspect of expressing care through digital media. Concerns for surveillance and privacy within family contexts also differ from discussions about corporate and government surveillance and big data (Farman, 2013; Andrejevic, 2006; Cincotta et al, 2011).

Marwick (2012) poses a perspective on social surveillance which focuses on everyday interactions. She argues that social surveillance assumes 'power differentials evident in everyday interactions rather than the hierarchical power relationships assumed in much of the surveillance literature' (Marwick, 2012, p 378). Marwick identifies some of the common notions of surveillance such as lateral (Andrejevic, 2006), participatory (Albrechtslund, 2008), social searching (Ellison et al, 2007) and social (Joinson, 2008; Tokunaga, 2011). As she notes, social surveillance differs from traditional models insofar as it is focused around micro-level, decentralized, reciprocal interactions between individuals.

More recently, in a special issue on 'infancy online', *Social Media & Society* considered some of the implications that posting infant pictures publicly, especially by microcelebrities, will have on the future of the infant. Recall the 1960s movie directed by Michael Powell entitled *Peeping Tom*. In the movie we meet the adult, Mark Lewis, a murdering byproduct of his psychiatrist father's experiments that were constantly filmed. Mark frames his life and his murders constantly in and through the cinema lens. What does it mean to document a life online? Will it become like the 1998 film *The Truman Show*, in which the reality and screen culture merge? As Tama Leaver (2017, p 3) eloquently argues, the phenomenon of infancy online is creating new types of 'intimate surveillance' we are yet to realize fully.

Benign social surveillance through social media platforms enables new ways of enacting care. The locative function on Facebook, for example, allows friends (and relatives) to monitor and care at a distance. And family groups in WhatsApp allow parents to participate in conversations equally with their children (whether they choose to do so or not). Mobile media provides creative and playful ways to manage intimate intergenerational relationships at a distance that differs from previous ways of managing transnational relationships, as well as ones within close proximity.

Prior to digital media, showing care through exchange involved the circulation of goods as well as communication through letters and phone calls. Research, particularly in contexts where women make up significant numbers in transnational labour, such as the Philippines, Indonesia and the Caribbean, has explored how care has been expressed through sending barrels of branded goods to frequent use of calling cards to, more recently, 'always on' use of webcams (Crawford, 2003; Horst, 2006; Olwig, 2007; Madianou and Miller, 2012). Yet other scholars have noted, in contexts where women have not migrated for labour, women still invest the majority of time and effort into caring at a distance, or contribute to doing most of the 'kinwork' (Baldassar, 2007b; di Leonardo, 1987).

By kinwork, di Leonardo (1987, p 442) refers to the:

> conception, maintenance, and ritual celebration of cross-household kin ties, including visits, letters, telephone

calls, presents and cards to kin; the organization of holiday gatherings; the creation and maintenance of quasi-kin relations; decisions to neglect or to intensify particular ties; [and the] mental work of reflection about all these activities.

She further emphasizes the time, attention and skill invested in maintaining these different, often asymmetrical relationships and the 'sense of family' created. Yet kinwork is also characterized by both altruism and self-interest, where the emotional consequences include cooperation and competition, guilt and gratification (di Leonardo, 1987, p 443). In relation to families separated by distance, Baldassar (2007b, p 392) extends kinwork to the efforts made in 'staying in touch': that is, 'visiting, writing letters, making phone calls, organizing reunions, celebrations and holidays, keeping family albums and sharing photos, and sending gifts and cards'.

The kinds of effort invested in staying in touch and caring at a distance might also include more 'hands on' forms of care, including practical, financial and personal. However, our fieldwork in Melbourne revealed that caring at a distance relies less on financial assistance, gifts and remittances, and more on care as emotional and moral support, and creating a sense of intimate co-presence. In the section that follows, we detail different categories of family relationships, alongside significant findings around how social media platforms and digital media for communications were used, illustrated through stories. We wish to highlight that digital media alleviates some of the obligations related to caring at a distance and also how it intersects with gender and power relations that reside in different categories of family relationships.

Families in Melbourne: kinship and boundary work

It has been established so far that mobile media provokes rethinking privacy, disclosure and publicness. Mobile media also allows a 'portability of care' that is constantly present (Baldassar, 2017). There is some continuity on the emphasis of exchange as an expression of care within transnational relationships, where instead of sending goods, it is now more common to send messages, images and links, especially within family groups on WhatsApp. Constant contact also has implications for family relationships that are more local. The frequency of interactions through banter, chatting, posting and commenting on images posted to platforms such as Facebook positively acknowledges the importance of these relationships by checking in, even when exchanges might not be about anything in particular (see Horst and Miller, 2005).

This section provides ethnographic case studies that illustrate the different ways surveillance is intertwined with other expressions of care within categories of family relationships. We provide examples from data collection in 13 households in Melbourne. The examples we draw on here are nuclear families with parents and children living within the same household, children who are now adults living nearby and, in one household, where the teenage child has recently moved abroad.

Our first example of a relationship challenges some of the frequent observations that mobile and social media become a source of tension and jealousy within intimate relationships (Miller, 2011). Instead, navigating privacy and disclosure over social media platforms such as Facebook becomes a mode of bonding and showing concern for the respective individuals as well as the relationship. Yana and Nathan minimize what they post to Facebook, however, Yana tries to post 'enough' for her parents and siblings interstate to keep them updated with their family life in Melbourne.

Yana is 38 years old and has one son from a previous relationship, Mark, who is in primary school. They live with her current partner Nathan, who works in hospitality as a sous chef. Nathan generally is not an avid user of social media, he has a Facebook profile, which he rarely posts to or checks and has downloaded WhatsApp to communicate with one of his friends who lives overseas. His immediate family lives nearby, they see each other regularly and he contacts them with phone calls and text messages. Yana, on the other hand, is originally from Sydney and her parents, brothers and sisters as well as their extended family all still live interstate. As Yana notes:

'I find Facebook as a way to connect and see what's happening, it makes you feel less super far away. And I like to post fun stuff. Just some of Marky, Mark and I went out to eat. A friend's wedding. I pretty much just have it because I moved from Sydney and just for my family to sort of see Mark grow up really.'

Although Yana and Mark do not see her family often, the pressure to visit appears to be alleviated through the sense of constant contact Facebook provides. Yana rarely posts photos other than family ones. Scrolling through photos on her phone, there are several food photos she has taken, but hasn't posted to social media. "So I just took pictures of it but this won't go on Facebook or anything like that but everyone at work has seen it but I won't post that because to me it's private. It's just, I don't know." Her friends at work know that Nathan is a chef and their family meals during the week are close to restaurant quality, so there is an element of self-deprecation at not wanting to come across as showing off, as Yana rarely does the family cooking. Instead, Yana frames her withholding of posting meals Nathan has cooked as:

> 'It's kind of nice to sort of stand around and talk about it rather than just display it and sort of put it out there. Because then I'll tell them like, okay, so this here that's a lotus flower with tuna and it's edible flowers and they're like, "Oh my God, wow." So they'll ask what each thing is and it's just a bit of fun.'

For Yana, platforms such as Facebook are more for keeping her family connected than for nurturing her relationships with peers. She is also the 'digital custodian' while Mark is in primary school. For another couple, Kathy and Daniel, whose teenage daughter is now living in Canada, several platforms become the source of frequent negotiation, as both parents and daughter use social media between their different social circles.

Kathy and Daniel lived for several years as 'digital resistors' – that is, they opted out of using media because digital communication technologies represent a lifestyle that is in opposition to their immediate way of life and values. 'Media refusal' is also related to lifestyle choices, as political and social commentary on media consumption and 'conspicuous non-consumption' (Portwood-Stacer, 2012). Baumer et al (2015) argue that such kinds of conspicuous non-usage are also expressive of socio-cultural identity. Kathy explains:

> 'We lived in her early years in quite an isolated community in Canada, and did the whole self-sustaining thing, so sustainability thing. And it was just a choice not to have a television. And then travelled for a couple of years and then it was on the south coast of New South Wales in sort of an alternative community.'

While their daughter Rita was a child, Kathy and David did not own a television, desktop or laptop. When she became a teenager and they moved to Melbourne, Kathy continues, "[we] put her into private school, put her in a warm Melbourne scene, and we had to get a television quick so that she could catch up with what the rest of the world was doing". Although they agreed with the ethos of sustainable living, Kathy and Daniel felt that it was unfair to disconnect Rita from her peers and so, once in Melbourne, they bought a television, laptops and smartphones.

Now Rita is 19 and has returned to Canada for a gap year, living with a family and working. Rita video calls her parents on Facetime with her iPhone every two days. Daniel and Kathy appreciate that although they would like her to have her independence, it is Rita who initiates contact with them most of the time, via Facetime or WhatsApp. Daniel commented on a call that they would leave Rita to have her space and she replied "no". Kathy reassures him, "She doesn't want space, she is very happy to have lots of contact".

Having grown up with social media as a teenager, Rita also 'fits' calling her parents around her work travelling time. She often calls home to or from work, which is reassuring to Daniel and Cathy regarding her daily movements. Kathy and Rita also often exchange photos on WhatsApp, especially if either are shopping or eating out. Photos exchanged between transnational family members can constitute 'evidence' that relatives are safe, emotionally well and are meeting the aspirations of upward mobility that accompanies migration (Hall, 1991; Lustig, 2004). Yet the constant contact afforded by locative and mobile media also results in the desire to self-monitor posting content that causes tensions or envy.

For Patrick and Esther, a couple in their 60s, maintaining a sense of privacy from other family members is not as much a concern as neither of them post to social media regularly. Instead, Esther frequently looks at her daughter Jasmine's profile even though she lives nearby, and her nieces' and nephews' posts as they still live in Malaysia. Esther is on WhatsApp and is part of two groups, one for her former classmates from Malaysia and one for her family in Melbourne. Members of the former classmates group frequently send old photos, memes with greetings and humour and the more local group mainly uses WhatsApp to coordinate catch-ups. Esther describes that sometimes the classmates group sends so many images across the day that it eats into her pre-paid data limit and she has to mute the conversation. Although she deletes images frequently, chats with members of the group one-to-one and seldom participates in the group chat herself, she says she wouldn't leave the group altogether, because it would seem 'rude'. Esther's presence as benign hanging around resonates with other studies of cultural aspects of mobile phone usage where retaining several contacts even though there is little communication with them still acknowledges that those contacts are included in the same social networks (Horst and Miller, 2005).

Esther is also on Facebook for Messenger, which she uses to chat and video call relatives overseas. Patrick's relatives in India are also Facebook friends with Esther and mainly contact her when they want to enquire about him. Patrick insists he is not on Facebook, Skype or any other social media. Yet, similarly to Yana, Esther is a kind of 'digital custodian' for the household, where Patrick is on social media through her. Patrick describes, "Esther goes to work and I use the tablet for my crossword and so on, but I look at Facebook occasionally. Especially if [his daughter] Jasmine has put up a photo of the cats. I see some of the things my cousins' children put up from India, but I'm not all that interested". In Esther and Patrick's household, there is more continuity with Esther as responsible for most of the 'kinwork', including staying in touch with relatives through mobile media.

WhatsApp groups were fairly common with transnational families and members of the group could span three generations. Chua is in his mid-70s and lives in the same suburb as his two daughters, whom he babysits for regularly. He has a Facebook profile, but says he doesn't browse or post to it regularly; he is most active in his family WhatsApp with his siblings and in-laws, and nieces and nephews in Malaysia, England and the US. The group is fairly active with messages exchanged at least once a day and the most common types of images circulated of different family members together, food and travel.

Yet family members including Chua also regularly exchange links to Christian websites, with daily Bible readings and religious reflections. Although the members do not comment on these posts directly, the regular circulation of links to religious web pages also reinforces a wider sense of sociality, beyond the immediate relationships between family members. By engaging in wider sociality based on religious beliefs, Chua also maintains some of the kinwork of staying in touch, which draws attention to how digital media challenges the gender roles of who does the work of the family.

In these concluding stories, two different teenagers – Jessica who was introduced at the beginning of the chapter and Mel who is also 19 – illustrate how care at a distance is enacted by youth for whom social media was ubiquitous from primary school. These final stories highlight the importance of the future orientations for considering different implications of the intersection of mobile media and expressions of care from an intergenerational perspective. For some of the older participants described above, social media is simply an add-on to other forms of caring at a distance. For these teenagers, being embedded in various media ecologies implies that uses of media has always been imbricated with experiences of emotions, especially in relation to platforms with visual affordances.

Growing up in Melbourne as an only child, Jessica's parents have taken her on overseas family holidays from a very young age. She is mindful that she has travelled more than her peers at school, but also more than her cousins and older relatives overseas. In addition to her upcoming exchange in New York, Jessica says that her short-term aspirations include more travelling while she is at university. "[I want to go to] places I haven't been, so Europe, broader Asia. And I'd like to go back, this sounds like such a spoiled kid, but I would love to go back to the Maldives. I had an amazing time there. Beaches and stuff." She sees a lot of posts on Facebook and her classmates from high school have a Messenger group as well, but she disables the locative functions.

'Yeah, like initially, I change the settings so like Facebook and Messenger doesn't know the location... more for people... I don't really feel it's necessary that they know where I am. Like sometimes I'll feel like I'm showing off if I show them where I am so I don't want them to think I'm showing off because I've put where I am. Like one time I was in LA and I didn't realize it was on and a friend asked you're in LA, how is it? Which is nice because it was a nice conversation topic, but after that I turned it off. Because I didn't really want to show off or anything.'

The concern to not come across as 'showing off', especially to relatives overseas who are on Facebook, counters many of the popular assumptions that teenagers are becoming more narcissistic because of social media. On the one hand, Jessica and her peers were subject to these kinds of discourses growing up, and therefore they circulate images in their Messenger group more than sharing them on their profiles.

Mel, on the other hand, uses the circulation of images, quotes and links among her meditation group friends, as a support group that facilitates self-care. Several of the women in the group are older and have children. We have included friendship as a category of relationships as much of the energy invested into friendships results in relationships that can be closer to an individual than other kinship-based relationships (Allan, 1989; Bell and Coleman, 1999; Pahl, 2000).

Mel lives with her father and has two part-time jobs, while she is saving up to go overseas. She explains, "We have a meditation group of girls [on Viber] so I'm part of that and we just keep each other updated, like post links to meditation websites or upcoming events and things like that which are good to know about". When inspirational quotes or memes appear on Mel's Facebook feed, she screen captures them and saves them to a 'Quotes' album in her images folder on her phone. Some of these she shares to the group.

> 'It makes a difference in the sense of having a security I
> guess. I don't really think about it so much, but I guess
> if I was to stop and think about it, knowing that other
> people feel like this, it's not just me. A lot of the work I do
> is interactive but it's actually quote solo, so I don't work
> in a team. When I'm cleaning now I'm pretty much by
> myself because the family's out and the kids' parties I'm the
> entertainer so I'm about facilitating, I don't so much work
> side by side with somebody else. So it's kind of good to
> have that dialogue in my head going it's alright, keep going
> or whatever it is… or like yeah you did great.'

The circulation of these 'handy reminders' function in a similar way to the circulation of religious posts that appeared in the story of Chua. By tapping into a wider sociality in the sense of Benedict Anderson's 'imagined community' (1991), expressing care moves beyond immediate, dyadic relationships and reinforces a sense of collective solidarity based on shared emotional experiences. This area, facilitated by mobile and social media, deserves more inquiry as to the dimensions of expressions of care within different categories of relationships.

Conclusion

This chapter began by establishing how surveillance and privacy have different implications within the context of intergenerational family relationships. We posed the framework of 'digital kinship', which provides a life course perspective to take into account the differing roles, positions, meanings and contexts over a person's life span that impact upon and influence how an individual navigates being embedded in these wider set of relationships, through digital media. We examined the notion of kinwork to examine how women were traditionally responsible for the ritual and routine work of maintaining family bonds and suggested the ubiquity of mobile and social media might challenge these more gendered roles drawing on the example of Chua, but also, as seen with Esther and Patrick, may present a continuity of kinwork as predominantly women's work.

We then illustrated how care and intimacy are interwoven with and through digital media practices. Often, as seen with Yana and Nathan, surveillance and control is less about the asymmetries within dyadic or intimate relationships, but are more related to how the nuclear unit negotiated extended family and networks.

Because of the socioeconomic factors related to our sample in Melbourne, 'caring for', that is the provision of financial and other resources, is less prominent than 'caring about', where expressions of care also highlights the efforts invested in relationships between individuals who are not closely related. As platforms for media for communication increase, so too do judgements from others around how a person uses media to navigate a relationship. The intersection between expressions of care and mobile media therefore draws attention to the persistence of the moral value of preserving and constantly acknowledging different categories of family relationships.

In brief

1. New forms of surveillance in the context of intergenerational family relationships are less concerned about privacy and data in relation to corporations and governments and are more concerned with expressing 'caring about' family members.

2. 'Friendly' surveillance advances literatures on types of social surveillance (Marwick, 2012) and what Leaver (2017) has described as 'intimate surveillance' to draw attention to the complexities of power and care in familial relationships (Hjorth et al, 2016).

3. 'Kinwork' highlights the routine and ritual work of kinship that is mainly enacted through the efforts made by women to maintain family relationships (di Leonardo, 1987; Baldassar, 2007a, 2007b, 2016).

4. 'Digital kinship' draws on families based on biology and structure as well as relationships that are created and maintained (Carsten, 2003). It considers the 'digital' in relation to kinship, offering a perspective that reveals how kinship moves in and out of 'online' and 'offline' spaces (Hjorth et al, forthcoming).

Note

[1] *Locating the Mobile* is an Australian Research Council Linkage project, partnered with Intel, Keio University and Fudan University with Chief Investigators: Larissa Hjorth, Heather Horst, Sarah Pink, Genevieve Bell, PIs: Fumitoshi Kato and Baohua Zhou and researchers Jolynna Sinanan and Kana Ohashi.

References

Albrechtslund, A. (2008) 'Online social networking as participatory surveillance', *First Monday*, 13(3), https://doi.org/10.5210/fm.v13i3.2142

Allan, G. A. (1989) *Friendship: Developing a Sociological Perspective*, Hemel Hempstead: Harvester Wheatsheaf.

Anderson, B. (1991) *Imagined Communities: Reflections on the Origin and Spread of Nationalism*, London: Verso.

Andrejevic, M. (2006) 'The discipline of watching: Detection, risk, and lateral surveillance', *Critical Studies in Media Communication*, 23(5): 391–407, https://doi.org/10.1080/07393180601046147

Baldassar, L. (2007a) 'Transnational families and aged care: The mobility of care and the migrancy of ageing', *Journal of Ethnic and Migration Studies*, 33(2): 275-297, https://doi.org/10.1080/13691830601154252

Baldassar, L. (2007b) 'Transnational families and the provision of moral and emotional support: The relationship between truth and distance', *Identities: Global Studies in Culture and Power*, 14(4): 385–409, https://doi.org/10.1080/10702890701578423

Baldassar, L. (2016) 'Mobilities and communication technologies: Transforming care in family life', in M. Kilkey and E. Palenga-Möllenbeck (eds) *Family Life in an Age of Migration and Mobility: Global Perspectives through the Life Course*, London: Palgrave Macmillan, pp 19–42.

Baldassar, L. (2017) *The Impact of New Media on Transnational Care: The Century-long Italian–Australian Migrant Case*, Public lecture given at RMIT University, Melbourne, 4 May.

Baumer, E. P., Ames, M. G., Burrell, J., Brubaker, J. R. and Dourish, P. (2015) 'Why study technology non-use?', *First Monday*, 20(11), http://journals.uic.edu/ojs/index.php/fm/article/view/6310/5137

Bell, S. and Coleman, S. (eds) (1999) *The Anthropology of Friendship*, Oxford: Berg.

Burrows, B. (2017) 'YouTube kids: The app economy and mobile parenting', *Social Media & Society*, 3(8): 1–8, https://doi.org/10.1177/2056305117707189

Carsten, J. (2000) '"Knowing where you've come from": Ruptures and continuities of time and kinship in narratives of adoption reunions', *Journal of the Royal Anthropological Institute*, 6(4): 687-703, https://doi.org/10.1111/1467-9655.00040

Carsten, J (2003) *After Kinship*, Cambridge: Cambridge University Press.

Carsten, J. (2007) 'Connections and disconnections of memory and kinship in narratives of adoption reunions in Scotland' in J. Carsten (ed) *Ghosts of Memory: Essays on Remembrance and Relatedness*, Malden, Blackwell, pp 83-103.

Cincotta, K., Ashford, K. and Michael, K. (2011) 'The new privacy predators', *Women's Health*, 11(00), www. purehacking. com/sites/default/files/uploads/2011

City of Melbourne, (2013) 'Census of land use and employment', www.melbourne.vic.gov.au/about-melbourne/research-and-statistics/city-economy/census-land-use-employment/pages/clue-data-and-reports.aspx

Clark, L. S. (2012) *The Parent App: Understanding Families in the Digital Age*, Oxford: Oxford University Press.

Conradson, D. and McKay, D. (2007) 'Translocal subjectivities: Mobility, connection, emotion', *Mobilities*, 2(2): 167-174, https://doi.org/10.1080/17450100701381524

Crawford, C. (2003) '"Sending love in a barrel": The making of transnational Caribbean families in Canada', *Canadian Woman Studies*, 22(3-4): 104-110.

De Souza e Silva, A. and Frith, J. (2012) *Mobile Interfaces in Public Spaces: Locational Privacy, Control, and Urban Sociability*, London: Routledge.

Di Leonardo, M. (1987) 'The female world of cards and holidays: Women, families, and the work of kinship', *Signs: Journal of Women in Culture and Society*, 12(3): 440-453, www.jstor.org/stable/3174331

Dourish, P. and Anderson, K. (2006) 'Collective information practice: Exploring privacy and security as social and cultural phenomena', *Human–Computer Interaction*, 21(3): 319-342, https://doi.org/10.1207/s15327051hci2103_2

Ellison, N. B., Steinfield, C. and Lampe, C. (2007) 'The benefits of Facebook "friends": Social capital and college students' use of online social network sites', *Journal of Computer⬚Mediated Communication*, 12(4): 1143-1168, https://doi.org/10.1111/j.1083-6101.2007.00367.x

Farman, J. (2013) *Mobile Interface Theory: Embodied Space and Locative Media*, London: Routledge.

Gazzard, A. (2011) 'Location, location, location: Collecting space and place in mobile media', *Convergence*, 17(4): 405-417, https://doi.org/10.1177/1354856511414344

Godelier, M. (2012) *The Metamorphosis of Kinship*, London: Verso Books.

Hall, S. (1991) 'Reconstruction work: Images of post-war black settlement', in J. Spence and P. Holland (eds) *Family Snaps: The Meanings of Domestic Photography*, London: Virago, pp 152–164.

Hjorth, L. (2007) 'Snapshots of *almost* contact: The rise of camera phone practices and a case study in Seoul, Korea', *Continuum,* 21(2): 227-238, https://doi.org/10.1080/10304310701278140

Hjorth, L. (2008) 'Being real in the mobile reel: A case study on convergent mobile media as domesticated new media in Seoul, South Korea', *Convergence*, 14(1): 91-104, https://doi.org/10.1177/1354856507084421

Hjorth, L., Richardson, I. and Balmford, W. (2016) 'Careful surveillance and pet wearables: At home with animals', *The Conversation*, 5 September, https://theconversation.com/careful-surveillance-and-pet-wearables-at-home-with-animals-63883

Hjorth, L., Pink, S., Horst, H., Kato, F., Zhou, B., Sinanan, J. and Ohashi, K. (forthcoming) *Locating the Mobile*, New York: Palgrave Macmillan.

Horst, H.A., (2006) 'The blessings and burdens of communication: Cell phones in Jamaican transnational social fields', *Global Networks*, 6(2): 143-159, https://doi.org/10.1111/j.1471-0374.2006.00138.x

Horst, H. A. (2012) 'New media technologies in everyday life', in D. Miller and H. A. Horst (eds) *Digital Anthropology*, Oxford: Berg, pp 61-79.

Horst, H. and Miller, D (2005) 'From kinship to link-up: Cell phones and social networking in Jamaica', *Current Anthropology*, 46(5): 755-778, https://doi.org/10.1086/432650

Joinson, A. N. (2008) 'Looking at, looking up or keeping up with people? Motives and use of Facebook', in *Proceedings of the SIGCHI Conference on Human Factors in Computing Systems*, New York: ACM, pp 1027-1036, https://doi.org/10.1145/1357054.1357213

Leaver, T. (2017) 'Intimate surveillance: Normalizing parental monitoring and mediation of infants online', *Social Media + Society*, 3(2): 1–10, https://doi.org/10.1177/2056305117707192

Lupton, D. and Williamson, B. (2017) 'The datafied child: The dataveillance of children and implications for their rights', *New Media & Society*, 19(5): 780-79, https://doi.org/10.1177/1461444816686328

Lustig, D. F. (2004) 'Baby pictures: Family, consumerism and exchange among teen mothers in the USA', *Childhood, 11(2): 175–193,* https://doi.org/10.1177/0907568204043055

Lynch, K. and McLaughlin, E. (1995) 'Caring labour and love labour', in P. Clancy, S. Drudy, K. Lynch and L. O'Dowd (eds) *Irish Society: Sociological Perspectives*, Dublin: Institute of Public Administration, pp 250–292.

Madianou, M. (2016) 'Ambient co-presence: Transnational family practices in polymedia environments', *Global Networks*, 16(2): 183-201, https://doi.org/10.1111/glob.12105

Madianou, M. (2017) '"Doing family" at a distance: Transnational family practices in polymedia environments', in L. Hjorth, H. A. Horst, A. Galloway and G. Bell (eds) *The Routledge Companion to Digital Ethnography*, New York: Routledge, pp 102-110.

Madianou, M. and Miller, D. (2012) *Migration and New Media*, London: Routledge.

Marwick, A. (2012) 'The public domain: Social surveillance in everyday life', *Surveillance and Society*, 9(4): 378–393, https://ojs. library.queensu.ca/index.php/surveillance-and-society/article/view/ pub_dom/pub_dom

McKay, D. (2007) '"Sending dollars shows feeling" – emotions and economies in Filipino migration', *Mobilities*, 2(2): 175-194, https:// doi.org/10.1080/17450100701381532

Miller, D. (2011) *Tales from Facebook*, Cambridge: Polity.

Morgan, D. (1996) *Family Connections*, Cambridge: Polity.

Nedelcu, M. and Wyss, M. (2016) '"Doing family" through ICT-mediated ordinary co-presence: transnational communication practices of Romanian migrants in Switzerland', *Global Networks*, 16(2): 202-218, https://doi.org/10.1111/glob.12110

Olwig, K. F. (2007) *Caribbean Journeys: An Ethnography of Migration and Home in Three Family Networks*, Durham, NC: Duke University Press.

Pahl, R. (2000) *On Friendship*, Cambridge: Polity.

Peletz, M. G. (1995) 'Kinship studies in late twentieth-century anthropology', *Annual Review of Anthropology*, 24(1): 343-372, www. jstor.org/stable/2155941

Portwood-Stacer, L. (2012) 'Media refusal and conspicuous non-consumption: The performative and political dimensions of Facebook abstention', *New Media & Society*, 15(7): 1041-1057, https://doi. org/10.1177/1461444812465139

Prøitz, L. (2007) *The Mobile Phone Turn: A Study of Gender, Sexuality and Subjectivity in Young People's Mobile Phone Practices*, PhD thesis, University of Oslo: Faculty of Humanities Unipub, www.duo. uio.no/bitstream/handle/10852/27243/NY_314_Proitz_hele. pdf?sequence=2

Sengupta, S. (2012) '"Big brother"? No, it's parents', *New York Times*, 25 June, http://tinyurl.com/aysm5ud

Tokunaga, R. S. (2011) 'Social networking site or social surveillance site? Understanding the use of interpersonal electronic surveillance in romantic relationships', *Computers in Human Behavior*, 27(2): 705–713, https://doi.org/10.1016/j.chb.2010.08.014

Wajcman, J., Bittman, M. and Brown, J. (2008) 'Families without borders: Mobile phones, connectedness and work–home divisions', *Sociology*, 41(4): 635–652.

Wilding, R. (2007) 'Transnational ethnographies and anthropological imaginings of migrancy', *Journal of Ethnic and Migration Studies*, 33(2): 331–348, https://doi.org/10.1080/13691830601154310

Wilding, R. (2017) '*Multimedia, Mobility and the Digital Southeast Asian Family*', Workshop held at LaTrobe University, Melbourne, 20 April to 21 April, www.latrobe.edu.au/__data/assets/pdf_file/0007/792367/Multimedia-Workshop-Abstracts-FINAL.pdf

Wilken, R. (2012) 'Locative media: From specialized preoccupation to mainstream fascination', *Convergence*, 18(3): 243–247, https://doi.org/10.1177/1354856512444375

Wilken, R. and Goggin, G. (eds) (2015) *Locative Media*, London: Routledge.

Yeates, N. (2004) 'Global care chains', *International Feminist Journal of Politics*, 6(3): 369–391, https://doi.org/10.1080/1461674042000235573

ELEVEN

Floating narratives: transnational families and digital storytelling

Catalina Arango Patiño

Introduction

According to the United Nations Population Fund (UNFPA, no date), in 2015 '3.3% of the world's population lived outside their country of origin'. This figure points to a large number of families on the move, a flux of volatile interactions, and a network of long-distance communications. Colombians are part of this phenomenon. Colombian migrations coincided with the outbreak of civil war, neoliberal reforms imposed by the government, and the growth of drug trafficking that started in the 1960s and which worsened throughout the 1980s and 1990s. The most recent wave of migration out of Colombia is ongoing and is largely comprised of people with high levels of education, and those from marginalized sectors of Colombian society. According to the Global Knowledge Partnership on Migration and Development more than 2.5 million Colombians (5.19% of the country's total population) lived abroad in 2013 (KNOMAD, 2016).

Several analyses have examined the political, economic, and social impacts of this mobility for Colombia and Colombians (see, for example, Ciurlo, 2012; Cárdenas and Mejía, 2006; Colombia Nos Une, 2004). Others have examined transformations of inner structures, roles, and dynamics of families within the context of Colombian international migration activities (Rivas Rivas and Gonzálvez Torralbo, 2009; Ciurlo, 2012). However, the relationship between information and communication technologies (ICTs) and storytelling as a practice of communication within transnational Colombian families remains relatively unstudied.

The argument advanced in this chapter is rooted in the idea that family is a social system in which individuals redefine their bonds through their own interactions (Turner and West, 2002). It follows, therefore, that through narratives, stories, and the practice of storytelling

201

itself families find ways to account, share, redefine and transform their own experiences. This perspective is anchored in a symbolic interaction approach to understanding family communication, and the notion of social construction, which views families as co-constructing their social realities through interactions and conversations. It also recognizes that families of immigrants experience a diasporic state of mind (Vertovec, 1997) while practising transnational interactions and building transnational social fields (Roudometof, 2005). The definition of transnational families adopted in this chapter draws from Bryceson and Vuorela's (2002, p 3) description of these families as collective entities who, despite living at a distance, remain linked while building some sort of 'collective welfare and unity' that helps them navigate between different national borders.

To date, analyses of family storytelling as a communication practice have been largely limited to 'traditional' moments in which families communicate, such as everyday face-to-face conversations (DeRoche, 1996), dinnertime conversations (Blum-Kulka, 1997), and special events in which traditional stories are shared (Marvin, 2004). We seek to interrogate a somewhat different landscape. When transnational families engage in processes of communication using ICTs, they seemingly traverse intricate domains of social engagement. In this context, oral language is important, but it is not the sole manner by which family narrates itself. Other modes of communication come into play, including online chats, videos, emoticons, audio messages, and digital photos. Voice is only one part of the multimodal constellation of available communication resources at one's disposal. Hence, a concern with technological affordances constitutes a core element of the analysis presented here.

The concept of affordances offers a means of understanding technologies 'as artifacts which may be both shaped by and shaping of the practices humans use in interaction with, around and through them' (Hutchby, 2001, p 441). Three technological affordances are linked to digital storytelling practices of the Colombian families described below. The first is *presence*. It is understood as the '"illusion of nonmediation" [that] occurs when a person fails to perceive or acknowledge the existence of a medium and responds as he/she would if the medium were not there' (Lombard and Ditton, 1997, np). The second is *interactivity*. It occurs when the perceptor is no longer mute because they also interpret, participate, interact, become the emitter, and create their own messages (Brea, 2007). The third affordance is *multimodality*. It refers to the incorporation of a variety of multimodal compositions and formats such as voice, music, text, graphics, and still or moving images into communicative processes (Lundby, 2008; also see Rowsell, 2013; Kress, 2010).

In helping individuals overcome the communicative barriers created by vast geographical distances, ICTs seemingly provide the social space where members of transnational families can maintain their communication as well as explore diverse modes and interactive alternatives to express their affection and common history. Storytelling, then, emerges as a crucial nexus at which families create and recreate themselves and their realities. The pervasiveness of transnational family storytelling in online spaces raises questions about the ways in which these narratives are created using digital processes, and whether and how family stories might be changing. With this in mind, a central question arising in this context is: How do ICTs catalyse and/or constrain storytelling within transnational families?

The discussion that follows consists of three main parts. The first presents the methodological approach employed to undertake the research study and the techniques used to collect and analyse the data. The second outlines the findings obtained during the fieldwork portion of the study. The third part summarizes the overall findings and offers an answer to the research question.

The method at hand

Studying Colombian transnational families is relevant to the analysis of family storytelling and transnational interactions in two ways. First, Colombia leads the World Bank's rankings of emigration among South American countries (2013 data), and is the top source of refugees (2014 data) from South America (KNOMAD, 2016). Tracking the consequences of mobile lifestyles at micro levels (that is, familial realms) contributes to understanding the new social meanings and interactions Colombians are building. Second, Colombian families seem to have a particular feature that facilitates the task of studying familial digital communication. According to Puyana et al (2009, p 103), Colombians have a social representation of themselves that is based on the 'familyhood' (*familismo* in Spanish). This is the tendency to idealize family as the only centre of emotional life. It follows, as a guiding assumption, that this sense of *familismo* most likely fosters frequent interactions at a distance among Colombian transnational family members that, in turn, encourages the practice of digital storytelling.

Six Colombian families with members in Montreal and Colombia took part in the empirical component of this study. Twelve adults based in Montreal and six who are based in Colombia, for a total of 18 participants. These participants comprised a convenience sample, where 'the researcher simply selects the cases that are at hand until the sample reaches a desired, designated size' (Powell and Connaway, 2004, p 68). This technique is particularly appropriate for research in which a lack of official records makes the studied population difficult to find and access (Weiss, 1994); which is the case when it comes to examining Colombian migrants. It must be noted, however, that convenience sampling cannot claim to be representative of the general population.

Two principal criteria for inclusion in the study were used, both of which were rooted in the definition of transnational families: (i) that the participant families maintain regular ICT-mediated communication through either computers or mobile phones; and (ii) that the families consume both Colombian and Canadian media, and/or retain working/academic ties with Colombia while living in Canada, and/or keep connected with friends and colleagues in Colombia, and/or maintain Colombian cultural (for example, food, music, literature) habits while incorporating new ones based on the new experiences in Canada, and/or frequently feel 'here and there'.

In order to collect the data required to answer the central research question, a series of in-depth, open-ended interviews were conducted with members of the participant families during August and September 2015. The confidentiality and anonymity of the participants were protected by the use of pseudonyms: Family A, G, L, R, S, and Z. Three members of each family participated in this study. They were named using a corresponding number: M1, 2, or 3 (1 being the Colombia-based member of the family). Once the interviews had been completed, three families spontaneously, and at their own behest, granted me access to their intimate familial digital interactions. Upon completion of the interview with the members of Family Z, these individuals carried on a Skype-based family conversation that they permitted me to observe. This post-interview sharing of stories lasted for approximately two hours. Two other families, L and R, gave me access to their respective families' WhatsApp chat groups for a period of one week, following the interview. The impromptu observations arising from these activities lacked the methodological rigour of formal ethnographic participant observation. Nonetheless, the information gleaned was a natural complement to the information gathered from the interviews.

The process of data analysis started with setting out the initial topics of discussion that, in turn, were key to creating the interview guide. Upon completing the interviews, the field notes from the informal observations and the recorded interviews were transcribed in their original language (Spanish) and then qualitatively analysed. Then, an additional reading of the transcripts was completed, looking for recurrent issues. The idea of finding recurrent issues is based on *open coding* and refers to the process of generating categories and properties for texts such as interview transcripts (Yin, 2011). The focus here was on identifying recurring common statements, ideas, phrases, and/or words expressed by the interviewees. Later, the recurrent common statements were reviewed to identify additional constituent elements relating to these issues such as the use of specific examples, cases or facts.

After visualizing the recurrent issues and the constituent elements, all the coded material was reviewed, looking for relational elements that can be understood as linkages among recurrent issues and constituent elements. This is known as *axial coding* (Yin, 2011). It is the process in which 'categories are systematically developed and linked with subcategories'. In other words, this was a process of contextualization: connecting and reconnecting, establishing relationships between different practices, constructing 'systems' out of ways of doing things that make sense only in relation to each other (Ferguson, 2011, p 198).

Digital storytelling within transnational families

The discussion presented in this section sets out the views of the participant families regarding the dynamics of their post-migration storytelling experiences, and is divided into four parts. The first examines the emerging polymedia environment (that is, the constellation of multiple devices and digital platforms that these families are building). This is followed by a discussion of the participant's perspectives about being present during their digital interactions, the possible creation of a liminal space (that is, a space 'in-between' that is not limited by geography), and how a contradictory sense of presence seems to exist among several family members. We then turn our attention to the ways in which family members navigate their communicative activities across platforms and stories, and the new modes by which stories are shared by the participant families.

Tech-linked

All participants reported using an array of communication platforms to engage in cross-border familial communication, including internet- and mobile phone-based platforms such as instant messaging (IM), social networking sites (SNS) and webcam via voice over internet protocol (VoIP). In other words, they talk, see, text, and send photos and videos to family members using diverse devices (computers and mobile phones) and platforms (more often WhatsApp, telephone by pre-paid cards and internet home phone, and Skype; less frequently Facebook, Facetime, and Viper). In so doing they are seemingly creating a polymedia environment (Madianou and Miller, 2012).

Although no specific questions about processes of domestication were posed during the interview sessions, and the members of the participant families did not explicitly articulate their experiences in this regard, the adoption and integration of ICTs into familial communicative activities implies a process in which these devices were brought home and embraced as part of the family dynamic. Expounding on this type of experience Family A, Member 1 described his family's experience as follows:

> 'We have lived through a time of change, but it feels that the change happened overnight. In the 1970s, D's grandfather and three of his aunts went to live in New York. Back then our communication was by letters. It was a little monthly letter that everyone expected to arrive. When D emigrated, our communication was based on a single phone call every Saturday. We got ready for that call and the rest of the week we had no contact. However, nowadays ... having this sort of communication via these very advanced texts and video platforms is a comfort, a cheer, a delight. You have to consider that now we have the other person on the other side of the screen, so close and so instant.'

Different devices, platforms, and apps have and are constantly being tested, used, and in some cases dismissed. This process of exploration seemingly enables some participant family members (mostly the younger ones) to reach an understanding of the apparent advantages and disadvantages of different technologies in relation to their respective familial communication practices. The diversity of perspectives reported aligns with Wilding's (2006, p 134) claim that ICTs are not all '"sunny day" technologies'. All interviewees suggested that the platforms they use shape their conversations and processes of storytelling.

WhatsApp. Eleven members of the participant families reported using WhatsApp as one of their main applications for communicating at a distance. There was a pervasive sense that WhatsApp reminds them of their conversations when they were in Colombia. Instant, handy, informal, easy to use, are qualities the interviewees attributed to this app. Moreover, it is precisely these qualities that the interviewees reported as enabling them to have constant and simultaneous communication with many members of their respective families.

Telephone. As reported by seven members of the participant families, telephone has always been there; mostly in the initial years of their migration when Internet was not as easy to access as it is now. In fact, two participants reported using only telephone because their parents do not have the technological skills to deal with other platforms. These two interviewees recognized that communication by telephone is limited because it is strictly restricted to the voice and there is no further exploration of other modes such as nonverbal expressions or images. Despite its inherent limitations, Family L – Member 1 reported feeling more comfortable using the telephone than any other platform, "The phone makes me go back in time when they were here, three blocks away."

Skype. The interviewees' perspectives about VoIP platforms were contradictory. The main point of contention centred on whether the use of Skype increases loneliness or facilitates having conversations that are sensorily expanded. Two interviewees expressed views supporting the former and six advocated for the latter. Expressing the loneliness view, Family L, Member 1 pointed out:

> 'I know that everyone is crazy about Skype saying that it is great. I have a colleague whose daughter is in Atlanta and has one-year-old twins. She gets connected every day at 5 p.m. and she sees the children ... I am not satisfied with that. I am not satisfied with the ritual of seeing them, no, I am more of, being there physically, not being there technologically.'

In contrast to this view, members of Family S spoke of the intimacy-enhancing qualities of both Skype- and Xbox-based familial communications.

Member 1:	'Skype, video is more practical. You can see the expression of the other and be in the context of the story.'
Member 2:	'I have Skype in my Xbox and 90% of the times when we talk we are sitting on the couch and it is

more familiar, yes, more private, more like being at home… They can see everything because the camera moves if I move. It is a different experience. I like it better.'

Their storytelling now: all about being present

During the interview sessions, it quickly became apparent that for all the members of five participant families communication via ICTs means staying in touch to share daily life. The members of the sixth family, L, reported using ICTs only to inform each other about the latest events. To this end, the members of five participant families reported that, in their exchanges, family members cook, eat, do household chores, help each other with homework, or play with the kids together.

Family Z, Member 2: 'I talk to my mom as if we were in her kitchen.'
Family Z, Member 1: 'Oh yes, yes. What happens is that they have never left. They are here…'
Family Z, Member 2: 'In other words, when we talk, we are so connected that we have conversations such as the ones we used to have. The same fluidity, the same detail, as if we were there…'

The communication experiences outlined above seemingly echo Peñaranda Cólera's (2010) notion of transnational coexistence insofar as the interviewees' comments allude to experiencing technological proximity and connected presence. Two aspects of this transnational coexistence are pertinent to the discussion: the creation of a liminal space and a contradictory sense of presence.

First, the analysis of data reveals an apparent creation of a liminal space, a space in between, both here and there. Upon completion of the interview with Family Z, its members spontaneously granted access to a Skype-based family conversation. At one point in this conversation, Family Z's three-year-old daughter was playing in the living room. Suddenly, in Colombia, her little cousin approached the camera and said hello. Back in Montreal, the daughter ran towards the computer to say hello as well. The cousin said "A long-distance hug!!!" They moved closer to each other and each of them hugged the computer.

In the light of the spontaneous practices of the little girls from Family Z, it seems plausible that for these individuals, at least, the concept of distance needs to be re-conceptualized. Caron and Caronia's (2007) concept of delocalization, or the notion that space is becoming mobile, seems latent in the dynamics of daily communication of these interview participants. When Family Z's daughter and her cousin hug each other virtually, they seem to be neither here nor there. For a short instance of spontaneous becoming these two children were in an ephemeral space in which they could be together.

The information emerging from the interviews with members of five participant families suggests that concepts such as far and close, here and there, are somewhat fluid for these individuals. They each maintained that although home is in Montreal, when they engage with distant family members via platforms such as WhatsApp and Skype, the reach of their home seemingly expands beyond a particular edifice in a particular location. Indeed, the views expressed by these individuals imply that, for them, home is transformed to include phenomenological experiences that can be extended to other spheres where feelings of safety, trust, freedom, community, and love also reside.

Another noteworthy aspect of this apparent liminal space is that all members from four of the participant families (A, L, R, and Z) reported that their current conversations and storytelling have somehow been altered after relatives living in Montreal have returned to Colombia for vacation or relatives living in Colombia have visited Montreal.

These interviewees seemingly evoke/relive/recreate the spaces where they had lived or visited when engaging in digitally mediated conversations at a distance. Their responses suggest a distinction between the imagined space (that is, the one that their relatives have described and explained but which the interviewees have never actually lived in and/or visited) and the evoked space (that is, the space that after being lived in and/or visited is recalled and relived by memories and stories). Bringing the evoking space into the conversation seems to invigorate the practice of storytelling among members of the participant families. Space, in other words, becomes alive: rooms may be re-occupied by recalling their smells, places may be gone over by bringing back memories and stories. In fact, the manner in which these individuals describe their technologically mediated long-distance communication practices resonates with Lombard and Ditton's (1997) notion of presence as transportation insofar as they are able to move from here to there and vice versa.

Second, the analysis reveals that a contradictory sense of presence is also latent within the participant families. Among the views expressed by members of the five families that identified as having experienced transnational coexistence, two contending perspectives emerged. The first, shared by 12 individuals, views ICTs as bridges connecting here and there. To this end, they reported frequently forgetting they are using a technological device to communicate and that they get lost in their memories and stories. In other words, Lombard and Ditton's (1997, p 9) 'the perceptual illusion of nonmediation' is a characteristic of their long-distance communicative practices with other family members.

One member of Family A, another from Family Z, along with Family L, Member 1, shared an opposing view. These three individuals expressed sensing a high level of disconnection from their families and the situations they are experiencing together when using ICTs to communicate at a distance. They reported not being able to let themselves succumb to the illusion of nonmediation. Instead, they remain keenly aware of the technical features of the devices mediating their long-distance communicative exchanges. Some of the issues they identified included the distortion/lack of sound or video, interferences, the speed of the internet connection, and a heightened sense of loneliness once the webcam is turned off.

Their narratives now: extractive interactivity

When describing the dynamics of their post-migration digital communication, ten members from five of the participant families reported frequently having multiple ongoing WhatsApp chats. These individuals stated that they created family chats to share news about the kids, family updates, and future plans.

The comments of these ten participants suggest that they segment their audiences into different chat groups in accordance with who is on the other side (that is, siblings, parents, cousins, aunts, and so on). It seems plausible therefore that narratives and stories are iteratively constructed and dispersed across different chat groups. In order to create a complete landscape of their families' narratives, members must seemingly gather each story, quilt them together in narratives, and create meaning from them all in a permanent ongoing conversation. This dynamic appears to align with Lunenfeld's (1999) notion of *extractive interactivity* insofar as the comments and observations of these interviewees suggest that they get involved in processes of non-stop 'hypertextual navigation' in which they search and create their family narratives by elaborating their own hypertexts and stitching together multiple stories.

All members of the participant families pointed out that their family narratives are seemingly rooted in numerous interwoven storylines that individuals consume and construct in putting together various story-related elements involving chat texts, videos, photos, and/or live exchanges. This individual work seemingly empowers each participant in the elaboration of family narratives while simultaneously giving rise to certain challenges. For instance, Family A, Member 2 and Family L, Member 2 noted that they each often receive WhatsApp texts from family members during their office hours, which they frequently decided to ignore. This failure to engage is sometimes a source of confusion with regard to the stories being told.

Likewise, members of Families A, G, and S mentioned that not every member of their respective families has the same technical abilities, which sometimes leads to their digitally mediated familial communications being constrained. This observation echoes the notion of digital divides (Paré, 2005; Paré and Smeltzer, 2013), especially regarding the importance of technological proficiency levels for facilitating family members accessing, searching, processing, using, and giving meaning to digital content. This raises the possibility that a lack of technological abilities may prevent some members from accessing all stories, creating new narratives, and/or being active participants in the digitally mediated storytelling activities of their respective families.

Their stories now: a multimodal transformation

According to all members of the participant families, when they were living in Colombia, family stories were mainly conveyed orally. In other words, verbal and nonverbal language were the main modes in face-to-face conversations. By contrast, all of the interviewees acknowledged that engaging in the sharing of photos, texts, emoticons, animations, graphic images such as memes, audio messages, and videos via WhatsApp have become commonplace in their post-migration communicative practices.

Families L and R both gave me access to their families' WhatsApp chat groups for a period of one week following the initial interview. The observations garnered from examining these exchanges sheds some light on the use of new modes during the digitally mediated conversations of these two families. One of the immediately noticeable aspects of these exchanges is that the messages in these chats are built using a common code that external observers are unlikely to fully understand. The participants in the exchanges frequently mentioned nicknames that give an intimate tone to the conversation. In addition, the participants share encrypted jokes whose meaning apparently evokes a complex history of offline conversations and previous encounters and experiences.

The creation of a shared code in these two families' WhatsApp chats can be seen as the way members of these particular families weave their narratives. These texts are an open door to other times and spaces in which the chat participants lived common experiences. Words and emoticons are not only online acts of communication but also portals to offline events that are continuously re-created and retold. In other words, it seems plausible that in this case texts can be considered as evocative stories that create a *cadavre exquis* (that is, a collection of words and images), an amalgam of memories and reminiscences that locate words beyond the chat, giving them a hypertextual character connected to alternative times and social spaces – evocative stories that shape a narrative that only those families can understand.

As the analysis of the chat logs revealed, each member of the six participant families reported sending photos and commenting them via WhatsApp. One particularly noteworthy facet of storytelling regarding family photos takes place when the photos are seen again at some future time. The observations of two interviewees from Family L are illustrative of this experience:

Member 2:   'Nowadays, sharing photos prevails. My mom, aunts, uncles, brother-and-sisters-in-laws, my parents-in-laws are carrying a photo, a video, or an audio of my kids all the time, although they do not live together.'

Member 1:   'It is true. Now I enjoy myself watching the pictures they send me… I show them to my co-workers, to my sister, to my mother-in-law… I tell them their stories.'

These responses seemingly resonate with Baldassar's (2008) suggestion that photos can become transnational objects embodying those who are somehow away. It is possible that the tangibility of these photos connects the one that keeps and re-sees them to the real body of the absent individual and conducts a sense of proximity. Further, the ways in which the interview participants reported treasuring, archiving, reusing and reliving photos, seem to support Sontag's (1990) claim that photographs are a way of imprisoning an inaccessible or remote reality, not only to reproduce the real but also to recycle it, create new usages, and assign new meanings.

An additional exploratory hypothesis that can be drawn is that, beyond their attributes as technical objects, photographs are complemented by a collective process of fluctuating meanings that allow them to be filled with stories. This may account for why these families discuss their photos; photos are sent to be seen, talked about, listened to, and, frequently, re-narrated. In this collective process of meaning-making, photos are likely to be touched and influenced by the one that sends them, the one that organizes and archives them, the one that narrates them, the one that re-sees them. In sum, it is in the act of mixing images with words, memories, pieces of the present, and family meanings that photographs seem to compile multiple modes of expression.

Conclusion

This chapter has examined the technologically mediated communication and digital storytelling practices of six Colombian families who immigrated to Canada in recent years. The starting point was the idea that emigrants may experience diaspora as a state of mind and transnationalism as a way of interacting, and use storytelling as the intersection to create and recreate themselves. The evidence presented suggests that the routine and consistent use of ICTs among the participant families influences in myriad ways how their respective members define stories, create narratives, as well as the practice of storytelling itself.

Exploring how different members of transnational families embrace and use ICTs during processes of migration becomes relevant to family and life course studies because it offers clues about the ways members of different ages experience and access technology. Parents, children, and relatives give meaning to digital contents depending on how they live the illusion of presence and engage with an orchestration of multimodal expressions. Likewise, members of transnational families expand their participation in processes of digital storytelling depending on their technological abilities and adaptability. These processes shed light on family interactions that occur in digital environments where space, time, and affection can transform their definition.

The views reported by one group of participant family members ($N = 12$) suggest that their storytelling processes are catalysed by ICTs in situations where presence is experienced and/or new multimodal forms of communication are explored. These individuals view the applications and platforms as both bridges connecting 'here with there' and as creating liminal social spaces for exchanging stories and narratives. Their physical space is seemingly transformed when family members admit one another into their homes via ICTs despite their bodies being miles away. The participants for whom the illusion of nonmediation, or presence, is activated report enjoying dinners together, throwing parties, celebrating traditions, and having intimate conversations while some family members are here and others are there. They appear to be able to connect themselves with the flux of stories while reliving some of the moments they, as families, treasure the most. According to the views expressed by these individuals, the recreation of familial moments and events via digital applications and platforms is particularly easy for younger members, who seem to adapt faster to technological environments.

The observations of the participant family members within this 'ICTs as catalyst' group also suggest that multimodality informs their storytelling practices. The information gathered from the interviews suggests that their family stories (i) now involve collective meanings created by everyone; (ii) reflect a shared code (that is, something that only the family can understand); and (iii) involve new modes of expression and representation beyond verbal language and face-to-face interaction. For these participants, technologically mediated communicative exchanges contribute to the creation of new kinds of stories that are nourished by the mundane character of the transnational coexistence these families experience.

The views expressed by a second, smaller, group of participants ($N = 6$) points to the potential for technological mediation to constrain family storytelling, especially in situations where ICTs are seen to disrupt the connection between 'here and there' and/or when extractive interactivity cannot be practised by everyone. Interviewees who reported viewing technology as an obstacle to interpersonal communication and who refute the possibility of an illusion of nonmediation perceive digital communicative applications and platforms as constraints on familial storytelling. This is where different roles, positions, meanings, and contexts over a family member's life span seem to make a difference in the way digital storytelling is experienced. For these individuals, the physical distance separating them from loved ones is like an abyss that impedes any sense of direct connection. While recognizing ICTs as key mediums for communication with their family members, technological malfunctions such as noise, interference, slow connection, and poor-quality video are constant reminders of physical separation. Although most of the participants' parents who remain in Colombia have apparently adapted well to the use of ICTs, half of them reported experiencing a heightened sense of loneliness when long-distance VoIP-based conversations come to an end and Skype is switched off. They also are unable to set aside the impossibility of touch, and/or the lack of depth in WhatsApp-based conversations with family members. Further, a strong sense of nostalgia pervaded their responses insofar as they reported missing the physical presence of their family member, preferring face-to-face conversations above virtual interactions. For these individuals, stories and narratives lose their spontaneity, natural warmness, and closeness when they are mediated by technology.

They also point out that the process of having to build multiple narratives across different applications and platforms (that is, extractive interactivity), entails a heightened level of effort that can be interrupted for any number of reasons which, in turn, risks rendering family narratives incomplete or otherwise unfinished. Equally problematic in their view is the diverse range of technical competencies and skills within families, with some individuals (elderly members) often feeling overwhelmed by the fast pace of technological change. This, in turn, raises the possibility of in-family segregation with regard to awareness of ongoing familial stories.

In summary, the findings reported in this chapter suggest that technological mediation is indeed shaping family storytelling insofar as ICTs appear to be facilitating new modes of expression as well as catalysing and supporting the creation of liminal spaces. However, common narratives are not equally grasped by all individuals because technological skills, adaptability, and context have an important influence on the ways in which individual family members connect and transform their digital stories.

In brief

1. Findings suggest that concepts such as far and near, here and there, are somewhat fluid for the participant families. When communicating with distant family members via ICTs, the reach of their home seemingly expands beyond a physical location.

2. Participants apparently get themselves involved in processes of non-stop 'hypertextual navigation' or extractive interactivity in which they search and create their family narratives by elaborating their own hypertexts and stitching together multiple stories.

3. All interviewees acknowledged that engaging in the sharing of photos, texts, emoticons, animations, graphic images such as memes, audio messages, and videos via WhatsApp have become commonplace in their communicative practices since migration. It has become a multimodal exploration.

4. The findings suggest that technological mediation is indeed shaping family storytelling. A group of 12 participants suggests that ICTs *catalyse* storytelling in situations where presence and multimodality is experienced.

5. Six participants say that ICTs *constrain* family storytelling when the illusion of nonmediation does not take place. They also claim that building multiple narratives across different platforms entails a heightened level of technological skills that not all members possess.

References

Baldassar, L. (2008) 'Missing kin and longing to be together: Emotions and the construction of co-presence in transnational relationships', *Journal of Intercultural Studies*, 29(3): 247–266, https://doi.org/10.1080/07256860802169196

Blum-Kulka, S. (1997) *Dinner Talk: Cultural Patterns of Sociability and Socialization in Family Discourse*, Mahwah, NJ: L. Erlbaum.

Brea, J. (2007) *Cultura_Ram. Mutaciones de la cultura en la era de su distribución electrónica,* Barcelona: Editorial Gedisa.

Bryceson, D. F. and Vuorela, U. (2002) *The Transnational Family: New European Frontiers and Global Networks*, Oxford: Berg.

Cárdenas, M. and Mejía, C. (2006) 'Migraciones internacionales en Colombia: ¿Qué sabemos?', Repositorio Institucional Fedesarrollo, www.repository.fedesarrollo.org.co/handle/11445/810

Caron, A. H. and Caronia, L. (2007) *Moving Cultures: Mobile Communication in Everyday Life*, Montréal: McGill-Queen's University Press.

Ciurlo, A. (2012) *Migración colombiana hacia Italia: un estudio exploratorio y de género sobre las familias trasnacionales*, www.cestim.it/sezioni/tesi/tesi_ciurlo_migracion_colombiana_hacia_itala_2012_2v.pdf

Colombia Nos Une. (2004) *Memorias Seminario sobre migración internacional colombiana y la conformación de comunidades transnacionales*, Bogotá: Ministerio de Relaciones Exteriores, http://repository.oim.org.co/bitstream/20.500.11788/211/1/COL-OIM%200076%202003.pdf

DeRoche, C. (1996) '"I learned things today that I never knew before": Oral history at the kitchen table', *Special Section: Immigrant Women. The Oral History Review*, 23(2): 45–61, https://doi.org/10.1093/ohr/23.2.45

Ferguson, J. (2011) 'Novelty and method reflections on global fieldwork', in S. Coleman and P. Von Hellermann (eds) *Multi-sited Ethnography: Problems and Possibilities in the Translocation of Research Methods*, New York: Routledge, pp 194–207.

Hutchby, I (2001) 'Technologies, texts and affordances', *Sociology*, 35(2): 441–456, www.jstor.org/stable/42856294

KNOMAD (2016) *Migration and Remittances Factbook*, World Bank Group, http://siteresources.worldbank.org/INTPROSPECTS/Resources/334934-1199807908806/4549025-1450455807487/Factbookpart1.pdf

Kress, G. (2010) *Multimodality: A Social Semiotic Approach to Contemporary Communication*, London: Routledge.

Lombard, M. and Ditton, T. (1997) 'At the heart of it all: The concept of presence', *Journal of Computer-Mediated Communication*, 3(2), https://doi.org/10.1111/j.1083-6101.1997.tb00072.x

Lundby, K. (2008) 'Introduction: Digital storytelling, mediatized stories', in K. Lundby (ed) *Digital Storytelling, Mediatized Stories: Self-representations in New Media*, New York: P. Lang, pp 1-17.

Lunenfeld, P. (1999) *Digital Dialectics. New Essays on New Media*, Cambridge, MA: MIT Press.

Madianou, M. and Miller, D. (2012) *Migration and New Media: Transnational Families and Polymedia*, Abingdon: Routledge.

Marvin, L. (2004) 'Why Mamiji cried: Telling stories and defining families', *Storytelling, Self, Society*, 1(1): 28-43, www.jstor.org/stable/41948943

Paré, D. (2005) 'The digital divide: Why the "the" is misleading', in A. Murray and M. Klang (eds) *Human Rights in the Digital Age*, London: Cavendish Publishing, pp 85-97.

Paré, D. and Smeltzer, S. (2013) 'ICTs as a catalyst for social justice? A capabilities perspective', in S. Ilcan (ed) *Mobilities, Knowledge, and Social Justice*, Montreal: McGill-Queens University Press, pp 320-339.

Peñaranda Cólera, M. (2010) '"Te escuchas aquí al lado". Usos de las tecnologías de información y la comunicación en contextos migratorios transnacionales', *Athenea Digital. Revista de pensamiento e investigación social*, 0(19): 239-248, https://doi.org/10.5565/rev/athenead/v0n19.787

Powell, R. and Connaway, L. S. (2004) *Basic Research Methods for Librarians*, Westport, CT: Libraries Unlimited.

Puyana, Y., Motoa, J. and Viviel, A. (2009) *Entre aquí y allá. Las familias colombianas transnacionales*, Bogotá: Fundación Esperanza.

Rivas Rivas, A. and Gonzálvez Torralbo, A. (2009) *Familias transnacionales colombianas. Transformaciones y permanencias en las relaciones familiares y de género*, www.reduniversitaria.es/ficheros/Familias%20transnacionales.pdf

Roudometof, V. (2005) 'Transnationalism, cosmopolitanism, and glocalization', *Current Sociology*, 53(1): 113-135, https://doi.org/10.1177/0011392105048291

Rowsell, J. (2013) *Working with Multimodality: Rethinking Literacy in a Digital Age*, London: Routledge.

Sontag, S. (1990) *On Photography*, New York, Toronto: Anchor Books.

Turner, L. H. and West, R. (2002) *Perspectives on Family Communication*, Boston: McGraw Hill.

United Nations Population Fund (UNFPA) (no date), http://www.unfpa.org/migration

Vertovec, S. (1997) 'Three meanings of diaspora. Exemplified among South Asian religions', *Diaspora: A Journal of Transnational Studies*, 6(3): 277-299, https://doi.org/10.1353/dsp.1997.0010

Weiss, R. (1994) *Learning from Strangers: The Art and Method of Qualitative Interview Studies,* New York: Maxwell Macmillan International.

Wilding, R. (2006) 'Virtual intimacies? Families communicating across transnational contexts', *Global Networks*, 6(2): 125-142, https://doi.org/10.1111/j.1471-0374.2006.00137.x

Yin, R. (2011) *Qualitative Research from Start to Finish*, New York: Guilford Press.

TWELVE

Rescue chains and care talk among immigrants and their left-behind parents

Sondra Cuban

Introduction

I introduce a new framework that focuses on the communication developed by immigrants living in the United States to care for their aged left-behind parents and grandparents through information and communication technologies (ICTs). Their care was captured through communication chains they developed to rescue these family members who had health problems associated with ageing. These parents and grandparents, living in their natal countries, and their adult children residing abroad engaged in a type of talk through ICTs that was characterized by protecting, providing, and proving that the care was valued. The stories of ten participants are illuminated through a methodology that engages qualitative understandings of the complexity of long-distance care communication. These stories emerged from a study of 60 immigrant women from various countries living and working in Washington State and their communication with their left-behind families (Cuban, 2017). The parents, mostly in their late 60s and older had various problems associated with ageing, including dementia, vision loss, prostate problems, mobility difficulties, and falling injuries, as well as chronic diseases such as diabetes that had taken a toll over a long lifetime, with the participants struggling to care for them while abroad. Additionally, a number of these parents were impoverished and lived in rural areas, such as Oaxaca, where there was a lack of health and medical care services, transportation, and resources, as well as communications infrastructure. I started my research on this particular problem with the following questions: To what degree do family members care for one another through ICTs across the life course and with special attention to health problems associated with ageing? What are the issues involved in communicating about this care? While the most recent literature (Baldassar, 2016; Madianou, 2016) demonstrates that non-proximate care within transnational families shows bonding from abroad, the focus has been on the ICTs themselves. I argue that the exchange of transnational care between separated family members is contingent not only on the ICTs, but the talk with which the family members engage at a distance. ICTs in and of themselves do not and cannot deliver care, bond relations or families and due to their architecture are severely limited. Yet in the literature, it would appear that it is the technology platforms and applications that make long-distance connections possible rather than transnational family members and their uses of ICTs.

I therefore draw on an expanded definition of ICTs to illustrate how technologies are subject to gendered and privileged notions. My definition draws from the field of migration studies and includes a wider range of technologies, new and old, and differs from ICT terms used within the computer science and IT fields. For example, long-distance and fixed/landline telephones as well as mobile telephones have often been considered a softer 'pedestrian' and feminized form of communication compared to the more masculinized internet (Panangokos and Horst, 2006). The digital literacy literature does not pay enough attention to phone calls even though it is the most popular form of communication worldwide (Madianou, 2015). The phone call has been a 'victim of its success… suffering the fate of those unobtrusive every day objects and practices that get overlooked because of their ordinariness' (Kenning, 2007, p 172). Moreover, excluding phone calls (via landline telephones) would mean not including marginalized groups in society, especially poor, older, and rural users, often women who cannot afford the internet infrastructure or more sophisticated telecommunications networks in low-income as well as high-income countries. Mirca Madianou (2015, p 2) states that research that excludes populations that cannot or do not use social media and the internet contributes to 'social inequalities'. Therefore, this study, in focusing on the 'talk' between immigrants and left-behind older members, highlights how digital inequalities inherent in ICT usage and social inequalities go hand in hand to affect long-distance care provision.

The stories of ten participants demonstrate the tensions they experienced resulting from communicating about care for ageing parents in poor health. Julieta's story illustrates these complex issues.

Julieta

Julieta migrated from Oaxaca, Mexico to California "through the desert and with no papers" 14 years ago to join her siblings and work in the fields. After getting married she moved to rural Washington, where she had four children. Using phone cards she bought from the local Mexican store, she called her family in Mexico once a week "to know how they are doing, to help them". Mainly she spoke to her mother whose health problems required medical attention. She had a serious case of kidney stones, and due to knee problems she was unable to move around much. These problems were compounded by her caregiving to Julieta's brother who had an unknown illness and was constantly being rushed to the hospital. Julieta gave her mother advice about her brother and even sent supplements for her and for him, but the doctor explained to her mother that it was "not helpful". First her mother phoned Julieta who then called her back due to the cost; afterwards Julieta called one of her seven siblings in the US who relayed the news to the next one. They remitted to their mother, with Julieta noting, "It was just not enough". She wished she could directly help her since "talking on the phone and sending money isn't the same". Although Julieta had a computer, it had no camera and she didn't know how to use it. Besides, neither she nor her parents had broadband. By 39, Julieta felt torn between her mother and her children. Her teenage son, aware of the tensions, vowed: "Don't worry mom, when I am older I am going to fix your papers so you can come and go." But Julieta felt uneasy about his need to rescue her so she could rescue her mother. Because Julieta could not return, due to being undocumented, she circulated her mother's news throughout her US sibling network and secured the funds for her medical needs as well as for her brother. Julieta was caught between countries and generations as well as siblings. As is evident from this story, Julieta is not operating alone but among a network of family members all trying to rescue their mother and support her at the end of the life course in Oaxaca, Mexico, where older people are often dependent on their children for their survival.

Literature review

Although there is a small but burgeoning literature on ageing and long-distance caregiving through ICTs, there has been little attention to the processes of this type of communication at the end of the life course. Baldassar (2007) has found that aged caregiving across long distances involves different responses than for children. Caring at a distance for the aged can be framed in terms of 'capacities', which are about the abilities to care. Then there are 'obligations', which are cultural expectations such as filial norms between the generations, and next there are 'negotiated commitments', which are the ways family members engage with one another from afar (Baldassar, 2007, p 280). Macro, meso, and micro are also factors, like health institutions and services in a particular country for ageing citizens (macro), networks of caregiving for those at the end of the lifecycle (meso), and micro levels such as family histories of diseases and life-cycle stages. Much of the care that happens with older parents is characterized by 'distant crisis care' (Baldassar, 2014, p 391). The crisis care often occurs through phone calls, which are useful for direct help in the form of remittances, as well as cheering up, and finding out information. The phone call may give more sense of 'being in close contact' (Baldassar, 2014, p 393) than internet-based conversations. Wilding (2006) for example found that the existence of health problems and disabilities affects the uses of newer communication systems and devices; older left-behind members can go from 'sunny day[s]' to bleak moods in the absence of support to navigate or afford these systems. Therefore even the newest ICT-based systems 'may never be enough to completely substitute for physical contact' (Bacigalupe and Cámara, 2012, p 1429). They only 'create a *semblance* of family life' (Parrenas, 2005, p 334). Still, other research shows that those who lack digital affordances (including digital literacy levels, devices, and infrastructure), like many older persons, ensure that their adult children assist them (Kang, 2012). More often than not, though, the transnational family research on care and ICTs is optimistic, especially when multimedia formats, containing audio/visual features in real time, such as Skype, are used. These ICTs, when used on a frequent basis, enable members to have a sense of 'connected presence' (Licoppe 2004, p 135) and hence become 'virtual families' (Wilding, 2006, p 138); adult mothers communicating through Skype with their immigrant children see and hear them, which lends a sense of reassurance about their relationship and reduces their anxiety (Longhurst, 2013).

The life-course literature on ageing in transnational families includes ICTs in care delivery but does not focus on the technologies so much as the human connections and the complications involved in distant elder care (Basa et al, 2011; Bevan and Sparks, 2011; Krzyżowski and Mucha, 2014; Sun, 2012; Sharma and Kemp, 2012). Generally, 'cross-border elder care' is a largely unmapped subject in migration studies (Sun, 2012, p 1241). These researchers find that caring for left-behind aged parents involves special responses and challenges, including rules governing norms for care (Sun, 2012). Bevan and Sparks (2011) see caregiving for older persons as difficult because of the geographic distance, which is the strongest predictor of interaction frequency. Likewise, Baldassar (2007, 2008) showed that visitations mediate long-distance caregiving activities, perceptions, and behaviours. In particular, assessing needs is the most challenging from far away so short visits can assist in knowing those needs and anticipating them in the future. The major supports immigrants give to their elderly parents are financial remittances for medical and other costs, followed by emotional support, and help with paperwork (Krzyżowski and Mucha, 2014). Yet the introduction of the internet can complicate care communications and provision. Kang (2012), for example, found that elderly mothers are excluded from conversations because their husbands, with more digital skills, dominated the digital devices. Kang referred to these elderly women as the 'silenced mothers' (Kang, 2012, p 152) and transnational communication as a 'gender ghetto' because of these women's digital exclusion.

Theories on care and ageing

Many immigrants feel a sense of filial piety and stress the importance of caring for their older parents (Sun, 2012). A number of the participants, like Julieta, grew up in rural areas when caring depended on kinship networks that centralized women's caring as part of the fabric of social life. Survival through communal caring was a norm and this collective view means women use interpersonal reasoning in their decision making, prioritizing relationships (Noddings, 1991, p 158; Fisher and Tronto, 1990).

Other researchers divide long-distance caring (Baldassar, 2008; Reynolds and Zontini, 2007) into two major aspects. *Caring about* means anticipating, recognizing, and identifying verbal and nonverbal needs (Tronto, 1998). *Caring for* means direct forms of delivering care, such as when 'someone assumes responsibility to meet a need that has been identified... [including] organizing, marshaling resources or personnel (Tronto, 1998, p 15). Most of the literature however focuses exclusively on *caring for* (Baldassar, 2014), with a distinct giver and receiver rather than an exchange of care over space and time, through multiple parties. This is primarily due to the attention given to the dyadic migrated mother and left-behind child within the 'global care chain' research (Hochschild, 2000). A newer 'care circulation theory' (Baldassar and Merla, 2014) shows care being exchanged across the globe between different family members and in diverse ways. This more open-ended and functional perspective lends greater agency to transnational family members and integrates the ICTs into their interactions through a mediation approach (Madianou and Miller, 2012).

I introduce a new framework, transnational ICT-based communication chains, or TICCs (Cuban, 2017), that accounts for the efficient and ingenious systems that transnational families develop for communicating through ICTs during health crises. The framework draws heavily from the human communications literature, which focuses on small group communication patterns (Galvin et al, 2014). Although four chains have been identified in this research, for the purpose of this chapter I focus on one type that was the most prevalent, the 'Line'. The 'Line' represents a grapevine, whereby one group member at the head of it passes on information and news to another, and so on. Most of the women dealing with crises like health problems of their parents at a distance, utilized the Line. The Line was specifically for rescuing these parents in health crises and I refer to it hereafter as *a rescue chain*. This rescue chain delivered needed care support and news in a timely way, through a step-wise method of communicating urgent information and providing help to a member in need. Julieta's actions illustrate it as she safeguarded her mother by calling her and then patch-worked resources among siblings to secure immediate remittances to send across the border. She did this through the phone, which everyone possessed.

As Julieta's example illustrates, caring from far away involves communication work to keep and maintain the relationship and the conversations surrounding the care (Reynolds and Zontini, 2007). Picking up the phone and calling or texting along the chain were therapeutic interventions in and of themselves and involved emotional and digital work to relate at a distance as well as eradicate or reduce health/medical problems or symptoms. This talk was important for family members to bond around a member who was physically suffering. The talk involved *extra* work to engage the siblings in the rescue chain, so as to make the care robust. The longer the participants used the ICTs to engage in rescue chain work, the more they were able to negotiate complex problems, selecting particular people to focus on, especially when there was a clear need, and working out times and places to talk. At the same time, the sense of absence was important in acknowledging the lack of physical and geographic proximity; conversations could be confusing to participants because of the distortions inherent in long-distance ICT-based communication;

for example, those siblings at the end of Julieta's rescue chain were less engaged.

Within this rescue chain, I show that the participants and their families engaged in three types of interrelated communication surrounding health care: protecting, providing, and proving. First, the participants and their families sought *protection* for the person in crisis. This ranged from listening and comforting, to fixing safe networks to 'anchor' that member. Withholding of information was also important in protecting the person in crisis, which meant not articulating difficulties of one's own. Second, family members *provided* care for medical needs directly, through sending medicine or health-related funds, medical materials or information, interacting with medical professionals, and/or giving medical or health care advice. Last, to check on the value and appropriateness of the care provided, family members were *proving* the extent to which the caring they had exchanged had improved the situation of the member in need and the degree to which the problem was resolved (or not). Proving could be a challenge. Julieta, for example, found that the funds pooled together by her siblings were 'not enough', while other participants called their parents on 'public phones' that were not private enough to share personal information.

It is important to note that neither the rescue chain nor the care talk were solutions to caring for ageing parents at a distance. The rescue chain (Line) provided emergency support for a family member in need, and voice calls were often used to determine that need and its fulfilment. Yet because of the step-by-step oral/aural calls, those members at the end of the chain could receive ambiguous messages. Also, as we shall see with the women's stories, protecting, providing, and especially proving the care was worthwhile through ICTs was made difficult due to digital affordances, the geographical distance, as well as the chain of command of people who all had different opinions and perspectives.

Methods and sources

The larger study used a reflexive methodology that integrated the perspectives of the researcher who had lived abroad and communicated with her transnational family for a number of years, as well as those informants who were part of the research process. In a sense, we, as a research team, were both insiders and outsiders to transnational care communication processes.

Data collection

The interviews were biographical and focused on the details of the participants' ICT-based communication surrounding care not only with family outside the US but also family residing within it. The interview instrument was tailored to capture these deeper meanings of long-distance care communication. It was semi-structured and served as a guide so that the participants could develop their stories (Siedman, 2013). Most interviews were conducted in the native languages so that the participants could express themselves in comfortable and authentic ways.

Data analysis

Narrative analysis is well suited for topics like transnational family communication, which is not much studied. A Riessman analysis (1993) was used to focus on the rich emotional landscapes of the participants communicating within their family members from afar. This model emphasizes the voices of the storytellers. It also encompasses images and metaphors with phrases that participants use. Importantly, it captures the 'talk organized around consequential events' of actors who make meaning from these events, including their cultural understandings (Riessman, 1993, p 3).

Sample size and selection

The participants were selected through snowball sampling where one person leads to another (Siedman, 2013), and which was dependent on the informants of the study; recruiting undocumented immigrants to participate in research is difficult for an outsider. Further sampling in different geographic locations and networks enabled me to gain a representative sample of immigrants across Washington State. This sample also represented various nationalities within Washington, especially Mexicans, one of the largest groups (Brown and Lopez, 2013), and which is reflected in the larger sample as well as this sub-sample. Many of the participants were caring in some way for left-behind family and the ten women discussed in this chapter are representative.

Findings

All of the participants deployed the rescue chain to care for their parents with medical problems. Siblings, both local and abroad, were part of the chain and either initiated it or followed the efforts of the participant in pooling resources, giving feedback to the person at the head of the rescue efforts, and creating safety nets for the parents and other members in need. The care talk the participants engaged in as they rescued their parents focused on protecting, providing, and proving that their care at a distance was worthwhile. This care talk was evident in each of the ten narratives. One participant explained why she constantly called her parents: "To call if they need money – we send money or call if someone is sick." Another participant recalled both difficulties and rewards: "With my mom more than anything I send her money and also I need to hear her to know she is well…. Sometimes she feels bad and sometimes she doesn't answer the phone and sometimes she is not there when she is at the doctor's office." This communication through the rescue chains they created via the ICTs was far from ideal, and struggles were the norm as the participants and their siblings tried to anticipate needs in order to provide for the parents, safeguard their interests to protect them, and finally to prove to themselves, the person in need, and the rest of the family that the care was meaningful. Mercy's story illustrates the complexities associated with care talk through the rescue chain.

Mercy

Mercy, in her 30s, was from Nairobi, Kenya, the middle of many siblings. Due to a lack of family funds Mercy could not afford college and instead volunteered in the slums of Nairobi where she meet a nun who offered her training and the promise of a career. She rationalized, "Well, I am a Christian and they were giving health care training… I was able to do a lot of things". The nun connected her with an American pastor, who needed a domestic in-house caregiver for his family in the US, and believing it would boost her career, she migrated. However when he harassed her and Mercy confronted him he said that "I was the problem and told me to leave". She escaped to live with a friend and then afterwards moved to New York to be with one of her brothers living there. This relationship was important since one of her sisters in Kenya had just died, which was "a big blow… we were very close in age" and Mercy could not attend her funeral because she lacked a green card: "If I left, I could not come back… it was very difficult." After that, the patriarch of the family, her father, was no longer functioning well. She discovered that "my father has dementia – he can't really make the head of household decisions really well". This led to her mother initiating daily calls to Mercy. Mercy explained, "She calls all the time… she will call like at 2 in the morning, or midnight". This led to Mercy taking on the role of financial provider and protector of her parents. The oldest brother in New York could not make these financial decisions in the father's cognitive absence, pushing the mother to constantly ask Mercy for advice and funds. She said, "he is getting older, his memory is becoming a bit blurred. He is suffering from mild dementia… he just spends his time at home with my mom". Mercy found that communicating with her 69-year-old father was difficult.

> 'I communicate with my dad almost every time I call my mom, but it's usually pretty brief because his memory is not very good and so he has a hard time remembering where I am again, what I am doing, and so it is almost like a new conversation every time I call him.'

As a paid caregiver in the US and an unpaid caregiver to her family, Mercy balanced her Kenyan parents' resources and support from abroad with her own growing family in the US.

With her father's absence in family decision making, the phone calls to Kenya became emotionally intense as the siblings negotiated a new head of family. Mercy described these calls as part of "fighting not physically but a lot of verbal exchange". This was especially the case around the land that her family owned in Kenya and disagreements about wanting to sell it for the proceeds for their parents. Every time there was a 'financial strain' in the family Mercy had to "figure out a way to solve the financial problem" because her mother, she described, was demanding and "loud". She added, "So the closer you are, the bigger the fight so it usually is so much drama", Mercy solved the problems by sending her parents as much money as she could as well as pushing her siblings to send some as well. She discovered that one person calling another was better than family conference calls. Yet even these one-to-one conversations could interrupt time with her infant son, and she did not see him much because of her work schedule. She described the tension:

> 'When I come home from work, I want to focus on my son, because I haven't seen him all day and he, of course, demands my attention… if the phone is constantly ringing,

someone wants to talk to me... I would rather talk to them when I can focus on them and you know my son won't start screaming in my ear.'

Mercy felt obligated to take her family's calls because "I am from a culture where you have gone through so much already in life that small inconveniences don't seem that big". Her mother and father, who lived on a farm, did not have access to the internet so the phone was important for communicating with them. Still Mercy said her mother "calls at whatever time... they do not understand when you put relationships aside to perform tasks so when you tell them 'I am busy right now I can't talk to you' they get offended". She felt that her Kenyan side of the family did not understand how much she sacrificed in order to provide and protect them from future financial disasters. She attested: "It took almost two years to finish paying for my car, but I don't tell them that because they still wouldn't understand."

Mercy's long-distance care communication, as with the other nine participants, was characterized by protecting them by withholding information about their own difficulties, providing for them financially by sending money and pressuring siblings to do the same, and engaging with them on the phone, to learn if the care was in place and working. Every call made or returned could however reactivate the rescue chain; Mercy's calls ended in demands for more money, for example. A broader analysis of the participants' care talk within the rescue chain through ICTs revealed:

1. *Ambiguous messaging and meanings through long-distance phone call contact.* Mercy for example, as with other participants, could not fully discern the needs of her father through the brief phone conversations they had which were coloured by his lack of referential memory, not to mention the background noise of her mother's 'loud' requests for finances. Being far away it was difficult for Mercy to detect what he was feeling and thinking, and she resigned herself to the limited conversations. Her mother was the only means by which she really knew how he was doing so satisfying her need for funds was important in connecting to her father. The stress of communicating with him and her mother from a distance was like an 'ambiguous loss' (Falicov, 2002, p 274), which is a sense of losing a key part of the family: Mercy lost her father to dementia and had to compensate for his role in the family without a sense of closure of his condition or emotional closeness. Although the phone was used by all of the participants as the best means of accuracy and precision by putting

voice and words together to form a rescue chain, it often led to confusing interactions, as 'contact and connection are not the same thing' (Hannaford, 2015, p 46). Mercy found it difficult to talk directly with her father and therefore could not verify if he was okay, and thus whether she or her family was either.

2. *The participants' care judgements were based on the least unpleasant choice.* Mercy, for example, had no choice other than to send her mother the money in the absence of her father's financial acumen, rather than deny it if she were to stay in the family as a respected member. So she complied with her mother's requests. Mercy's care behaviours and dispositions were characterized then as 'cruel optimism' (Berlant, 2006, p 21), which is 'a relation of attachment to comprised conditions of possibility'. What was difficult about Mercy's attachment to her family was not only the threat of the loss of the family if she did not comply with their financial requests or form rescue chains to supply funds but also the loss of herself in the world as a care provider and protector. By separating herself physically from her family but providing financially for them through patch-working resources in the US, she thought she could make good on her promises to everyone. Her care talk to them was nonetheless highly problematic. Due to the global inequities, being 'here' in the US meant supporting family 'there'. By talking with their parents, they were able to be *there*, albeit to a limited extent.

3. *A sacrificial persistence defined by filial piety of daughters and their ageing parents.* Mercy, in her 30s, was supporting her parents 30 years older who could no longer work. She did not want to sell the land her father owned and decided instead to work hard to support both sides of the family in Kenya and the US. As a result, like many of the other participants, she felt divided at the same time that she was internally attached (Menjívar, 2000). This communication could produce 'trauma through separation' especially for those who were very far away like Mercy, or were undocumented, like Julieta (Abrego, 2014, p 68). Like Mercy, who could not attend her sister's funeral, or Julieta who could not see her mother or brother, many of the women experienced permanent separation, especially from parents who were too old or ill to migrate. Yet the participants' rescue networks were divided precisely to distribute support for care, material and emotional, and they were enduring over time and for life and death decisions (Menjívar, 2000). Yet the heads of the chains were constantly in a dilemma, putting their own self-determination last, especially in working for subsistence wages to rescue everyone else.

Conclusion

Among the ten participants, nearly all of them had children, a number of whom lived with them in the US. Like both Julieta and Mercy, they felt torn between generations and siblings and had to make sacrificial decisions, especially in light of medical problems of their parents that threatened livelihoods and relations; this created internal tension in the deals they made surrounding their care. Their care talk was determined more by an 'ambient presence,' which is 'an increased awareness of the everyday lives and activities of significant others through the background presence of ubiquitous media environments' (Madianou, 2016, p 183). Each family member in the chain had a 'peripheral awareness' of the emotions of distant others rather than a central understanding of their needs (Madianou, 2016 p 183). This sense of separation and distance, and the tensions to resolve problems through the rescue chains, never went away.

This tension can be tied in directly to tightened immigration policies that physically separate family members from one another. These issues tend to be neglected within the ICT-based literature, that make the communication novel. US immigration policies limited the participants' abilities to be with their families in the flesh and they did not have a *right to family unity*, which is protected by international human rights. Computer-mediated conversations alone did not compensate for being with an aged parent. Similarly, critical research on ageing shows the disembodied nature of using new technologies to aid older persons living at home and needing care (Roberts et al, 2012). Furthermore, the dependence on immigrants, like many of the participants, to give care in high-income countries creates a care drain in more marginalized parts of the world. One parent of a participant in Oaxaca, for example, told her daughter that she wished she could be "a bird to fly" to see her grandchildren in Washington. However, she could not afford it in cost, let alone her duties as caregiver for her father and her husband's father, without direct help from her children, who had all migrated. Therefore, this chapter raises questions about the importance of care at a distance and the role of ICTs in bridging care between transnational family members, specifically adult immigrant children and their older left-behind parents. This research points to the fact that technologies do not and will not resolve distance in caring practices among families. In a number of cases, particularly in rural regions in Mexico or Kenya, for example, as Julieta and Mercy's cases demonstrate, the parents did not have full access to different forms of communication, and were dependent exclusively on landline phones for contact with their children. Much of the ICT-based literature does not account for the lack of digital affordances and its effects on relations and communications between separated family members. Also, it assumes that the newest communication systems compensate for geographic distance. I showed that family members do adjust to these restraints by creating rescue chains to anticipate care needs, ensure the care is delivered, and check on its value. Yet it was problematic. My research also indicates that there may be new ways that immigration and communication policies can ease the burden on immigrant daughters and their ageing parents in a way that builds on the communication chains they have already established.

In brief

This study shows:

1. A sacrificial persistence defined by filial piety of daughters and their ageing parents.
2. Immigrants and their siblings, locally and abroad, form rescue chains to deliver care to ageing left-behind parents with health problems through ICTs.
3. The rescue chain communication involves 'care talk' that is characterized by providing, protecting, and proving the care needs of the person in crisis were addressed.

References

Abrego, J. L. (2014) *Sacrificing Families: Navigating Laws, Labor, and Love across Borders*, Stanford, CA: Stanford University Press.

Bacigalupe, G. and Cámara, M. (2012) 'Transnational families and social technologies: Reassessing immigration psychology', *Journal of Ethnic and Migration Studies*, 38 (9): 1425–1438, https://doi.org/10.1080/1369183X.2012.698211

Baldassar, L. (2007) 'Transnational families and aged care: The mobility of care and the migrancy of ageing', *Journal of Ethnic and Migration Studies*, 33(2): 275–297, https://doi.org/10.1080/13691830601154252

Baldassar, L. (2008) 'Missing kin and longing to be together: Emotions and the construction of co-presence in transnational relationships', *Journal of Intercultural Studies*, 29(3): 247–266, https://doi.org/10.1080/07256860802169196

Baldassar, L. (2014) 'Too sick to move: Distant 'crisis' care in transnational families', *International Review of Sociology*, 24(39): 391–405, https://doi.org/10.1080/03906701.2014.954328

Baldassar, L. (2016) 'De-monizing distance in mobile family lives: Co-presence, care circulation and polymedia as vibrant matter', *Global Networks*, 16(2): 145–163, https://doi.org/10.1111/glob.12109

Baldassar, L. and Merla, L. (2014) 'Introduction: Transnational family caregiving through the lens of circulation', in L. Baldassar and L. Merla (eds) *Transnational Families, Migration and the Circulation of Care: Understanding Mobility and Absence in Family Life*, New York: Routledge, pp 3–23.

Basa, C., Harcourt, W. and Zarro, A. (2011) 'Remittances and transnational families in Italy and the Philippines: Breaking the global care chain', *Gender & Development*, 19(1): 11–22, https://doi.org/10.1080/13552074.2011.554196

Berlant, L. (2006) 'Cruel Optimism', *A Journal of Feminist Cultural Studies*, 17(3): 20–36, https://doi.org/10.1215/10407391-2006-009

Bevan, J. L. and Sparks, L. (2011) 'Communication in the context of long-distance family caregiving: An integrated review and practical applications', *Patient Education and Counseling*, 85(1): 26–30, https://doi.org/10.1016/j.pec.2010.08.003

Brown, A. and Lopez, M. H. (July 2013) 'Mapping the Latino population by state, county, and city', Pew Research Center, www.pewhispanic.org/2013/08/29/mapping-the-latino-population-by-state-county-and-city/

Cuban, S. (2017) *Transnational Family Communication: Immigrants and ICTs*, New York: Palgrave Macmillan.

Falicov, J. C. (2002) 'Ambiguous loss: Risk and resilience in Latino immigrant families', in M. Suarez-Orozco and M. Paez (eds) *Latinos: Remaking America*, Berkeley, CA: University of California Press, pp 274–288.

Fisher, B. and Tronto, J. (1990) 'Towards a feminist theory of care', in E. Abel and M. Nelson (eds) *Circles of Care: Work and Identity in Women's Lives*, Albany, NY: State University of New York Press, pp 35–62.

Galvin, M. K., Braithwaite, O. D. and Bylund, L. C. (2014) *Family Communication: Cohesion and Change*, New York: Routledge.

Hannaford, D. (2015) 'Technologies of the spouse: Intimate surveillance in Senegalese transnational marriages', *Global Networks*, 15(1): 43–59, https://doi.org/10.1111/glob.12045

Hochschild, A. R. (2000) 'Global care chains and emotional surplus value', in W. Hutton and A. Giddens (eds) *On the Edge: Living with Global Capitalism*, London: Jonathan Cape, pp 130–146.

Kang, T. (2012) 'Gendered media, changing intimacy: Internet-mediated transnational communication in the family sphere', *Media, Culture and Society*, 34(2): 146-161, https://doi.org/10.1177/0163443711430755

Kenning, M. (2007) *ICT and Language Learning: From Print to the Mobile Phone*, Basingstoke: Palgrave Macmillan.

Krzyżowski, Ł. and Mucha, J. (2014) 'Transnational caregiving in turbulent times: Polish migrants in Iceland and their elderly parents in Poland', *International Sociology*, 29(1): 22–37, https://doi.org/10.1177/0268580913515287

Licoppe, C. (2004) '"Connected" presence: The emergence of a new repertoire for managing social relationships in a changing communication technoscope', *Society and Space*, 22(1): 135-156, https://doi.org/10.1068/d323t

Longhurst, R. (2013) 'Using Skype to mother: Bodies, emotions, visuality, and screens', *Environment and Planning D: Society and Space*, 31(4): 664-679, https://doi.org/10.1068/d20111

Madianou, M. (2015) 'Digital inequality and second-order disasters: Social media in the typhoon Haiyan recovery', *Social Media + Society*, 1(2): 1-11, https://doi.org/10.1177/2056305115603386

Madianou, M. (2016) 'Ambient, co-presence: Transnational family practices in polymedia environments', *Global Networks*, 16(2): 183-201, https://doi.org/10.1111/glob.12105

Madianou, M. and Miller, D. (2012) *Migration and Families and Polymedia*, London: Routledge.

Menjivar, C. (2000) *Fragmented Ties: Salvadorian Immigrant Networks in America*, Berkley, CA: University of California Press.

Noddings, N. (1991) 'Stories in dialogue: Caring and interpersonal reasoning' in C. Witherell and N. Noddings (eds) *Stories Lives Tell: Narrative and Dialogue in Education*, New York: Teachers College Press, pp 157-170.

Panangokos, A.N. and Horst, H. A. (2006) 'Return to cyberia: Technology and the social worlds of transnational migrants', *Global Networks*, 6(2): 109-124, https://doi.org/10.1111/j.1471-0374.2006.00136.x

Parrenas, R. (2005) 'Long distance intimacy: Class, gender and intergenerational relations between mothers and children in Filipino transnational families', *Global Networks*, 5(4): 317–336, https://doi.org/10.1111/j.1471-0374.2005.00122.x

Reynolds, T. and Zontini, E. (2007) 'Assessing social capital and care provision in minority ethnic communities: A comparative study of Caribbean and Italian transnational families', in R. Edwards, J. Franklin and J. Holland (eds) *Assessing Social Capital: Concept, Policy and Practice*, Newcastle, UK: Cambridge Scholars Press, pp 217-233.

Riessman, C. K. (1993) *Narrative Analysis*, Newbury Park, CA: Sage.

Roberts, C., Mort, M. and Milligan, C. (2012) 'Calling for care: "Disembodied" work, teleoperators and older people living at home', *Sociology*, 46(3): 490–506, https://doi.org/10.1177/0038038511422551

Sharma, K. and Kemp, C.L. (2012) '"One should follow the wind": Individualized filial piety and support exchanges in Indian immigrant families in the United States', *Journal of Aging Studies*, 26(2): 129–139, https://doi.org/10.1016/j.jaging.2011.10.003

Siedman, I. (2013) *Interviewing as Qualitative Research: A Guide for Researchers in Education and Social Sciences*, New York: Teachers College Press.

Sun, K. E. (2012) 'Fashioning the reciprocal norms of elder care: A case of immigrants in the United States and their parents in Taiwan', *Journal of Family Issues*, 33(9): 1240–1271, https://doi.org/10.1177/0192513X12445564

Tronto, J. C. (1998) 'An ethic care', *Generations*, 22(3): 15-20.

Wilding, R. (2006) 'Virtual intimacies. Families communicating across transnational contexts', *Global Networks*, 6(2): 125-142, https://doi.org/10.1111/j.1471-0374.2006.00137.x

'Wherever you go, wherever you are, I am with you ... connected with my mobile': the use of mobile text messages for the maintenance of family and romantic relations

Bernadette Kneidinger-Müller

Relationship maintenance in the age of mobile communication

Relationship maintenance is a fundamental need of all humans (Baumeister and Leary, 1995). Keeping in touch with family members, romantic partners, close friends, and even acquaintances forms one of the main motivations for the everyday exchange of personal information. Individuals want to know what happens in the lives of their loved ones. Conversely, individuals want to inform other people about their own everyday experiences, thoughts, and feelings. Interpersonal communication forms the basic condition for any form of relationship maintenance. In the past, such everyday interactions have been mainly limited to face-to-face communication. The introduction of various forms of communication media has changed forms of interaction (de Souza e Silva, 2006; Ling and Yttri, 2002; Urry, 2007). Without going into detail about the usage habits of written communication sent via conventional mail or changing interaction habits because of landline telephony, this chapter addresses new communication modes in the age of mobile phones with internet connections. The so-called smartphones change communication practices in three aspects: they stimulate mobilization, flexibility, and individualization of interpersonal communication (de Souza e Silva, 2006; Ling and Yttri, 2002; Urry, 2007).

Mobile phones set aside the limitations of landline telephony by making individual communication available independent of one's current location. One does not have to stay at home to call another person or to receive a call because people's smartphones are always with them. This mobilization of interpersonal communication creates flexibility of interactions and everyday management (Ling and Yttri, 2002).

It is not only the location of making or receiving a call that becomes more flexible because of mobile phones but also the modes of communication, especially with the new option of computer-mediated communication that becomes available because of smartphones with internet connections. A smartphone offers not only the ability to make a telephone call but also the opportunity to exchange text messages with others or to use one of the main forms of computer-mediated communication, such as writing an email, commenting on social networking sites, or even sending (audiovisual) messages via a mobile messaging application.

The third fundamental change results from mobile phones and smartphones representing very personal devices. Whereas landline telephony connects households with one another, mobile telephony connects individuals. A smartphone is hardly ever shared by a number of people, but forms a very personal device belonging to one specific person. Therefore, if you get someone's mobile phone number, you can be quite sure that you will actually reach that specific person rather than a roommate, a family member, or anyone else. Teenagers, in particular, appreciate their smartphones because they allow them to keep in contact with their peer group without their parents needing to notice their interactions (Ito, 2001; Kasesniemi and Rautiainen, 2002). The individualization of mobile communication is also expressed in the fact that the applications and content available on a smartphone can be adjusted to personal needs and usage habits. Therefore, even for adults, the smartphone forms a very personal device that not only contains personal information and conversations but also fits individual usage needs (Fortunati, 2010).

Considering the increased mobilization, flexibility, and individualization, interpersonal communication via mobile phones can be described as having four characteristics that are important to understand for an analysis of their usage for relationship maintenance.

First, mobile phones increase the availability of their users. Katz and Aakhus (2002) discuss this under the term 'perpetual contact', which becomes possible because of the omnipresence of mobile phones. Turkle (2008) talks about a society of 'tethered selves' referring to the 24-hour connectedness of individuals. This perpetual connection not only supports relationship maintenance (Vincent, 2010, p 166) but can also cause feelings of stress and pressure (Bailey and Konstan, 2006; Knop et al, 2015).

Second, this perpetual mobile connection blurs the differences between physical presence and absence. Licoppe (2004) names it a 'connected presence', and Gergen (2002) discusses it using the key term 'absence presence'. Communication via mobile phone does not require the physical presence of the interaction partner. Even people who are at different locations are available as interaction partners independent of time and place because they can be reached via their mobile phones.

Third, the perpetual connectivity causes a 'doubling of space' (Scannell, 1996) or the appearance of 'hybrid spaces' (de Souza e Silva, 2006). The perpetual availability of mobile interaction partners creates parallel communication spheres that exist simultaneously with the traditional face-to-face communication with physically present people. This 'doubling of space' becomes especially obvious in situations where face-to-face conversations are interrupted by incoming calls or text messages on mobile phones. The individual has to coordinate simultaneously the interaction situation with the physically present communication partner and the physically absent caller on the mobile phone because of this 'invasive' character of mobile communication (Rettie, 2009, p 428).

Lastly, as the fourth characteristic, smartphones, in particular, lead to a 'multimodal connectedness' (Chan, 2014) by offering the opportunity not only to call a person but also to communicate via many other forms of written or verbal communication. This plurality of communicative options creates a new usage habit that Isaacs et al (2012) call 'channel blending', which describes the shift between different communication channels during one conversation. For example, users start an interaction using a text message but switch to a phone call when they notice that a topic has become too complicated to be explained in text messages.

These four characteristics describe how smartphones have changed the conditions for everyday communication. This chapter will put a special focus on text-based communication via mobile phones because previous research has mainly focused on mobile communication via traditional mobile phones (without internet connections); usage of phone calls or short message service (SMS); or general usage habits (see Faulkner and Culwin, 2005; Grellhesl and Punyanunt-Carter, 2012; Pettigrew, 2009).

On the contrary, this study analyses the new opportunities offered by internet-connected smartphones and discusses how different relationship types influence the specific communication habits involved in using a smartphone. The texting habits between family members and romantic couples will be compared with those between close friends or acquaintances. Over the life course, these different relationship groups are assigned different levels of significance: whereas for teenagers and young adults friends are highly important interaction partners, in older age groups the significance of family members and romantic partners increases (Antonucci et al, 2004). Therefore, it will be interesting to see how mobile communication is used differently for these three groups of related persons.

Methods

The data collection for this study took place as a part of a research-teaching course at a German university in June 2015. The project combines data from a quantitative diary study and follow-up qualitative interviews with 24 smartphone users aged between 20 and 30 years. Fourteen women and ten men were asked to record for three predefined days (a Friday, Sunday, and Tuesday) all incoming and outgoing SMS and text messages in their preferred mobile messaging application using a diary sheet with predefined categories (computed as an Excel file). In total, 3,224 messages were recorded over the three days from the 24 participants. After the diary period, all the participants were asked in guided face-to-face interviews about their general smartphone usage habits and experiences. All interviews were transcribed and analysed using quantitative content analysis (Mayring, 2008). The diary data was processed and analysed using the software package SPSS 23.0.

Results

Smartphones as everyday companions

The interviews confirm the assumption that the smartphone becomes an everyday companion for the majority of users. Fourteen participants reported being available 24 hours a day, and an additional three were available at least during daytime hours. A 21-year-old woman describes her usage as follows:

> 'When I'm sitting at my laptop, I look at my phone. When I'm talking with other people, I look at my phone. When I'm watching TV, I look at my phone. Even while I'm cooking, I look at my phone [laughing]. So actually, I'm looking at my phone the whole time.'

The technological availability combined with one's own perpetual availability influences the expectations about the social availability of others (see Grintner et al, 2006; Ling, 2004), as described in the statement of a 27-year-old man: "If I know that the person always carries around his smartphone with himself, then I really expect his availability."

This is especially the case in close relationships, such as romantic relationships or relationships with family members. According to a 30-year-old man, "The closer the relationship – with my partner, my family, or close friends – the higher my expectation to get an immediate response".

In nearly all interviews, the young adults named perpetual availability as a significant factor for having a smartphone. They want to be available for their loved ones and – vice versa – appreciate the opportunity to reach these people independently of their location. It can be supposed that for a generation that is used to mobile devices that allow constant contact with others, the importance of mobile availability will remain or even increase when they get older.

Smartphones are quite a recent technological development; therefore, we can only try to conjecture the changing significance of mobile availability over the life course. What we can do now is look at different usage habits depending on different types of interaction partners. Whereas teenagers use their smartphones mainly for the perpetual interaction with their peer group (Lenhart et al, 2010), young adults additionally appreciate the mobile availability with family members, especially if they have already left their parental homes. For parents, smartphones can be an important tool to coordinate childcare with their partners or stay in contact with their children while they are at work (Oksman and Turtiainen, 2004). And for elderly people, mobile phones – or, for the technophiles, even the smartphones – give a feeling of safety because they can always reach someone when they have their mobile with them (Kang and Jung, 2014; Ling and Yttri, 2002). Therefore, this study explores differences in text message usage habits in the communication of young adults with different relationship groups.

The age group between 20 and 30 years is of special interest because members of this generation get used to mobile communication during their teenage years, and now many of them are experiencing profound change in their living situation by starting to work or attending a university, which is often connected with moving out of the parental home. Therefore, it can be supposed that the smartphone becomes a significant tool for keeping in contact with family members, romantic partners, or close friends, especially if geographic distance makes face-to-face interactions happen less frequently.

The communication partners

Based on the diary data, the number of messages exchanged between different relationship groups was analysed. Table 13.1 shows that 45% of all recorded messages are transmitted between close friends, followed by 27% between romantic partners, 13% between acquaintances, and 8% for family communication (6% of the messages are exchanged in other relationship types or with unknown people). By analysing these numbers, the special role of the romantic partner becomes obvious. Whereas a group of close friends consists − in most cases − of more people, a single person represents a romantic partner. Thus, 27% of all messages are actually exchanged with this specific individual, whereas 45% of the messages exchanged in close friendships refer to communication with more than just one person. Additionally, a close look at the data reveals interesting gender differences. The diaries of the women reveal that they are communicating with a very heterogeneous network, including acquaintances (16%; men: 9%) and family members (10%; men: 6%) as frequent interaction partners. Men focus their conversations significantly more on close friends (64%) than on women (29%). By contrast, the highest proportion of female text messages (35%) is exchanges with romantic partners (men only: 19%).

These data confirm the assumption that young adults use mobile communication not only for interactions with their peer groups but also for family conversations or interactions with romantic partners.

Table 13.1 Percentage of messages exchanged between different relationship types

	Men (N = 1499)	Women (N = 1714)	Total (N = 3213)
Close friends	63.8%	28.9%	45.2%
Partner	18.7%	35.0%	27.4%
Acquaintances	9.4%	16.0%	12.9%
Family	5.9%	9.7%	8.0%
Others	2.1%	9.9%	6.3%
Unknown person	0.0%	0.5%	0.2%

The content of the messages

In the diaries, the content of each message was coded using predefined categories. This data was used to answer if different contents are transmitted in the text messages depending on the relationship type. The analysis (Table 13.2) highlights some interesting differences between the four relationship groups. In romantic relationships and between family members, text messages are mainly used for the exchange of everyday private information: 46% of all the messages exchanged with family members and 49% of the messages between romantic partners represent 'private news'. By contrast, only 25% of the messages exchanged in close friendships and 37% of the messages between acquaintances contain private information. Most frequently used are text messages in close relationships for arranging private appointments (31%). In the interaction with acquaintances, this forms the second most common content (17%). Completely different is the usage in romantic or family relationships, where text messages are hardly ever used to arrange private appointments (romantic partner: 9%; family: 8%). Text messages as a tool for mobile 'small talk' appear to be relevant for all types of relationships, but they seem to be especially important in close friendships (26%; family: 21%; romantic partner: 19%; acquaintances: 14%). Interestingly, writing about personal sensitivities only forms important content in mobile conversations with partners (10%) or close friends (8%) but is not so important in interactions with family members (3%). Other content categories that are recorded are inquiries, work appointments, starting or ending conversations, greetings, and wishes. All these categories have small relevance in everyday conversations via text messages.

Besides the relationship type, even the geographic distance between the interaction partners influences the content of what is exchanged via text. With people living nearby, text messages are obviously used more frequently for the organization of face-to-face meetings. On the contrary, with people living farther apart, text messages are used to exchange information about everyday experiences to create the feeling of sharing one's life with another. In these cases, text messages have a significant function for relationship maintenance, as some participants explained in the interviews:

'With a friend living close by, I text about appointments, when we will meet each other … or we make small talk and exchange jokes. With those friends living away, I exchange questions about how they are doing, their general sensitivities ... or try to make them participate in my life.' (Woman, 28 years)

Table 13.2. Content of text messages

	Family	Partner	Close friends	Acquaintances	Others	Total
Information (private)	45.7%	48.7%	25.1%	37.1%	42.1%	35.8%
Small talk	21.1%	19.0%	26.1%	14.2%	6.9%	20.9%
Appointments (private)	7.8%	8.5%	30.7%	17.3%	6.9%	19.5%
Exchange of sensitivities	3.1%	10.2%	8.3%	6.3%	2.0%	7.7%
Other contents	7.0%	6.1%	4.6%	8.9%	21.3%	6.8%
Enquiry	6.6%	2.2%	1.0%	3.4%	2.0%	2.1%
Appointments (work)	/	1.4%	0.5%	6.3%	4.5%	1.9%
Information (work)	/	1.7%	0.6%	2.9%	11.4%	1.8%
Start/end conversation	0.8%	0.9%	2.3%	1.9%	2.5%	1.7%
Greetings/ wishes	7.8%	1.4%	1.0%	1.7%	0.5%	1.7%

According to a 22-year-old woman, "The smartphone is very important for me because I'm alone here now, and my friends and family live at a distance".

These statements implicitly describe a different relevance of mobile communication for relationship maintenance with family and friends because of changing living conditions that are a part of the individual life course – in this case, moving to another town, which means leaving parents, siblings, and at least some friends behind.

Other fundamental life changes that may not influence the place of residence but the time that is available for face-to-face meetings could be, for example, becoming a parent, getting a new job, or receiving new responsibilities (for example, taking care of an elderly family member). Such life-changing events could also influence the importance of mobile communication (Smoreda and Licoppe, 1999).

Further longitudinal studies will have to address the impacts of life-changing events on mobile communication behaviour in more detail.

Motivations for texting

All participants were asked why they were using text-based communication via smartphones. In many cases, relationship maintenance is one of the main motives for using a smartphone for interaction. This was named as one of the main advantages of smartphone communication:

> 'It's a big advantage that you can stay in contact with different people permanently and easily ... you can overcome distances ... and so you really get the feeling that you always know what happens in the lives of others.' (Woman, 24 years)

In particular, users appreciate the variety of mobile communication options because it permits perpetual contact with loved ones:

> 'The smartphone allows me to stay in contact with other people without the need to call them ... I can send them pictures and so on ... you can use it when you are not able to call.' (Woman, 25 years)

Messaging applications were preferred not only because of the opportunities to include audiovisual material in the messages and the more unobtrusive form of contact compared to a phone call (Pettigrew, 2009) but also because of the specific form of easy-going, fast conversation. Via text messages, even news with little significance can be shared, which normally would not be a reason to call someone. Therefore, text messages increase the information that is exchanged between interaction partners. According to a 23-year-old man, "For me, the smartphone represents fast, easy-going conversation ... things that you write quickly – things that don't have much significance."

Another interesting result of the interviews was that many participants reported using the automated notifications about the online status of a person that are displayed in many mobile messaging applications as additional information about a person's life. If a user does not disable the function, applications – such as WhatsApp – automatically display the time of the last application usage of a contacted person. Additionally, little tick marks indicate that a message has been sent (one grey tick), has been received by the contacted person (two grey ticks), or has been opened (two blue ticks). Participants use these 'little signals' as information 'between the lines', allowing them to make assumptions about the current situation – that is, the activities of a contacted person (see Church and de Oliveira, 2013; O'Hara et al, 2014). The automated information can substitute or supplement the actual communication. It works as a substitute when the time of the last online presence of a user is interpreted as proof that everything is fine with the person.

> 'Sometimes it only matters if you know that the person has read the message ... you get the feeling that the person is okay because she has been online. Nothing happened to her while she was driving in her car, for example.' (Woman, 24 years)

The automated notifications supplement the main communication when the displayed ticks (or lack thereof) indicate that the contacted person has not received or has not opened an urgent message. This information is used to switch the communication channel to increase the chance that a (urgent) message will reach the contacted person in time. According to a 22-year-old woman, "It's a somewhat urgent situation, and then you see that the person isn't online and no blue ticks appear in WhatsApp. Then I decide to call the person. That's how I do it".

Such information could be helpful for all age groups and the maintenance of various relationship types. For example, parents could find it helpful to see the time of the last online usage of their child to know whether he or she is fine. Children could see, based on the displayed checks, whether their parents are available via text message or whether they should instead call them if something urgent has to be said. Little research has been done on the phenomenon of the everyday interpretation of such digital traces of smartphone users. It would be interesting to see how the usage and interpretation of such automated usage signs change over the life course and what advantages or even risks the users experience by looking at such information 'between the lines'.

Smartphones as a threat to relationships – some critiques

Besides the advantages of smartphones, the interviews also show criticism. In some conditions, smartphones are actually experienced as a threat to relationships. Some participants fear that the perpetual contact via mobile phones could devalue face-to-face interactions. According to a 30-year-old man, "Because you are permanently available ... the personal contact isn't as valued as it should be because you get the feeling of being in contact, and therefore, you don't have to meet each other anymore".

Others discuss the phenomenon of 'hybrid spaces' as a problem for relationship maintenance, especially if the smartphone is regularly used during face-to-face interactions. This seems to be a frequent experience because one out of five sent messages (21%) recorded in the diaries was written in the presence of face-to-face interaction partners. Despite – or maybe because of – the everyday occurrence of such usage habits, many participants perceive such communication behaviour as impolite and disturbing. According to a 27-year-old man, "I perceive such habits as very impolite because the attention should be with the physically present conversation partner and not on other channels".

A comparison of texting in the presence of others depending on the relationship with the mobile interaction partner (Table 13.3) reveals that family members (12%) and romantic partners (16%) tend to be less frequently contacted while face-to-face interaction partners are present than close friends (29%) or acquaintances (27%).

Table 13.3 Texting in the presence of face-to-face interaction partners

N = 1323	Family	Partner	Close friends	Acquaintances	Total
In co-presence	11.8%	15.6%	28.8%	26.8%	21.1%
Without co-presence	88.2%	84.4%	71.2%	73.2%	78.9%
Total	100.0%	100.0%	100.0%	100.0%	100.0%

Consequently, the perpetual availability creates an increased competition for the attention of interaction partners. Meeting someone in person does not automatically mean an exclusive interaction situation because each ongoing conversation could be immediately interrupted by incoming phone calls or text messages received on the smartphone.

The perpetual contact not only increases the pressure on relationships by creating such problematic interaction situations, but also leads to a kind of availability pressure (Church and de Oliveira, 2013; Hall and Baym, 2012; Knop et al, 2015; Mieczakowski et al, 2011; Quan-Haase and Collins, 2008). If a contacted person does not answer a call or text message immediately, this could be interpreted as a neglect or even devaluation of the relationship (Church and de Oliveira, 2013;

Licoppe, 2004). This is especially the case if it is assumed that the contacted person is able to look at their smartphone, as this 30-year-old man describes: "If I know that a person has nothing to do the whole weekend and still doesn't answer, it's really not cool. In this case, I know where I'm placed on the friendship hierarchy."

The technological availability made possible by modern smartphones increases the expectations of social availability (Boneva et al, 2006; Ling and Yttri, 2002). This is especially true for interactions in close relationships such as between family members, romantic partners, or close friends.

Limitations of the study

The selected qualitative approach allows a better insight into the individual usage habits and experiences of smartphone users. Nevertheless, it has to be emphasized that the discussed findings cannot be transferred without constraints to mobile phone users in general. Therefore, one limitation of the study is based on the selection of the interview participants, who belong to a specific age group. Further research needs to replicate the study with a sample of participants that is more mixed in terms of age and educational background.

Another limitation results from the self-report diary data. It cannot be validated whether the reported communication behaviour represents the individual communication process entirely. Depending on individual, social, and contextual factors, some participants might not have recorded all incoming and outcome messages. This can be seen as a general problem of self-report diary studies. Nevertheless, the combination of diary study with follow-up interviews allows a kind of recheck of the diary data by comparing it with the usage habits described in the interviews.

Discussion

Mobile phones and smartphones are used by large portions of modern societies and form important tools for everyday communication, especially in the age groups up to 65 years (Pew Research Center, 2017). The wide distribution of mobile phones and their nature as a personal device often creates the impression that anyone is just one call or one message away. If you need something, want to know how someone is, or want to share experiences, thoughts, or questions with one of your loved ones immediately, you just have to use your mobile phone.

Similar to other technological developments, this high level of mobile connectivity in our society has two sides to it. Many users name the perpetual contact because of their smartphone as a reason to buy a smartphone, which they now really appreciate. But the perpetual availability is also experienced as a disadvantage when it leads to a feeling of pressure for constant availability to fulfil the expectations of families, partners, or friends.

The data in this study confirm the constant presence of smartphones in the lives of young adults. Many of them cannot imagine a life without their device in hand, which allows them to keep in touch with others 24 hours a day. In contrast to the findings about the texting behaviour of teenagers whose mobile phone usage is mainly focused on interaction with their peer group (Ito, 2001; Kasesniemi and Rautiainen, 2002), the findings indicate that as they become older, the new 'multimodal connectedness' is used not only for everyday interaction with close friends but also for relationship maintenance with family members or romantic partners. Smartphones and their option of exchanging text messages, which can be used for asynchronous communication independent of time or place, are helpful in sharing everyday experiences with loved ones. This becomes especially important if face-to-face interactions cannot be realized regularly because of geographical distances between interaction partners or for other reasons.

Over the life course, various events could cause geographical changes for individuals, which could increase the significance of mobile-mediated communication. The participants in this study represent the group of young adults aged between 20 and 30 years. Many of them have already left their parental homes, so they live more or less far away from their families. Smartphones help them keep in contact with their parents or siblings. The news of the day is no longer exchanged at the dinner table but via phone calls or specifically text messages that allow for the inclusion of audio-visual materials such as photos or videos that intensify the experiences of sharing one's life with another. This is especially the case if the photos and videos are shared directly from a situation where the individual would like to inform their relatives. This visual material allows for a new form of 'live life participation' without the need for co-presence. Many participants spontaneously indicated that smartphones help overcome distance and create a feeling of presence even during periods of physical absence.

But besides such positive experiences, smartphones and text messages are also seen as risks for relationships, especially if the mobile communication is used as a substitute for theoretically possible face-to-face interactions. It is not only families with teenagers that are familiar with the situation where text messages are used for communication inside the same household just to save the effort of going downstairs and telling the person what they want to say.

Mobile phones are a great option for relationship maintenance when they help fill in communication gaps caused by geographic distances or other reasons. But mobile communication includes some risks for relationship quality if: (1) they cause increased competition between face-to-face interaction partners and mobile-connected individuals (parallel communication); (2) users feel pressure to be available for others 24 hours a day; or (3) nonresponses to mobile messages or calls are interpreted as a devaluation of the relationship.

Perpetual mobile availability is a recent phenomenon; therefore, no data are available to allow an analysis of how it influences the usage of mobile phones in family relationships over the life course. But the findings of this study, which was focused on young adults – an age group that is likely to experience some fundamental life changes, such as moving out of the parental home, starting work or school, and establishing new relationships – can provide insights on how life-changing events can influence the importance of mobile communication for maintenance of different types of relationships.

In brief

1. Written communication via smartphones is not only used for the organization of everyday tasks but for relationship maintenance over distance.
2. Smartphones are everyday companions of many users and allow perpetual contact with loved ones, independent of time or space.
3. Young adults use text messages for different purposes depending on the relationship type that connects them with their interaction partner.
4. Texting with family members or a romantic partner happens less frequently in the presence of face-to-face interaction partners than texting with friends or acquaintances.

References

Antonucci, T., Akiyama, H. and Takahasi, K. (2004) 'Attachment and close relationships across life span', *Attachment & Human Development*, 6(4): 353–370, https://doi.org/10.1080/1461673042000303136

Bailey, B. P. and Konstan, J. A. (2006) 'On the need for attention-aware systems: Measuring effects of interruption on task performance, error rate, and affective state', *Computers in Human Behavior*, 22(4): 685–708, https://doi.org/10.1016/j.chb.2005.12.009

Baumeister, R. F. and Leary, M. R. (1995) 'The need to belong: Desire of interpersonal attachments as a fundamental human motivation', *Psychological Bulletin*, 117(3): 497–529, https://dx.doi.org/10.1037/0033-2909.117.3.497

Boneva, B. S., Quinn, A., Kraut, R. E., Kiesler, S. and Shklovski, I. (2006) 'Teenage communication in the instant messaging era', in R.E. Kraut, N. Brynin and S. Kiesler (eds) *Computers, Phones, and the Internet: Domesticating Information Technology*, Oxford: Oxford University Press, pp 201–218.

Chan, M. (2014) 'Multimodal connectedness and quality of life: Examining the influences of technology adoption and interpersonal communication on well-being across the life span', *Journal of Computer-Mediated Communication*, 20(1): 3–18, https://dx.doi.org/10.1111/jcc4.12089

Church, K. and de Oliveira, R. (2013) 'What's up with WhatsApp? Comparing mobile instant messaging behaviors with traditional SMS', *Proceedings of the Mobile HCI 2013 – Collaboration and Communication*, Munich, Germany, 30 August, 352–361, www.ic.unicamp.br/~oliveira/doc/MHCI2013_Whats-up-with-whatsapp.pdf

De Souza e Silva, A. (2006) 'From cyber to hybrid: Mobile technologies as interfaces of hybrid spaces', *Space and Culture*, 9(3): 261–278, https://doi.org/10.1177/1206331206289022

Faulkner, X. and Culwin, F. (2005) 'When fingers do the talk: A study of text messaging', *Interacting with Computers*, 17(2): 167–185, https://doi.org/10.1016/j.intcom.2004.11.002

Fortunati, L. (2010) 'A discourse around theories on new media', in J. R. Höflich, G. F. Kircher, C. Linke and I. Schlote (eds) *Mobile Media and the Change of Everyday Life*, Frankfurt: Peter Lang, pp 19–39.

Gergen, K. J. (2002) 'The challenge of absent presence', in J. Katz and M. Aakhus (eds) *Perpetual Contact: Mobile Communication, Private Talk, Public Performance*, Cambridge: Cambridge University Press, pp 227–241.

Grellhesl, M. and Punyanunt-Carter, N.M. (2012) 'Using the uses and gratifications theory to understand gratifications sought through text messaging practices of male and female undergraduate students', *Computers in Human Behavior*, 28(6): 2175–2181, https://doi.org/10.1016/j.chb.2012.06.024

Grintner, R.E., Palen, L. and Eldridge, M. (2006) 'Chatting with teenagers: Considering the place of chat technologies in teen life', *ACM Transactions on Computer–Human Interaction*, 13(4): 423-447, https://doi.org/10.1145/1188816.1188817

Hall, J.A. and Baym, N. K. (2012) 'Calling and texting (too much): Mobile maintenance expectations, (over)dependence, entrapment, and friendship satisfaction', *New Media & Society*, 14(2): 316-331, https://doi.org/10.1177/1461444811415047

Isaacs, E., Szymanski, P., Yamauchi, Y., Glasnapp, J. and Iwamoto, K. (2012) 'Integrating local and remote worlds through channel blending', *Proceedings of the CSCW'12 on Computer Supported Cooperative Work*, Seattle, Washington, DC, https://doi.org/10.1145/2145204.2145299

Ito, M. (2001) 'Mobile phones, Japanese youth, and the replacement of social contact', in *Proceedings of the Annual Meeting for the Society for the Social Studies of Science*, Cambridge, MA, www.itofisher.com/PEOPLE/mito/Ito.4S2001.mobile.pdf

Kang, S. and Jung, J. (2014) 'Mobile communication for human needs: A comparison of smartphone use between the US and Korea', *Computers in Human Behavior*, 35: 376-387, https://doi.org/10.1016/j.chb.2014.03.024

Kasesniemi, E. L. and Rautiainen, P. (2002) 'Mobile culture of children and teenagers in Finland', in J. E. Katz and M. Aakhus (eds) *Perpetual Contact: Mobile Communication, Private Talk, Public Performance*, Cambridge: Cambridge University Press, pp 170-192.

Katz, J. E. and Aakhus, M. (2002) *Perpetual Contact. Mobile Communication, Private Talk, Public Performance*, Cambridge: Cambridge University Press.

Knop, K., Hefner, D., Schmitt, S. and Vorderer, P. (2015) *Mediatisierung mobil. Handy- und Internetnutzung von Kindern und Jugendlichen*, Leipzig: Vistas, Schriftenreihe Medienforschung der Landesanstalt für Medien Nordrhein-Westfalen (LfM), Band 77.

Lenhart, A., Ling, R., Campbell, S. and Purcell, K. (2010) *Teens and Mobile Phones*, Pew Research Center, http://www.pewinternet.org/2010/04/20/teens-and-mobile-phones/

Licoppe, C. (2004) '"Connected Presence': The emergence of a new repertoire for managing social relationships in a changing communication technoscape', *Environment and Planning D: Society and Space*, 22(1): 135-156, https://doi.org/10.1068/d323t

Ling, R. (2004) *The Mobile Connection*, San Francisco, CA: Elsevier.

Ling, R. and Yttri, B. (2002) 'Hyper-coordination via mobile phones in Norway', in J. Katz and M. Aakhus (eds) *Perpetual Contact: Mobile Communication, Private Talk, Public Performance*, Cambridge: Cambridge University Press, pp 139-169.

Mayring, P. (2008) *Qualitative Inhaltsanalyse. Grundlagen und Techniken* (10th ed), Weinheim: Beltz.

Mieczakowski, A., Goldhaber, T. and Clarkson, J. (2011) *Culture, Communication and Change: Report on an Investigation of the Use and Impact of Modern Media and Technology in Our Lives*, Cambridge: University of Cambridge.

O'Hara, K., Massimi, M., Harper, R., Rubens, S. and Morris, J. (2014) 'Everyday dwelling with WhatsApp', *Proceedings of the CSCW 2014, Mobile Apps for Enhancing Connectedness*, Baltimore, MD, pp 1131-1143, https://doi.org/10.1145/2531602.2531679

Oksman, V. and Turtiainen, J. (2004) 'Mobile communication as a social stage: Meanings of mobile communication in everyday life among teenagers in Finland', *New Media & Society*, 6(3): 319-339, https://doi.org/10.1177/1461444804042518

Pettigrew, J. (2009) 'Text messaging and connectedness within close interpersonal relationships', *Marriage & Family Review*, 45(6-8): 697-716, https://doi.org/10.1080/01494920903224269

Pew Research Center (2017) *Mobile Fact Sheet*, www.pewinternet.org/fact-sheet/mobile/

Quan-Haase, A. and Collins, J. L. (2008). 'I'm there, but I might not want to talk to you', *Information, Communication & Society*, 11(4): 526-543, https://doi.org/10.1080/13691180801999043

Rettie, R. (2009) 'Mobile phone communication: Extending Goffman to mediated interaction', *Sociology*, 43(3): 421-438, https://doi.org/10.1177/0038038509103197

Scannell, P. (1996) *Radio, Television and Modern Life: A Phenomenological Approach*, Oxford, UK: Blackwell.

Smoreda, Z. and Licoppe, C. (1999) 'La téléphonie résidentielle de foyers: Réseaux de sociabilité et cycle de vie', Paper for the conference *Usage and Services in Telecommunications*, 7-9 June, Arcachon.

Turkle, S. (2008) 'Always-on/always-on-you: The tethered self', in J. E. Katz (ed) *Handbook of Mobile Communication Studies*, Cambridge, MA: MIT, pp 121-138.

Urry, J. (2007) *Mobilities*, Cambridge: Polity Press.

Vincent, J. (2010) 'Living with mobile phones', in J. R. Höflich, G. F. Kircher, C. Linke and I. Schlote (eds) *Mobile Media and the Change of Everyday Life*, Frankfurt: Peter Lang, pp 155-170.

FOURTEEN

Permeability of work-family borders: effects of information and communication technologies on work-family conflict at the childcare stage in Japan

Yuka Sakamoto

Introduction

Childcare stage in Japan

In Japan, life transitions to childcare stages are often difficult, especially for women who try to continue their vocational career. From the 1980s to 2000s, while the overall female employment rate increased, the employment rate of women with young children remained low. Only recently have nationwide statistics begun to show that the ratio of women continuing to work before and after the birth of their first child has increased from 30% to 40% (Japanese National Institute of Population and Social Security Research, 2016). However, 17.1% of women leave their jobs upon marriage, and 33.9% upon the birth of their first child (Japanese National Institute of Population and Social Security Research, 2016); even now it is not uncommon for Japanese women to retire due to family responsibilities.

A major factor behind this situation is that people have not been allowed appropriate arrangements to allow them to combine work and family. The percentage of people working 60 hours per week or more was 10% in 2008 and 7.8% in 2016. In particular, the percentage of male workers in their thirties, corresponding to the childcare stage, stands at 20% for 2008 and 14.7% for 2016 (Japanese Ministry of Internal affairs and Communications, 2008, 2016b). In addition to the significant trend of full-time workers in Japan working long hours, in many cases a considerable commute time is required when living in one of the three major metropolitan areas: Tokyo, Osaka and Nagoya (Nagase and Moriizumi, 2011). The adoption of flexible working time systems is needed especially for workers at the childcare stage (Cabinet Office Government of Japan, 2015).

Telework adoption and ICTs

In recent years, there have been reports that many large Japanese companies have introduced teleworking (Japanese Ministry of Internal Affairs and Communications, 2015). While the share of teleworkers was less than 5% of all employees in 2008–2010, it was 12.5% in 2012 (Japanese Land, Infrastructure and Transportation, 2013) and 16.2% in 2016 (Japanese Ministry of Internal Affairs and Communications, 2016a).

A major trigger of this development was the Great Tōhoku earthquake of 11 March 2011. The widespread paralysis of public transportation and disruption to distribution networks in the immediate aftermath of the earthquake made a large number of companies recognize the importance of teleworking. Many of these companies have introduced home-based teleworking as part of their business plans (BCP) after 2011 (Japanese Ministry of Land, Infrastructure & Transport, 2013). In addition, the Act on Advancing Measures to Support Raising Next-Generation Children (Japanese Ministry of Health, Labour and Welfare, 2012) and the Work-Style Reform promoted by Prime Minister Shinzo Abe (Prime Minister of Japan and His Cabinet, 2016) provide a boost to adopting various work–life balancing programmes, including teleworking.

Diffusion of ICTs

The growing adoption of teleworking is due to an increasingly widespread use of information and communication technologies (ICTs). Especially in recent years, small, easily portable equipment, such as smartphones, have become pervasive in developed countries, facilitating real-time communication. The ratio of household smartphone penetration increased from 16.2% in 2011 to 71.8% in 2016 (Japanese Ministry of Internal affairs and communications, 2016). Not only devices (that is, smartphones, tablet computers) but also various groupware, applications or internet services, including chat applications, instant messengers, video calls and calendars, have also become very popular. This development of digital media enables us to access information at any time and from any location.

One of the features of these ICTs is fewer time and location restraints in communication. Sophisticated access to digitized information through ICTs also allows workers to address work-related activities or concerns from anywhere. Improved mobility and accessibility are extending the reach of work, including, of course, at home.

Literature review

Effect of ICTs on work-family life balance

To date, evaluations of the effect of ICTs on work–family life balance are divided. Whereas some researchers report positive influences providing resources for managing work–family life balance, some have found a negative impact that extends the reach of work to the family/intimate domain. Work extension is positively linked to increases in productivity and pace of life (Chesley, 2010), but also to work stress (Mano and Mesch, 2010).

With respect to research focusing on the positive effect of ICTs, the personal digital assistant (PDA) is regarded as a personal agency to control the work-family boundary by users (Golden and Geisler, 2007) and help workers to achieve greater balance between work and personal life (Cousins and Robey, 2005). Many workers positively evaluate the flexibility gained through the use of ICTs, although they tend to work longer (Derks and Bakker, 2010). Kennedy and Wellman (2007) found that ICTs have afforded mutual awareness, integration and support between the work domain and the family domain. Wajcman et al (2008) claimed that ICTs encouraged deeper contacts with intimates rather than having a primary influence on work–family life balance.

Regarding the negative impact of ICTs, ICT-enabled work arrangements tend to increase extra and supplemental work (Derks and Bakker, 2010; Fenner and Renn, 2010; Middleton, 2008), and thus blur the boundaries that separate work and home (Leung and Zhang, 2017). More permeable boundaries between work and home, facilitated by ICT use, were associated with not only an increase in the distress of workers but also a decrease in family satisfaction (Chesley, 2005; Middleton, 2008). As for smartphone users, Jarvenpaa and Lang (2005) indicated increased work pressure and an inability to separate work/personal life and keep their distance from work. Furthermore, Derks and Bakker (2014) showed that smartphone use, work–home interference, and burnout were positively related.

Telework and work-family life balance

The effect of ICTs is often treated together with flexible work arrangements such as telework, rather than examining the impact of its technological element independently. However, the implications of telework are also contested. Telework has been associated with benefits for workers, such as decreased work-family conflict (WFC) (Sakamoto and Spinks, 2008; Hill et al, 2003), but can also bring about risks of strain spillover from work to home (Peters and van der Lippe, 2007), or increased family-work conflict (Golden et al, 2006). Demerouti et al (2014) pointed out the importance of an adoption strategy since research showed both pros and cons of new ways of working. Kossek et al (2006) indicated the significance of work flexibility for psychological rather than for physical reasons (that is, temporal and spatial). More research is necessary to clarify the complexity of flexible work arrangements. As ICTs continue to develop, evidence supporting its influence on work extension and work-family domains is needed.

Theoretical framework and hypotheses

The purpose of this study is to explore the positive and negative effects of ICTs on work-family life balance at the childcare stage, focusing on the effect of ICTs and home-working arrangements. Specifically, the effects of ICTs on the permeability of work-family borders are examined empirically, applying the work-family border theory presented by Clark (2000). We consider the influence of ICTs, such as small laptops, smartphones, tablets, video calls and instant messenger services – technologies that enable instant and easy access to work.

Clark (2000) presents a comprehensive theory to understand the complex interaction between work and family by focusing on the borders between the two domains. Clark's border theory offers useful concepts and propositions to treat the effects of ICTs on the permeability of work-family borders.

According to this theory, people daily cross borders between the two domains of work and family. Assessment of work-life balance is influenced by the characteristics of the border (that is, permeability, strength, flexibility) between the work domain and the family domain. 'Permeability', the main concept of this chapter, is defined as 'the degree to which elements from other domains may enter' (Clark, 2000, p 756). The physical, temporal and psychological aspects of borders are taken into account. These concepts, developed by Clark, are appropriate to examine the impact of ICTs, which tend to weaken the temporal and other restrictions of communication.

Clark (2000) suggests that 'other domain awareness' of work and family members facilitates work–family balance, so that factors affecting the increase of awareness of the other domain, such as border-crossing communication, are considered to be important. In this study, we propose four factors, namely the degree of use of ICTs (that is, variety of applications used, frequency of use), the physical permeability of borders, the temporal psychological permeability of borders, and border-crossing communication, as the key elements facilitating work–family life balance.

Figure 14.1 shows the conceptual model of this study applying the concepts of border theory, which explains the occurrence of work–family conflict originally caused by the usage of ICTs. Much of the previous work on WFC addressing telework environment does not reflect the effect of ICT itself, nor does it fully reflect the supplemental nature of work that is extending beyond office hours and office borders (Middleton, 2008). We scope the influence of ICTs separately and demonstrate the relationship explicitly between ICTs and the permeability of work–family borders as a result of work extension.

Figure 14.1 Conceptual model predicting work–family conflict

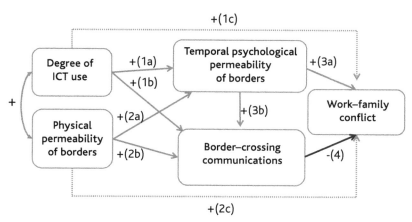

Note: Each character in brackets corresponds to the working hypotheses; positive and negative signs indicate their predicted impact.

We predict that ICT in itself is neither a demand nor a resource (Derks and Bakker, 2010), but acts to increase border permeability. Since ICT users are more likely to work at home than non-users and vice versa (Sakamoto, 2009), we assume a strong positive correlation between the degree of ICT use and physical permeability of borders as well as frequency of home-working.

However, the degree of ICT use does not have a direct effect on WFC, since we assume that ICTs serve as a trigger to increase border permeability and border-crossing communications. Applying these findings and assumptions, the following hypotheses are offered.

Although ICTs have no direct effect on WFC, an indirect, contradictory effect will be shown through two pathways:

> H1. Increased WFC through greater border permeability around the family.

> H2. Reduced WFC through greater frequency of border-crossing communication.

These research hypotheses can be subdivided into the following working hypotheses:

> 1. A higher frequency of ICT use will, (a) increase the permeability of temporal and psychological borders; (b) increase the frequency of border-crossing communication; (c) have no direct effect on WFC.

> 2. Greater physical permeability of borders (higher frequency of home-working) will (a) increase the permeability of temporal and psychological borders; (b) increase the frequency of border-crossing communication; (c) have no direct effect on WFC.

> 3. Greater permeability of temporal and psychological borders will (a) exacerbate WFC; (b) increase the frequency of border-crossing communication.

> 4. Frequent border-crossing communication will decrease WFC.

Regarding the effect of border permeability on WFC, Sakamoto and Spinks (2008) reported that although the WFC of Japanese home-based workers is lower than that of those who commute to work, due to their shorter work hours, the presence/absence of home-based work does not have a direct impact on WFC after controlling for work hours. This suggests that border permeability may trigger WFC in Japanese home-based work settings. We therefore predict that increased permeability of temporal psychological borders increases WFC. Kossel et al (2006) also found that boundary management strategies that were higher on integration led to greater family-work conflict. Finally, we also predict that the influence of border crossing communications on WFC will be negative as Clark (2000) suggests.

Method

Sample

Data used for this study derive from a web questionnaire survey conducted in February 2013 with a sample of 20-49-year-old working parents, who reside in the three major metropolitan areas of Tokyo, Osaka and Nagoya. The data set is provided in Table 14.1.

Random sampling was conducted from the registered monitors/participants of an online research company, who matched the specified criteria. The valid sample size excluding short time response and/or inappropriate answers was 300 (150 males and 150 females). Regarding the degree of ICT usage, all survey subjects are not only internet users, but also use a wide variety of ICTs.

Table 14.1 Dataset outline

Survey type	Cross-sectional survey
Survey subjects	20-49-year-old working parents, who reside in the three major metropolitan areas of Tokyo, Osaka and Nagoya
Sampling	Random sampling from registered participants of an online research company
Survey method	Web questionnaire survey
Survey period	18-21 February 2013
Valid sample size (rate)	300 (15.5%)
Number of emails sent	1,936

Measures

Measures of the main concepts were in Likert-type response format. Though all of the original measures were on a scale from one to five, we changed to four-level scales in order to avoid the strong tendency of Japanese respondents to select the middle option.

WFC: The WFC scale is Kanai's (2000) ten-item scale, which includes 'My work interrupts family life' and 'I'm busy both with my work and housework'. The scale assesses work interference with family (WIF) and time-based WFC. Kanai (2000) reported an α coefficient ranging from 0.93 to 0.95, including the dimension of work interference with family.

Permeability around family: A Japanese version of the five-item permeability scale (Clark, 2002) was created but transformed into a six-item permeability scale. Although the 'Work-Family Integration-Blurring Scale' suggested by Desrochers et al (2005) was another option, we preferred Clark's scale (2002) because of its focus on behavioural aspects. Based on her empirical results, however, Clark (2002) points out that this scale could have various meanings, the most reasonable explanation being 'defencelessness to work invading home'. Sample items include: 'I receive work-related calls while I am at home', 'I stop in the middle of my home activities to address a work concern'. The item 'I have work-related items at my home' was not used. Clark (2002) reported the α for the six items at 0.89, assessing temporal and psychological permeability of the border around the family.

Communication with family about work: The communication scale was also derived from Clark's (2002) scale. The Japanese version includes two dimensions of communication, namely domain as obligation and domain as a centre of activities. Clark (2002) identified only one principal component for these two dimensions, and the coefficient α for all eight items was 0.86. The Japanese version conflated five items, including 'I talk about my work schedule with my family' and 'I share pleasant things that happened at work with my family'.

Degree of ICT use: This was measured with four items on a six-point scale. The share of using recent devices for work was very low, so we used the frequency of recent applications for measuring the degree of ICT use. We asked 'How often do you use the ICTs listed below for business purposes?' (1 = never; 6 = almost every day including weekends). Table 14.2, in the next section, provides a list of the ICTs.

Frequency of home-working: This measure assessed the physical permeability of borders around the family. Our measure included three items of home-working frequency as shown in Table 14.2. Respondents selected six level options from 'Never (= 1)' to 'More than five times per week (= 6)'.

Results

Descriptive statistics

Table 14.2 presents the range, α coefficient of internal consistency for the entire sample, and descriptive statistics calculated by gender. While WFC and permeability around family did not differ by gender, female

Table 14.2 Descriptive statistics

		Range	α	Male ($n = 150$)		Female ($n = 150$)		
				M	SD	M	SD	
1	Work-family conflict (WFC)	10-40	0.927	24.24	6.91	23.94	6.35	
2	Temporal, psychological permeability	5-20	0.881	11.33	2.89	11.23	3.34	
3	Communication frequency with family	5-20	0.902	13.40	3.62	14.51	3.48	**
Frequency of home-working								
4	During daytime on weekdays	1-6		1.69	1.58	1.71	1.60	
5	On weekends	1-6	(0.632)	1.56	.90	1.26	.65	**
6	10 pm-7 am	1-6		1.44	.89	1.22	.71	*
Degree of ICT use								
7	Instant messenger	1-6		1.73	1.50	1.23	.93	**
8	Video call, Video conference	1-6		1.39	.79	1.04	.23	***
9	Electronic conference room, Bulletin board	1-6	(0.655)	1.66	1.35	1.14	.67	***
10	Scheduler	1-6		2.91	2.06	1.52	1.34	***

*$p < 0.05$; **$p < 0.01$; ***$p < 0.001$ (*t*-test).

communication frequency with family about work was significantly higher than for males.

Overall, the level of home-working frequency was low, and there was no difference between the frequency of daytime home-working on weekdays for males and females. However, males showed a significantly higher frequency of out-of-hours home-working. The general degree of ICT use was also low, with female use being significantly lower than males across all items.

Since the α reliability of WFC, permeability around family and communication scales was high, we used an aggregate scale for these concepts in the structural equation modelling (SEM) analysis. However, the α coefficient of frequency of home-working and degree of ICT use was not high, so latent variables for these concepts were created instead of using aggregate scales.

SEM multiple group analysis

Figure 14.2 shows the standardized path coefficients of the theoretical model for the male and female sub-samples with multiple group analysis. We based the analytic procedure for testing our model on Vandenberg and Lance's (2000) structural equation modelling method for testing scale invariance across different samples. The result of an omnibus test of measurement invariance suggests that the variance–covariance matrix including items from all scales was not invariant across male and female sub-samples. The proposed model of two groups without constraint yielded a chi-square of 70.276 with 56 degrees of freedom. The GFI (Goodness of fit index) of 0.96 and the RMSEA (Root mean square error of approximation) of 0.29 (no greater than 0.05) show that our hypothesized model without measurement invariance fits the data well.

The estimated values of factor loadings for both the latent construct degree of ICTs and frequency of home-working were significant at $p < 0.001$. As noted before, the factor weights were significantly different between the male and female sub-samples. A large difference was observed especially in the factor loadings for frequency of home-working. Although every weight on items for frequency of home-working was high for females, the weight of 'during daytime on weekdays' was low for males.

Turning to each path coefficient, temporal and psychological permeability significantly increased WFC for both males and females. However, the degree of ICT use had a non-significant positive effect on temporal and psychological permeability. Frequency of home-working, that is physical permeability around family, showed a positive

Figure 14.2 Standardized path coefficients of conceptual model

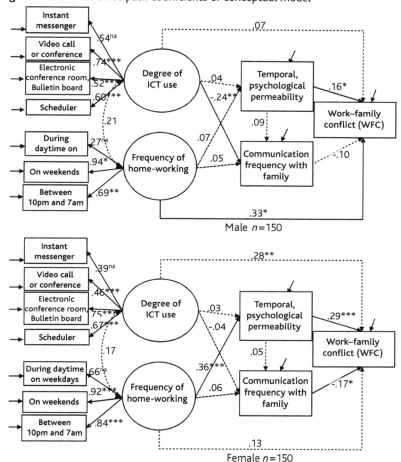

Male n=150

Female n=150

Note: All coefficients are standardized, estimated by maximum likelihood and computed with AMOS.
$\chi 2(56)=70.276$: GFI=.958 AGFI=.917 RMSEA=.029. *p<.05 **p<.01 ***p<.001 (two-tailed tests)

influence on temporal and psychological permeability. However, this relationship was only significant for females. In contrast, frequency of home-working significantly increased WFC for males.

Regarding the impact of communication frequency, although a significant relationship was only observed for females, more frequent communication decreased WFC as expected. However, the impact of ICT use on communication frequency was not positive, but showed a negative direction, contrary to our prediction. Nevertheless, the negative influence of ICT use on communication frequency was significant for males. Both the effect of frequency of home-working and temporal psychological permeability on communication frequency was positive but non-significant for male and female sub-samples.

Discussion

This study analysed the effect of ICTs on work–family conflict, focusing on the mediating effect of work–family permeability and border-crossing communication. Hypotheses concerning the impact of permeability and communication on WFC were generally supported. Whereas increased temporal and psychological permeability around family strengthens WFC, more frequent communication decreases it. Increased physical permeability as well as frequency of home-working also directly exacerbates WFC, especially for males and contrary to our prediction.

Consistent with earlier studies by Clark (2002) and Desrochers et al (2005), two types of permeability tended to increase WFC. Longer work hours correlated to temporal psychological permeability particularly for males. In other words, an increase in permeability of borders reflects a greater amount of out-of-hours working. As Clark (2002) pointed out, permeability of home border may be a result of the individual's lack of control over work invading home.

Hypotheses concerning the effect of ICTs were not supported. Contrary to our prediction, ICTs had a direct negative effect on WFC especially for females. Along with permeability of borders, frequent use of ICTs may be a mirror of more demanding work. Moreover, ICTs did not increase communication with family about work issues. This means that real-time and visual contact from work members with home did not trigger communication with family members about work. Overall, the results for ICTs do not show a positive impact on work–family life balance, but suggest, if anything, a negative impact.

As such, particularly in the childcare stage, reducing the amount of work or total work hours may be needed instead of limited flexibility such as timing or place of work. As Leung and Zhang (2017) demonstrated, controlling ICT use and its permeability in the home domain are important to prevent the negative effects of telework.

Despite these findings, the measurement validity or the influence of the degree of ICT use for business needs to be reviewed. ICTs are not used very much at work even though our survey panels are comprised of internet users living in the three metropolitans areas of Tokyo, Osaka and Nagoya. In fact, about half of respondents did not even use traditional ICTs such as desktop PCs or email for work. According to the empirical research of Wajcman et al (2008), the mobile phone encourages deeper contact with intimate ties. Though the smartphone has rapidly been diffused in Japan, this may tend to be used not for business purposes but for communication and/or amusement purposes with family/intimates.

Findings from the data on workers at the childcare stage imply that border-crossing communication acts to reduce WFC, although ICTs did not act as a catalyst. So far, the importance of border-crossing communication has not been noted in Japanese work–family research, so this result offers empirical support for Clark's (2000) border theory and brings a new perspective to Japanese work–family research and practice. If Japanese workers realize the importance of border-crossing communications and use ICTs for that kind of communications, ICTs can connect families.

To sum up, in a life stage associated with considerable amounts of housework and childcare, work reduction and frequent border-crossing communication are important means for decreasing WFC, while time and spatial flexibility seem to be secondary means. Despite limitations (for example, cross-sectional survey, the measurement validity of the degree of ICT use), these empirical results contribute to an understanding of the impact of ICTs on work–family life balance and suggest the need for effective measures to facilitate work–family life balance during the childcare stage.

In brief

1. New types of portable devices, various applications and internet services have become popular in Japan, which facilitate real-time communication and allow workers to address work concerns from anywhere.

2. Flexible work arrangements such as telework, involving less commuting time and greater scheduling flexibility, are needed because of the recent rise of dual-earner families in Japan.

3. This study examines the effect of recent ICTs on the permeability of work-family borders and on work-family conflict (WFC) at the childcare stage, by drawing on work-family border theory.

4. Results of structural equation modelling show that WFC increased with greater permeability of borders, and tended to decrease with more frequent border-crossing communication with family.

5. However, the degree of ICT use did not show a strong effect on increases in border permeability or communication frequency; but it directly increased WFC, suggesting that the degree of ICT use at work may be a mirror of more demanding work.

Acknowledgements

This research was funded by Grant-in-Aid for Scientific Research (C), Grant No. 22530425.

References

Cabinet Office Government of Japan (2015) *2015nen Shoushika Shakai Hakusho* [2015 declining birthrate white paper], Tokyo: Nikkei Insatsu, www8.cao.go.jp/shoushi/shoushika/whitepaper/measures/english/w-2015/index.html

Clark, S. C. (2000) 'Work/family border theory: A new theory of work/family balance', *Human Relations*, 53(6): 747–770, https://doi.org/10.1177/0018726700536001

Clark, S. C. (2002) 'Communicating across the work/home border', *Community, Work & Family*, 5(1): 23–48, https://doi.org/10.1080/13668800020006802

Cousins, K. C. and Robey, D. (2005) 'Human agency in a wireless world: Patterns of technology use in nomadic computing environments', *Information and Organization*, 15(2): 151–180, https://doi.org/10.1016/j.infoandorg.2005.02.008

Chesley, N. (2005) 'Blurring boundaries? Linking technology use, spillover, individual distress, and family satisfaction', *Journal of Marriage and Family*, 67: 1237–1248, https://doi.org/10.1111/j.1741-3737.2005.00213.x

Chesley, N. (2010) 'Technology use and employee assessments of productivity, workload, and pace of life', *Information, Communication & Society*, 13(4): 485–514, https://doi.org/10.1080/13691180903473806

Demerouti, E., Derks, D., Lieke, L. and Bakker, A. B. (2014) 'New ways of working: Impact on working conditions, work-family balance, and well-being', in C. Korunka and P. Hoonakker (eds) *The Impact of ICT on Quality of Working Life*, Dordrecht: Springer, pp 123–141.

Derks, D. and Bakker, A. (2010) 'The impact of e-mail communication on organizational life', *Cyberpsychology: Journal of Psychosocial Research on Cyberspace*, 4(1): https://cyberpsychology.eu/article/view/4233/3277

Derks, D. and Bakker A. (2014) 'Smartphone use, work–home interference, and burnout: A diary study on the role of recovery', *Applied Psychology*, 63(3): 411–440, https://doi.org/10.1111/j.1464-0597.2012.00530.x

Desrochers, S., Hilton, J. M. and Larwood, L. (2005) 'Preliminary validation of the work-family integration blurring scale', *Journal of Family Issues*, 26(4): 442–466, https://doi.org/10.1177/0192513X04272438

Fenner, G. and Renn, R. (2010) 'Technology assisted supplemental work and work-family conflict: The role of instrumentality beliefs, organizational expectations and time management', *Human Relations*, 63(1): 63-82, https://doi.org/10.1177/0018726709351064

Golden, A. G. and Geisler, C. (2007) 'Work-life boundary management and the personal digital assistant', *Human Relations,* 60(3): 519-551, https://doi.org/10.1177/0018726707076698

Golden, T. D., Veiga, J. F. and Simsek, Z. (2006) 'Telecommuting's differential impact on work-family conflict: Is there no place like home?', *Journal of Applied Psychology*, 91(6): 1340-1350, https://doi.org/10.1037/0021-9010.91.6.1340

Hill, E. J., Ferris, M. and Martinson, V. (2003) 'Does it matter where you work? A comparison of how three work venues (traditional office, virtual office, and home office) influence aspects of work and personal/family life', *Journal of Vocational Behavior*, 63(2): 220-241, https://doi.org/10.1016/S0001-8791(03)00042-3

Japanese Ministry of Health, Labour and Welfare. (2012) *Jisedai ikusei taisaku suishin hou* [Law for measures to support the development of the next generation], http://law.e-gov.go.jp/htmldata/H15/H15HO120.html

Japanese Ministry of Internal Affairs and Communications. (2008) *Roudouryoku chousa* [Labour force survey], www.stat.go.jp/data/roudou/report/2008/ft/index.htm

Japanese Ministry of Internal Affairs and Communications. (2015) *Jouhou tsushin hakusho* [White paper on information and communications in Japan], Tokyo: Nikkei Insatsu, www.soumu.go.jp/main_content/000380937.pdf

Japanese Ministry of Internal Affairs and Communications. (2016a) *Tshushin riyou doukou chosa* [Communications usage trend survey], www.soumu.go.jp/johotsusintokei/statistics/pdf/HR201600_001.pdf

Japanese Ministry of Internal Affairs and Communications. (2016b) *Roudouryoku chosa* [Labour force survey], www.stat.go.jp/data/roudou/report/2016/index.htm

Japanese Ministry of Land, Infrastructure and Transport. (2013) *2012 nen terewaku jinkou jittai chosa kekka* [Results of the 2012 Telework Population Survey], www.mlit.go.jp/crd/daisei/telework/docs/24telework_jinko_jittai_gaiyo.pdf

Japanese National Institute of Population and Social Security Research. (2016) *Gendai nihon no kekkon to shussan: dai 15 kai shussei doukou kihon chosa* [Marriage and childbirth in Japan today: The 15th Japanese National Fertility Survey], www.ipss.go.jp/ps-doukou/j/doukou15/NFS15_reportALL.pdf

Jarvenpaa, S. and Lang, K. (2005) 'Managing the paradoxes of mobile technology', *Information Systems Management Journal*, 22(4): 7–23, https://doi.org/10.1201/1078.10580530/45520.22.4.20050901/90026.2

Kanai, A. (2000) 'Waku famiri konfurikuto to mentaru herusu no kanrensei ni kansuru sinrigakuteki kousatu' [A psychological study on the relationship between work-family conflict and mental health], *kagaku kenkyuuhi hojokin kenkyu houkokusho* [Report of grant-in-aid for scientific research (no. 09610113)], Nagoya: Nagoya University.

Kennedy, T. L. M. and Wellman, B. (2007) 'The networked household', *Information, Communication & Society*, 10(5): 645-670, https://doi.org/10.1080/13691180701658012

Kossek, E. E., Lautsch, B. and Eaton, S. C. (2006) 'Telecommuting, control, and boundary management: Correlates of policy use and practice, job control, and work-family effectiveness', *Journal of Vocational Behavior*, 68(2): 347-367, https://doi.org/10.1016/j.jvb.2005.07.002

Leung, L. and Zhang, R. (2017) 'Mapping ICT use at home and telecommuting practices: A perspective from work/family border theory', *Telematics and Informatics*, 34(1): 385-396, https://doi.org/10.1016/j.tele.2016.06.001

Mano, R. S. and Mesch, G. S. (2010) 'E-mail characteristics, work performance and distress', *Computers in Human Behavior*, 26(1): 61-69, https://doi.org/10.1016/j.chb.2009.08.005

Middleton, C. A. (2008) 'Do mobile technologies enable work-life balance? Dual perspectives on BlackBerry usage for supplemental work', in D. Hislop (ed) *Mobility and Technology in the Workplace*, Abingdon: Routledge, pp 209-224.

Nagase, N. and Moriizumi, R. (2011) '1990 nendai kara 2000 nenndai ni daisotsu josei no shuugyou keizoku koudou ha dou kawatta ka: 26-33 sai wo taisho to shita kikitori chosa yori' [Work and family choices of higher educated Japanese women: The effects of changing labour practices of Japanese firms in the 1990s and 2000s], *Seikatsu shakai kagaku kenkyu* [Journal of social sciences and family studies], 17, 1-21.

Peters, P. and van der Lippe, T. (2007) 'The time-pressure reducing potential of telehomeworking: the Dutch case', *The International Journal of Human Resource Management*, 18(3): 430-447, https://doi.org/10.1080/09585190601167730

Prime Minister of Japan and His Cabinet. (2016) *Hatarakikata kaikaku jikko keikaku* [The outline of work-style reform], http://www.kantei.go.jp/jp/singi/hatarakikata/pdf/gaiyou_h290328.pdf

Sakamoto, Y. (2009) 'Jouhou tsushin gijutsu (ICT) ga hitobito no shugyo basho ni oyobosu eikyo: terewaku ha fukyu shite irunoka' [The impact of information and communications technology (ICT) on work places: Is telework making ground?]. *Nihon roudou kenkyu zasshi* [Japanese Journal of Labour Studies], 51(2), 91-105.

Sakamoto, Y. and Spinks, W. A. (2008) 'The impact of home-based telework on work-family conflict in the childcare stage', *The Journal of E-Working*, 2(2): 144-158.

Wajcman, J., Bittman, M. and Brown, J. E. (2008) 'Families without borders: Mobile phones, connectedness & work-home divisions', *Sociology*, 42(4): 635-652, https://doi.org/10.1177/0038038508091620

Vandenberg, R. J. and Lance, C. E. (2000) 'A review and synthesis of the measurement invariance literature: Suggestions, practices, and recommendations for organizational research', *Organizational Research Methods*, 3(1): 4–70, https://doi.org/10.1177/109442810031002

Digital connections and family practices

Elizabeth B. Silva

As digital technologies – used socially for information, communication or entertainment – allow for new ways of living social life and of knowing about it, it is increasingly significant that we inquire about the crucial matter of what the digital does to the ways we know about each other, how we live, and what social scientists can learn from and with the digital.

An important point for investigation of changes linked to digital connections is that there is no proper or clear boundary between what more traditional information and communication technology (ICT) is – and how we have so far referred to it – and the current digital technologies used for information and communication, which have fully moved into mainstream with the prominence of social media (Berker et al, 2005). In the process of social change, technological innovation and adoption happen unevenly and not concomitantly. What matters is that digitally powered technologies are increasingly around us, a daily component of our lives, whether we are engaged with it ourselves – moving across space and time, emailing, phoning, searching for information, tweeting – or by our simply being in contemporary settings, be they rural, urban, remote, cosmopolitan or traditional. Living in a digitally connected world affects all kinds of our social practices – and relationships. Family is one of those.

However, a focus on family does not claim specialness for the exploration of the digital. Here family is simply context, situation, and site for linkages of relationships. These have something to do with marriage, partnership, parenthood or kinship, be these formally or informally recognized (Morgan, 1996). While these relationships could be described in different ways, for example as unmarried people living together, biological parents caring for children, and so on, I focus on all sorts of relationships to do with family practices (involving people living together and 'doing' family), to inform a way of looking at domestic, everyday connections in flow, in movement (that is, not marked by legal or biological – or any other – frameworks). I privilege certain family connections in the reflections I make in this paper: intergenerational, sexual, intimate and fractured in space through migration and borders. I am unable to make any extensive elaboration about the use of theories of practice to think about digital connections. It seems sufficient to say that for 'practices', doing is emphasized over thinking, practical competence is stressed over strategic reasoning, and mutual or shared intelligibility prevails over personal/individual motivation. Importantly, practices precede individuals, they derive from, and generate effects at, both individual and societal levels. In this way, practices have institutional form, regulative interventions, conventions and rituals; they do not depend on conscious consideration for conduct and are interconnected with other entities in their field (or environment) (Warde, 2016), as evidenced in the various practices I discuss in this paper.

Current assessments of the roles of technological digital imprints invoke both their enrichment and hindrance to our current practices of living. The latter echoes more loudly and occupies my attention here. Are digital ICTs affecting our close relations in troubling ways? Are we changing into unsociable, individualistic beings unable to hold conversations, get out of doors and talk to each other? Are there any spaces of life still unmonitored by technological devices? What digital technologies do to our sexuality and intimacy? Could we still be parents, partners, children and friends who care for each other in unmediated ways – or have we become disabled in this capacity by the mediation of digital connections? Can we learn better about social life by using the capacities of digital technology and data?

I am unable to properly consider all of these concerns in this paper. My aim is to survey some of the academic and media engagement with these concerns regarding change over time in some key areas affecting family life. Let us begin by considering some of the major digital tools we currently use for relating to other people and the recent pace of these changes (see Table 15.1).

Emails are nowadays a normalized form of communication, having reached 3.7 billion users since January 2017, nearly 54% of the entire planet (The Radicati Group, 2017), while in 1997 it reached 10 million users. The number of mobile phone users was forecast to grow to 4.77 billion by the end of 2017 (Statista, 2015b), although the distribution worldwide is uneven, with Asia Pacific, the Middle East and Africa having the lowest numbers of users. In June 2017, the most popular social networking site in the world, Facebook, had 2 billion monthly active users (those who logged in during the last 30 days). This was

Table 15.1 Timeline of the most used contemporary ICT and platforms

Email
1972: first electronic email with the '@' signal.
1976: Queen Elizabeth II sends an email message on Arpanet, the first head of state to do so.
1996: Microsoft releases Internet Mail and News 1.0, features of Internet Explorer version 3, later renamed Outlook. A few companies – including Hotmail – begin to offer free, use-anywhere, internet email.
1997: about 10 million users worldwide have free web mail accounts.
2014–2019: 4.1 billion active accounts in 2014, expected 5.6 billion in 2019.[a]

Mobile phones
1983: first unveiled.
1992: first UK consumer phones; first text message on 03 December 1992.
2002: first Europe camera phone.
2007: iPhone launched, as the first consumer **smartphone**, a device to make telephone calls, with added features for web access, previously found only on a personal digital assistant or a computer.
2016: estimated 62.9% of the population worldwide owned a mobile phone.[b]

Laptop
1984: IBM announced its first Portable Personal Computer.
2010: **Tablets** sales amount to 19 million worldwide, growing since.
2019: estimates of 170 million laptops and 180 million tablets to ship worldwide.[c]

Skype
Launched August 2003, provides cost free instant online text message, phone and video chat.
2016: there were 74,000,000 skype users worldwide.[d]

Facebook
Social networking service launched in February 2004. **Facebook Chat** released in 2008, instant message one friend or multiple people. In 2011 incorporation of video and release of mobile app **Messenger**.
2017: Facebook users amount to more than 2 billion monthly (June).[e]

Myspace
developed 2006. Users could instant message with friends on their desktops, as well as online starting in 2009.
2008: peak number of users in December at 75.9 million. Decreased to 15 million in April 2016.[f]

WhatsApp
instant message, with text, photo, video, indicates the status of users – launched 2009.
2017 (July) more than 1.3 billion monthly users.[g]

Instagram
a photo-sharing social platform launched in October 2010. Video sharing was incorporated in June 2013.
2017 (Sept): more than 800 million users.[h]

Snapchat
launched September 2011. Ephemeral multimedia messages referred to as 'snaps'; snaps, consisting of a photo or a short video, which can be edited to include filters and effects, text captions, and drawings. Presented as the solution to stresses caused by the longevity of personal information on social media.
2017 (third quarter): 178 million daily users worldwide.[i]

Note: Technologies were developed and perfected slowly. Dates refer to significant moments of user connection and uptake.

[a] Statista (2015a); [b] Statista (2015b); [c] Statista (2017e); [d] Statistic Brain (2016); [e] Alexa (2017b); [f] Smith (2017); [g] Statista (2017d); [h] Statista (2017b); [i] Statista (2017c).

double the number in September 2012 (Statista, 2017a). While these digital information and communication technologies (d–ICT) include public connections of work, education, health and others, a lot of relationships of choice and of a familial kind are developed through them. The early 2000s marked the launch of major commercial platforms and devices – Skype, Facebook, iPhone – speedily propelling social media participation, already significant via email, distribution lists, discussion lists, internet chat and other online fora (Coleman, 2012).

The pace of technological change in information and communication and their consumption rates has been fast, reaching large numbers of people. This quickly extended usability in numbers to include extensive capability for monitoring, informing and analysing social life (Orton-Johnson and Prior, 2013; Marres, 2017). Research in this volume (Neves and Casimiro, 2018) shows that digital information and communication technologies, prevalent in all walks of life, connects families over the life course, affecting routines, relationships, ways of working and of doing intimacy, and privacy. Four main areas were found to relate to connections between dICT and families: intergenerational, intimate couple relationship, transnational or migrant families and life course (Casimiro and Nico, Chapter Eight in Neves and Casimiro, 2018). While I agree about these being prominent areas of connection, I frame my discussion of digital connections and family practices under two headings: (1) intergenerational connections, and (2) connections of sexuality, intimacy and over fractured spaces. A final section discusses research agendas, focusing on what we know, what we need to know and how to go about knowing. In this I claim for the use of multiple methods to develop knowledge about digital transformations in family practices and beyond, vital for current social sciences.

Intergenerational connections

As I write this chapter, the September 2017 issue of the US publication *The Atlantic* presents a piece by American academic psychologist Jean Twenge (2017a) claiming that social media is having a truly malign effect on the young. The article, 'Have Smartphones Destroyed a Generation?', follows a book she wrote, revealingly entitled *iGen. Why Today's Super-Connected Kids are Growing Up Less Rebellious, More Tolerant, Less Happy – and Completely Unprepared for Adulthood – and What that Means for the Rest of Us* (Twenge, 2017b). The book draws from data gathered from four large-scale nationally representative surveys of 11 million Americans since 1961. The iGeneration consists of teens and young adults born since 1995, the first generation to spend their entire adolescence in possession of smartphones. Social media and texting have replaced other activities, claims Twenge. iGen youth are together a lot but only virtually. According to Twenge, they experience unprecedented levels of anxiety, depression and loneliness. They are non-religious, have no community attachment, and show great safety concerns. iGen grows up more slowly than previous generations: 'eighteen-year-olds look and act like fifteen-year-olds used to' (Twenge, 2017b, p 3). Following publication of these data and claims, reactions from parents and experts abounded in the media (printed and online), exposing concerns over amounts of use, risks, the need for policies, control, precaution and, importantly for my reflections about this, about the quality of the research on which Twenge bases her claims.

In an interview in the 'Science & Tech' supplement of 'The New Review' in the UK Sunday broadsheet *The Observer*, Twenge (2017a) describes her engagement with the phenomenon. 'In 2013-14 I started to see some really sudden changes… I'd never seen anything like it… It's an absolutely stunning pattern… All the screen activities correlated with lower happiness.' The presentation Twenge (2017a, 2017b) makes of her work sounds sensationalist. Yet she also refers to brain development of teens requiring human interaction for development of social skills, and to screen engagement of one hour a day having no detrimental effect on mental health.

Controversies of these kinds mirror long-held views of opposing camps. On one side we find the conservative right claiming that technology leads to moral degradation of youth. On the other, progressives and technophiles try to unravel the complexity of the matter. I found similar stances in my research on domestic technology. In the dominant social sciences debates of the 1950-1960s concerns emerged that women's idleness, generated by the widespread consumption of household technologies, had left room for dangerous ideologies to creep into domestic life, generating family breakdown and crises in the wellbeing of family members. A number of feminist academic studies confronted these conservative views, showing, among other things, that technology had facilitated family life in the face of changes such as the growing employment of women outside of the home (Silva, 2002). In the contemporary context of digital technology the split between conservative and progressive views echoes similar arguments.

In the heat of this recent debate about smartphones, Alexandra Samuel (2017), a freelance researcher on technology, presented a comprehensive reading of Twenge's claims. Acknowledging the importance of Twenge's investigation and findings, Samuel explores the survey data. Reviewing 20 years of the *Monitoring the Future survey* series (Figure 15.1), used by Twenge, Samuel says that 'levels of happiness and unhappiness are largely constant, though we may be heading into a very modest (though not unprecedented) dip'. Similarly, longer length of screen use does not indicate significant unhappiness (Figure 15.2). There is no crisis. Moreover, teens who do not use smartphones show unhappiness. Considering data from the non-partisan Pew Research Center, based in Washington DC, about the growth of social media use in the US by age (Figure 15.3), Samuel shows that social network adoption bracketing the four years around the introduction of the iPhone indicates continued growth of teens' usage, and steady usage growth among 18-to-49-year-olds, whom she appropriately refers to as *parents*. An important intergenerational connection is raised. Samuel claims that smartphones and social media are good for 'tuning out' the children. When parents are distracted – something they welcome because children are less interesting than relating to peers or the adult world – parenting suffers. Backing her arguments with psychologist Zussman's (1980) experiment about parental distraction, she notes that encouragement suffers since control and sanction are easier to implement distractedly. Disputing Twenge's claims, Samuel suggests

Figure 15.1 Teen happiness

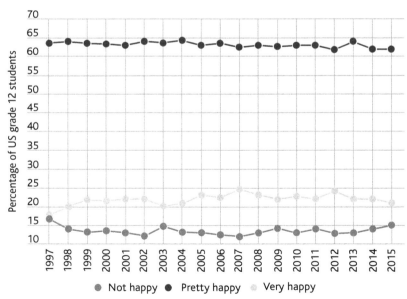

Source: Monitoring the Future grade 12 surveys. Reproduced with permission from the author, Alexandra Samuel (2017) available at:
https://daily.jstor.org/yes-smartphones-are-destroying-a-generation-but-not-of-kids/

Figure 15.2 Teen happiness levels

Source: Monitoring the Future grade 12 survey 2015. Reproduced with permission from the author, Alexandra Samuel (2017) available at:

https://daily.jstor.org/yes-smartphones-are-destroying-a-generation-but-not-of-kids/

Figure 15.3 Social media and parents

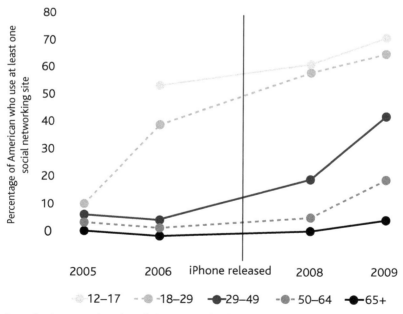

Source: Pew Internet and American Life Project. Reproduced with permission from the author, Alexandra Samuel (2017) available at:

https://daily.jstor.org/yes-smartphones-are-destroying-a-generation-but-not-of-kids/

that new models for ways of being online, for both adults and children, need to be created, whereby parents develop digital mentoring practices paying attention to what is enriching in required engagement of digital skills and connections. This implies regular talking, physical proximity and personal physical human interaction.

Various recent interventions add further to the privileged attention to – and disputes over – the wellbeing of children and teenagers, which are relevant to intergenerational changes and concerns of digital technology in family practices.

Evidence to the UK Select Committee Inquiry in 2017 into children's mental health includes that heavy use of screen devices (games, social media and television) lead to socio-emotional risks (Institute for Social and Economic Research, 2017). Yet the former head of GCHQ (Government Communications Headquarters) in the UK pleaded for children to spend more time online and to be trained in data coding from very young age, and learn vital cyber-skills (Farmer, 2017). According to Ofcom, the UK media regulator, reporting in early August 2017, children aged 5-15 were spending 15 hours a week online, a large increase from the previous year. The UK government children's commissioner commented on this, claiming that online sites and parents needed to take responsibility for the dangers (Savage, 2017).

It is claimed that children are encouraged – compelled, even – to increase their use of sites through features such as built-in games they engage with. For example, Snapchat currently uses Snapstreak, creating a streak when friends share photos over three consecutive days, but destroying it if a day is missed. Missing one day may ostracize a child, who would feel 'not liked'. After three years of existence, Snapchat's main app, Stories (a collection of snaps to tell a 'story'), that allows users to post photos and videos that disappear after 24 hours, has been cloned by WhatsApp, Instagram, Messenger and Facebook (Hern, 2017). While Snapchat's founders claimed that it presented 'a solution to stresses caused by the longevity of personal information on social media' (Gestalt Law), the ephemeral nature keeps faithful users ensnared. Information appears more enticing when it is volatile, offering non-ending renewal, and demanding engagement.

Although a strong intergenerational concern addresses the wellbeing of children, older people have also been considered. It is thought that the physical isolation of the elderly could potentially be overcome with access to social media. Also that their care, by family members or professionals, could be enhanced. Research by Quan-Haase and colleagues (Chapter Four in Neves and Casimiro, 2018) shows that technology can in many cases provide real support, and that the process of learning to operate devices provides welcoming socialization in itself. The fact that familiarity with digital devices is uneven complicates the productive potential of their use for this population. Peng and colleagues (Chapter Nine in Neves and Casimiro, 2018) show the skills deficit and low motivation of the older users of digital technologies. The potential is great in areas of finance, healthcare and recreation. Yet innovation is also required to address particular physical impairments such as loss of hearing, loss of sight and loss of mobility. Neves and colleagues (Chapter Seven in Neves and Casimiro, 2018) equally observe that the social disengagement, depression, functional decline and premature mortality found among the elderly living in institutions can be made better with the social connectedness opportunities offered by new technologies. This is corroborated by Cuban's (Chapter Twelve in Neves and Casimiro, 2018) focus on the management of separateness between ageing parents and their adult children, albeit this can include misunderstandings and ambiguous responses, created via technologically mediated long-distance care giving, which is a poor substitute for personal care.

Conflicts between generations stir up powerful emotions. Longitudinal studies are important to infer social change, in particular in periods of rapid change. The practices illustrated here are not of the young or the old alone. They are relational, with parents (including elderly parents) and children (young and teens), as well as other social agents (technological innovators included), being implicated. The conditions of socialization of children in the present are markedly different to that of parents socialized in a prior social world. Constant negotiations are needed, in particular due to the absence of wider sociocultural frames of reference for how to relate to – and with – the digital in all sorts of social spheres affected. Further complications are evident in other areas of social life, like sexuality, intimacy and in relation to spatial mobility, as discussed in the next section.

Connections of sexuality, intimacy, and over fractured spaces

The limits of privacy and respect to others, the revelation of the self, and the risks of too much sharing have been matters of concern in social media. Researchers have argued that pervasive disembodied encounters create boundlessness for individuals (Agger, 2012). Drawing from Virilio and Lotringer (2007), Du Preez (Chapter Five in Neves and Casimiro, 2018) remarks that vision technology provide too much to see, also taking over the function of sight, as it becomes a 'techno-prosthesis for perception'. This effect resembles those of some traditional technology. Describing the effects of high speed for race drivers, Lesley Hazleton writes in 'Whenever I Drive Fast' that after three seconds the driver's peripheral vision is completely blurred: 'He can only see straight ahead' (as cited in Zinsser, 1998, p 188). A bodily related philosophical assertion is that both too much speed and too much light are blinding (Virilio and Lotringer, 2007, p 98). DuPreez (2018) argues that effects rebound to life offline as the pressure to share online affects the flow and intensity of real-time sharing, which is also done in haste – and some detachment. Physical sexual engagement suffers similar processes.

Pornography, in the pre-internet days, separated makers of pornographic material and fans/users of them. These days bespoke porn flourishes. Fetishes of varied kinds are explored via customer porn, where clients write their own scripts and pay professional porn makers to shoot what they want. An illustration is the site PornHub, the world's currently 39th most popular on the web, which caters for an expanding new community (Alexa, 2017a). The anonymity of social media is seen to have allowed increased misogyny; porn changing the demeanour of men.

Having sex with robots has been a concern in recent television dramas such as *The Humans* (Channel 4 UK) or *Westworld* (Sky Atlantic remake of a 1970s movie), as well as in print media. This excites debate about the ways we live. Laura Bates (2017), founder of 'Everyday Sexism' wrote an essay for *The New York Times* expressing worry about the normalizing of rape as machines cannot give consent. Bates' essay relates to the launch of a sex robot named Roxxxy TrueCompanion, which changes into various 'personalities': Wild Wendy, S&M Susan and Frigid Farrah. The discussion is centred on the uses and vision about violence in sex related to boundaries between sexual fantasies, which may be gratified with a robot, and violence, which plausibly has nothing to do with the machine, which cannot consent to sex, being transposed to human sexual encounters. Yet, it is important to remember that the concern about robot is limited: sex dolls, which have existed a long time, as much as robots, do not either consent or refuse sex!

A relevant real-life illustration about sexuality and the digital is in an investigation I carried out (Silva, 2010). Related to the sexual lives of participants in my ethnographic study of home life, Lucey discovered various pornographic websites listed under her husband Henry's 'favourites' in his internet browser. The sites contained children's sexual exploitation and bestiality. In Lucey's words, they were 'racist, sexist, offensive, grotesque, unimaginable' (Silva, 2010, p 172). While Henry used the web for his sadomasochistic encounters, he claimed not to be a hard-porn user and would never transgress to the horrifying levels of the material Lucey found on his computer. Naively, in 2003, Henry believed nothing could be linked to his internet service provider (ISP), unaware that 'cookies' (identifiers on a user's machine employed to compile a history of browsing activities) constructed his digital profile on the web from his masochistic searches, expanding the field of his tastes, as cookies are designed to do.

Amid all this, there is a strong concern about the digital as surveillance both at public and private levels. Everyday activities are monitored and recordable to a high degree; movements are traced; search engines know our preferences and opinions; and we are invited to get ourselves known in exchange for knowledge about ourselves: when we wake up, how fast and where we walk can be registered and returned to us in statistical formats and appraisals, in self-knowledge formats. This surveillance resonates within family relationships: parental and partnering practices are affected.

Who has the right to spy on whom? 'Of Course Parents Have a Right to Spy on Their Kids' is Barbara Ellen's article title in *The Guardian* (2017), where she reports that a father with expertise in digital products created an app to force his 13-year-old son (distracted by video games) to respond to his calls or texts. The 'ReplyASAP' app locks a smartphone and sounds an alarm that only stops when the recipient replies by text. It enables tracking and controlling, it shows when a message is seen, and if a phone is turned off. Ellen's argument for the right of parental interference is based on the need of parents to *know* children are safe overriding the moral entitlement of privacy.

One can accept the argument that in certain cases spying relates to being concerned for someone's wellbeing. Yet in adult relationships, these are often connected to mistrust and control. Research on mobile phone use by couples show the negotiation of intimate relationships passing through the control by men – usually the norm – of women's movements being exacerbated by the surveillance potential of mobile technology (Silva, 2014). Geolocation services are currently built into smartphones. These are commonly designed to find lost or stolen phones; yet if someone knows the password to a person's cloud account, they can follow their movements constantly via the software. Spyware is cheap and easy to install in phones via computers or emails, allowing people to listen in and record calls, read texts, see photos and even watch someone via their phone's camera. These practices have been discussed in the media and cases of great distress have been documented (Williams, 2017). They have been given ambiguous labels such as 'intimate surveillance' (Leaver, 2017), or 'friendly surveillance'

(Marwick, 2012), yet a crucial component in them is power used for domination.

Academic literature on domestic work has pointed out the controlling use of spyware on nannies and maids (Sinanan and Hjorth, Chapter Ten in Neves and Casimiro, 2018). The regulation and disciplining of bodies and care practices grow with technological potential and the bringing together of disparate cultures in home care via the use of migrant services. As in other areas of social life, worthwhile and disruptive practices are found. Migration in the contemporary world does not involve the 'social death' of separateness experienced in the nineteenth century, argue Sinanan and Hjorth (2018). Nowadays, it is possible to 'do family' at a distance, giving and receiving care, maintaining intimacy, they say. Yet it is important to acknowledge the quality and limitations of contact. Likewise, Gillespie (2016) has found that mobile phones are extensively used in making, improving, generating family connections in the recent European refugee movements. Yet they empower and threaten refugees at the same time.

The issue of borders has featured strongly in matters of surveillance. Immigration targets and the displacement of people have been key foci. Refugees learn about routes and the cost of transport, which borders are open and which are closed, through their phones (Gillespie, 2016). They also learn about weather conditions for sea crossing (Gillespie, 2016). Phones empower but are also dangerous. Digital traces enable surveillance via GPS location by people or the governments refugees are trying to escape from. Social media interactions and networks can also be spied on. One indication is the recent European governments' attempts to take to task Facebook and Twitter for allowing fake accounts which intervened in election results with commentary and spread of one-sided opinions – said to be part of a wider attempt by Russia's President Putin to shape international politics. Digital surveillance encompasses very private and most public matters.

The media presents a number of cases affecting family relations on a daily basis, particularly in the UK currently facing Brexit negotiations. Some cases are ordinarily dealt with taking the digital as an integral participant. An illustration is a US surgeon hired by the NHS, with a British wife, who failed to get a visa for their two adopted children aged 10 and 12 (Hill, 2016). The Home Office letter sent to them, following an appeal, stated as one of the grounds for refusal that one of the parents could return to the US 'with the boys and stay in touch with the rest of the family through email and Skype'. The newspaper *The Guardian* quotes the family's solicitor saying 'It's unlawful for the Home Office to suggest modern forms of communication can be used to maintain a relationship between a minor child and a parent' (Hill, 2016). Regardless of the lawfulness of the case, it is curious to note how mainstream digital technologies have come to feature in legal cases.

Connections and disconnections abound in the digital-human interface, as illustrated in these stories. Many resolutions and negotiations are done on a case-by-case basis. These affect parents, children, partners, as well as national boundaries, movements of people and legal guidelines to the rights of the person and the politics of family relationships. Challenges are great for a renewed sociological imagination. Social science enquiry is fast working on these issues, recharging the sociological agenda to capture the array of matters affected by digital transformations.

Research agendas

A claim I have made in my work on technology is that their use, and indeed innovation patterns, are not an imposition – the material is not determining of sociocultural appropriations – but that adoption, uses and adaptations are part of a desire of how to live; it comes from us, our choices and abilities. My claim does not imply disregard for the effects of materiality in social life or the strong influence of corporative interests. My emphasis is on technology being taken up not by force, victimization or seduction, but rather by a desire for a way of living, a connection. Yet there are unintended consequences in technology adoption, as in other social engagements. Here is the crux of the problem, and where it is most useful to turn to social sciences knowledge.

I presented disputed interpretation about the effects of digital technologies on the young generation and on adults or older people considering social interaction and isolation as well as significant entanglements in sexuality, intimacy, surveillance, movements of bodies across space and changes over time. The illustration of various practices affecting personal and family relationships indicate interconnections of various fields with the uses and adoptions of the digital. It also shows some necessary regulative interventions of an institutional kind, currently in dispute. An understanding of the workings of power (institutional, corporative, in social divisions of age, gender, sexuality, class and ethnicity) appears key to capturing current dynamics of digital connections in family life: to learn about it, to curb potential disastrous effects, to bring to fruition productive ways of social engagement and flourishing ways of living with the digital.

What we know – what we need to know

Outlining various approaches to connections between families and technologies, Mauthner and Kazimierczak (Chapter Two in Neves and Casimiro, 2018) describe the posthumanist perspective as being one where these are not separate entities, being historically dynamically constituted in material and cultural practices. This is the way I researched the innovation patterns of household technologies in the twentieth century in the UK (Silva, 2010). My approach was adopted in the search for models to understand the specificities of a life course perspective regarding technology and family connections, as discussed by Mead and Neves Chapter Three in Neves and Casimiro, 2018) with a claim for the incorporation of the notion of 'technological nexus' to consider the intersections of social structures, technologies and the immediate contexts of deployment (Silva, 1999, p 57).

Can the digital be a device for intervention in social life and an instrument for its analysis? (Edwards et al, 2013; Marres and Weltevrede, 2013). Because the digital coordinates individuals' movements in time and space throughout the day to bond, share and plan, it should be possible to analyse family connections by means of the digital (Casimiro and Nico, 2018; in this volume). Storytelling is another way of doing family using the potential of digital technologies. According to Patiño (2018; Chapter Eight in this volume) the digital offers multimodality and liminal spaces, providing potentially rich explorations. Maddox (2018; Chapter Six in this volume) explores the prospect of 'digital methods' to study the life course. These interventions in knowing realistically express caution since consistency cannot be assumed either for different groups of people or longitudinally. Potential overrepresentation of people from certain locations are clearly a problem, as well as of certain characteristics of age, gender, race or wealth, as data carry the imprints of the devices, platform applications and attached users (boyd and Crawford, 2012; Driscoll and Walker, 2014). Moreover data is already classified in their own production process (Uprichard, 2013). Large data sets, collected by technological means, carry an array of methodological problems for researchers and create problems of interpretation. I considered some of these in a paper about 'What's [Yet] To Be Seen?' via video recordings (Silva, 2007), but I am unable to elaborate about this in detail here.

An important contextual issue regarding the generation of research material about the digital concerns the 'traces' left by different engagements – ontological perspectives, epistemological and methodological approaches – on the material of research. This is not a particular issue regarding family, or the digital. What we know about these relationships depends on what we seek to know and the instruments of our knowledge practices.

The salient questions I listed in the introduction refer to our changed sociability in face of the digital. Clearly the exploration depends on the models for being online and for being sociable that we seek to develop. This bears on our values about intergenerational relationality – the roles of parents for younger children, the care of the elderly parent – and in partnership – the sorts of intimate lives regarding sexual relations, privacy and sharing we desire to have. The heightened context of the digital interference via monitoring of our lives and the mediation of our relating is exacerbated by the absence of guidance about how to relate to each other and to these new things in our lives. While we want the digital to do certain things for us and our social living we are also concerned about it doing more than we can handle or differently than we wish. And our 'we' is a very extensive social field pervaded by interest and power (including state power) differences.

As Ricœur (1973) argues, texts – and I extend this to material gadgets and also data in general – are not just produced under certain material conditions embedded within sociocultural contexts, because texts – and gadgets and data – are also produced to do something. Regarding social science knowledge interventions in this field, this means that the research material – whether interview, text, online data or other artefact – becomes part of the context to be understood.

Material knowledge evidence can be re-observed, reanalysed and reinterpreted in different ways, but the coherence of the interpretation will depend on the fit of data with theoretical criteria involved in ontology, epistemology and methodology. It is important in this regard to note, as stressed by Hodder (1994, p 401), that material culture – and material artefacts to produce data – can 'speak back': interpretations can be challenged in view of interpretation of the context, in view of the 'traces' left in each iteration. Differing from Derrida's (1981) provocative assertion that meaning does not reside in the text, I maintain that while there is much more than the text itself, texts – as any research data – need to be understood in the context of their production and of their reading, of their reproduction and rereading. This implies situating the sociocultural context of a researcher's engagements with research material. Digital connections are particularly relevant for this.

Once what's yet to be known is identified, how to go about knowing?

How to go about knowing

Scripting refers to the ways in which social action is imprinted into technology whereby the technical apparatus demands particular actions from the user. I explored this notion extensively in my paper 'The cook, the cooker and the gendering of the kitchen' (Silva, 2000), discussed in detail by Mead and Neves (2018; Chapter Three in this volume). Digital platforms similarly 'script' action (see Akrich, 1992). They have a template of activity capturing data of particular kind: likes, clicks, heart shaped icons, following, flagging, sharing, quoting, and so on, which limit the scope of what interaction is mediated between users, the type of sociality created. The limitation is compounded by the format and structuring of data, always implicated in particular ontologies and their attached classification systems (Bowker and Star, 2000). Because of this scripting, it has been strongly claimed that the investigation of the ways in which people actually use technologies, and what they make of the use of the technologies at their disposal, is fundamental to understanding how they are embedded in sociability (Silva, 2000, 2007, 2010; Slater, 2002).

In her recent book on *Digital Sociology* Noortje Marres (2017) nicely invokes Max Weber's (1968) assertion that social enquiry must contend with the fact that the ideas people have about the social interact with what happens in it. This means that knowledge about social life and social life itself is inherently interactive (see Cicourel, 1964). For Marres (2017, p 19), this leads to an examination of how the social world is transformed by the very digital ways we currently have of knowing social life. For me, this means that technology use needs to be approached from the broad perspective attending to the architecture of the device/machine, the script/data produced, and the situation/ context in which action takes place, including the participation of other agents in a 'technological nexus' (Silva, 2000). This follows a strong claim that technology does not make people do things; that people adapt what they want to do to the capacities of the technology, but desires and capacities are balanced by the affordances particular to the socio-material context of living. Noortge Marres (2017, p 70), in my view, presents a similar argument regarding a 'holistic view on digital social life', saying that 'sociality is enacted with digital media technologies in various ways, varying across different settings and occasions... and... multiple entities participate in the configuration of sociality with digital media technologies: setting, data, contexts, methods'.

More specifically, how to go about knowing about digital connections and family practices is best devised through embracing the full range of research devices required by specific questions of investigation. My suggestion is that complex research questions require more than one method. This eclecticism provides the plausibility of interpretations in a coherent manner, from various angles, with a variety of methods.

References

Agger, B. (2012) *Oversharing: Presentations of Self in the Internet Age*, New York: Routledge, https://doi.org/10.4324/9781315732282

Akrich, M. (1992) 'The de-scription of technical objects', in W. Bijker and J. Law (eds) *Shaping Technology/Building Society*, Cambridge, MA: MIT Press, pp 205–24.

Alexa. (2017a) *Top Sites*, https://www.alexa.com/topsites

Alexa. (2017b) *Facebook.com Traffic Statistics*, https://www.alexa.com/siteinfo/facebook.com

Bates, L. (2017, July 17) 'The trouble with sex robots', *The New York Times – Opinion*, 17 July, https://www.nytimes.com/2017/07/17/opinion/sex-robots-consent.html

Berker, T., Hartmann, M. and Punie, Y. (2005) *Domestication of Media and Technology*, London: McGraw-Hill Education.

boyd, d. and Crawford K. (2012) 'Critical questions for big data: Provocations for a cultural, technological, and scholarly phenomenon', *Information, Communication & Society*, 15(5): 662–679, https://doi.org/10.1080/1369118x.2012.678878

Bowker, G. C. and Star, S. L. (2000) *Sorting Things Out: Classification and its Consequences*, Cambridge, MA: MIT Press.

Casimiro, C. and Nico, M. (2018) 'From object to instrument. Technologies as tools for family relations and family research', in B. B. Neves and C. Casimiro (eds), *Connected Families? Information & Communication Technologies, Generations, and the Life Course*, Bristol: Policy Press.

Cicourel, A. V. (1964) *Method and Measurement in Sociology*, New York: Free Press.

Coleman, G. (2012) *Hacker, Hoaxer, Whistleblower, Spy: The Many Faces of Anonymous*, London: Verso.

Cuban, S. (2017) *Transnational Family Communication: Immigrants and ICTs*, London: Palgrave Macmillan, https://doi.org/10.1057/978-1-137-58644-5

Cuban, S. (2018) 'Rescue chains and care talk among immigrants and their left-behind parents', in B. B. Neves and C. Casimiro (eds) *Connected Families? Information & Communication Technologies, Generations, and the Life Course*, Bristol: Policy Press.

Derrida, J. (1981) *Writing and Difference*, London: Routledge, https://doi.org/10.4324/9780203991787

Du Preez, A. (2018) 'Oversharing in the time of selfies: An aesthetics of disappearance', in B. B. Neves and C. Casimiro (eds) *Connected Families? Information & Communication Technologies, Generations, and the Life Course*, Bristol: Policy Press.

Ellen, B. (2017) 'Of course parents have a right to spy on their kids', *The Guardian – Parents and Parenting: Opinion*, 20 August, www.theguardian.com/commentisfree/2017/aug/20/parents-have-a-right-to-spy-on-their-children

Driscoll, K. and Walker, S. (2014) 'Working within a black box: Transparency in the collection and production of big Twitter data', *International Journal of Communication*, 8: 1745-1764, http://ijoc.org/index.php/ijoc/article/view/2171

Edwards, A., Housley, W., Williams, M., Sloan, L. and Williams, M. (2013) 'Digital social research, social media and the sociological imagination: Surrogacy, augmentation and re-orientation', *International Journal of Social Research Methodology*, 16(3): 245-260, https://doi.org/10.1080/13645579.2013.774185

Farmer, B. (2017) 'British children must spend more time online so they can "save the country", spy chief tells parents', *The Telegraph*, 7 August, www.telegraph.co.uk/news/2017/08/07/british-children-must-spend-time-online-can-save-country-spy/

Gestalt Law (no date) 'Snapchat screenshots: Copyright infringement', Gestalt Law, http://gestalt.law/snapchat-screenshots-copyright/, accessed 23 August 2017.

Gillespie, M. (2016) 'Phones – crucial to survival for refugees on the perilous route to Europe', *The Conversation*, 16 May, https://theconversation.com/phones-crucial-to-survival-for-refugees-on-the-perilous-route-to-europe-59428

Hern, A. (2017) 'Vanishing app: Snapchat struggles as Facebook bites back', *The Guardian*, 11 August, www.theguardian.com/technology/2017/aug/11/vanishing-app-snapchat-struggles-as-facebook-bites-back

Hill, A. (2016) 'US physician assistant may be forced to quit UK because of visa nightmare', *The Guardian – Immigration and Asylum*, 4 August, www.theguardian.com/uk-news/2017/aug/04/us-surgeon-may-be-forced-to-quit-uk-because-of-visa-nightmare

Hodder, I. (1994) 'The interpretation of documents and material culture', in N. Denzin and Y. Lincoln (eds) *Handbook of Qualitative Research*, London: Sage, pp 110-129.

Institute for Social and Economic Research. (2017) *Children and Young People's Mental Health: The Role of Education*, http://data.parliament.uk/writtenevidence/committeeevidence.svc/evidencedocument/health-committee/children-and-young-peoples-mental-healththe-role-of-education/written/45633.pdf

Leaver, T. (2017) 'Intimate surveillance: Normalizing parental monitoring and mediation of infants online', *Social Media + Society*, 3(2): 1-10, https://doi.org/10.1177/2056305117707192

Maddox, A. (2018) 'The application of digital methods in a life course approach to family studies', in B. B. Neves and C. Casimiro (eds) *Connected Families? Information & Communication Technologies, Generations, and the Life Course*, Bristol: Policy Press.

Marres, N. (2017) *Digital Sociology*, Cambridge: Polity.

Marres, N. and Waltevrede, E. (2013) 'Scraping the social? Issues in live social research', *Journal of Cultural Economy*, 6(3): 313-335, https://doi.org/10.1080/17530350.2013.772070

Marwick, A. (2012) 'The public domain: Social surveillance in everyday life', *Surveillance & Society*, 9(4): 378-393, https://ojs.library.queensu.ca/index.php/surveillance-and-society/article/view/pub_dom/pub_dom

Mauthner, N. and Kazimierczak, K. (2018) 'Theoretical perspectives on technology and society: Implications for understanding the relationship between ICTs and family life', in B. B. Neves and C. Casimiro (eds) *Connected Families? Information & Communication Technologies, Generations, and the Life Course*, Bristol: Policy Press.

Mead, G. and Neves, B. B. (2018) 'Recursive approaches to technology adoption, families, and the life course: Actor network theory and strong structuration theory', in B. B. Neves and C. Casimiro (eds) *Connected Families? Information & Communication Technologies, Generations, and the Life Course*, Bristol: Policy Press.

Morgan, D. (1996) *Family Connections: An Introduction to Family Studies*, London: Polity.

Neves, B. B., Baecker, R., Carvalho, D. and Sanders, A. (2018) 'Cross-disciplinary research methods to study technology use, family, and life course dynamics: Lessons from an action research project on social isolation and loneliness in later life', in B. B. Neves and C. Casimiro (eds) *Connected Families? Information & Communication Technologies, Generations, and the Life Course*, Bristol: Policy Press.

Orton-Johnson, K. and Prior, N. (2013) *Digital Sociology: Critical Perspectives*, Basingstoke: Palgrave Macmillan.

Patiño, C. A. (2018) 'Floating narratives: Transnational families and digital storytelling', in B. B. Neves and C. Casimiro (eds) *Connected Families? Information & Communication Technologies, Generations, and the Life Course*, Bristol: Policy Press.

Peng, S., Silverstein, M., Suitor, J. J., Gilligan, M., Hwang, W., Nam, S. and Routh, B. (2018) 'Use of communication technology to maintain intergenerational contact: Toward an understanding of "digital solidarity"', in B. B. Neves and C. Casimiro (eds) *Connected Families? Information & Communication Technologies, Generations, and the Life Course*, Bristol: Policy Press.

Quan-Haase, A., Wang, H., Wellman, B. and Zhang, R. (2018) 'Weaving family connections on and offline: The turn to networked individualism', in B. B. Neves and C. Casimiro (eds) *Connected Families? Information & Communication Technologies, Generations, and the Life Course*, Bristol: Policy Press.

The Radicati Group (2017) *Email Statistics Report, 2017–2021*, www.radicati.com/wp/wp-content/uploads/2017/01/Email-Statistics-Report-2017-2021-Executive-Summary.pdf

Ricœur, P. (1973) 'The model of the text: Meaningful action considered as text', *New Literary History*, 5(1): 91-117, https://doi.org/10.2307/468410

Samuel, A. (2017) 'Yes, smartphones are destroying a generation, but not of kids', *JSTOR Daily*, 8 August, https://daily.jstor.org/yes-smartphones-are-destroying-a-generation-but-not-of-kids/

Savage, M. (2017) 'Stop children bingeing on social media during holidays, parents urged', *The Guardian*, 5 August, www.theguardian.com/society/2017/aug/05/children-bingeing-social-media-anne-longfield-childrens-commissioner

Silva, E. B. (1999) 'Transforming housewifery: Practices, dispositions and technologies', in E. B. Silva and C. Smart (eds) *The 'New' Family?*, London: Sage, pp 46-65.

Silva, E. B. (2000) 'The cook, the cooker and the gendering of the kitchen', *The Sociological Review*, 48(4): 612-28, https://doi.org/10.1111/1467-954x.00235

Silva, E. B. (2002) 'Time and emotion in studies of household technologies', *Work, Employment & Society*, 16(2): 329-340, https://doi.org/10.1177/095001702400426866

Silva, E. B. (2007) 'What's [yet] to be seen? Re-using qualitative data', *Sociological Research Online*, 12(3), https://doi.org/10.5153/sro.1478

Silva, E. B. (2010) *Technology, Culture, Family: Influences on Home Life*, London: Palgrave Macmillan, https://doi.org/10.1057/9780230297029

Silva, S. R. (2014) '"24 hours on air": Gender and mobile phones in a Brazilian low-income neighbourhood', *International Journal of Gender, Science & Technology*, 6(1): 165-181, http://genderandset.open.ac.uk/index.php/genderandset/article/view/309/573

Sinanan, J. and Hjorth, L. (2018) 'Careful families and care as "kinwork": An intergenerational study of families and digital media use in Melbourne', in B. B. Neves & C. Casimiro (eds) *Connected Families? Information & Communication Technologies, Generations, and the Life Course*, Bristol: Policy Press.

Slater, D. (2002) 'Social relationships and identity online and offline', in L. Lievrouw and S. Livingstone (eds) *Handbook of New Media: Social Shaping and Consequences of ICT*, London: Sage, pp 533-546.

Smith, C. (2017) *19 MySpace Statistics and Facts Then and Now*, https://expandedramblings.com/index.php/myspace-stats-then-now/

Statista. (2015a) *Number of Active E-mail Accounts Worldwide from 2014 to 2019 (in Millions)*, www.statista.com/statistics/456519/forecast-number-of-active-email-accounts-worldwide/

Statista. (2015b) *Number of Mobile Phone Users Worldwide from 2013 to 2019 (in Billions)*, www.statista.com/statistics/274774/forecast-of-mobile-phone-users-worldwide/

Statista. (2017a) *Number of Monthly Active Facebook Users Worldwide as of 3rd Quarter 2017 (in Millions)*, https://www.statista.com/statistics/264810/number-of-monthly-active-facebook-users-worldwide/

Statista. (2017b) *Number of Monthly Active Instagram Users from January 2013 to September 2017 (in Millions)*, www.statista.com/statistics/253577/number-of-monthly-active-instagram-users/

Statista. (2017c) *Number of Daily Active Snapchat Users from 1st Quarter 2014 to 3rd Quarter 2017 (in Millions)*, www.statista.com/statistics/545967/snapchat-app-dau/

Statista. (2017d) *Number of Monthly Active WhatsApp Users Worldwide from April 2013 to July 2017 (in Millions)*, www.statista.com/statistics/260819/number-of-monthly-active-whatsapp-users/

Statista. (2017e) *Shipment Forecast of Laptops, Desktop PCs and Tablets Worldwide from 2010 to 2021 (in Million Units)*, www.statista.com/statistics/272595/global-shipments-forecast-for-tablets-laptops-and-desktop-pcs/

Statistic Brain. (2016) *Skype Company Statistics*, www.statisticbrain.com/skype-statistics/.

Twenge, J. (2017a) 'Are smartphones really making our children sad?', *The Guardian – The Observer*, 13 August, www.theguardian.com/technology/2017/aug/13/are-smartphones-really-making-our-children-sad

Twenge, J. (2017b) *IGen: Why Today's Super-connected Kids are Growing up Less Rebellious, More Tolerant, Less Happy – and Completely Unprepared for Adulthood – and What That Means for the Rest of Us*, New York: Simon and Schuster.

Uprichard, E. (2013) 'Describing description (and keeping causality): The case of academic articles on food and eating', *Sociology*, 47(2): 368–382, https://doi.org/10.1177/0038038512441279

Virilio, P. and Lotringer, S. (2007) *Pure War: Twenty-five Years Later*, New York: Semiotext(e).

Warde, A. (2016) *The Practice of Eating*, Cambridge: Polity.

Weber, M. (1968) *The Protestant Ethic and the Spirit of Capitalism* (T. Parsons, Trans.), London: George Allen & Unwin (Original work published 1905).

Williams, R. (2017) 'Spyware and smartphones: How abusive men track their partners', *The Guardian – Women*, 26 January, www.theguardian.com/lifeandstyle/2015/jan/25/spyware-smartphone-abusive-men-track-partners-domestic-violence

Zinsser, W. (1998) *On Writing Well*, New York: Harper Collins.

Zussman, J. U. (1980) 'Situational determinants of parental behavior: Effects of competing cognitive activity', *Child Development*, 51(3): 792–800, https://doi.org/10.2307/1129466

Index

References to tables and figures are in *italics*

9 781447 339946